CONTENTS

FOREWORD

First of all, let's get the questions out of the way:

'Is it necessary to write a book focussing of the achievements of a particular ethnic group, in a modern world full of freedoms and equality?'

'Isn't it a bit divisive to separate achievements of those who happen to belong to a particular ethnic group?'

My answer: I will concede each point, providing you and ten people you know can: name one Black inventor, one Black judge, one Black theatre director, and one Black scientist (who is not American[1]).

Unfortunately, while we may like to think that greatness has no nationality or ethnicity, this assertion is extremely hollow, when almost all the information we receive is to the contrary.

Of *Black Londoners: A History*, I have faith in readers of all nationalities, ethnic groups and religions, being able to celebrate with me and appreciate the achievement of remarkable individuals who happen to be Black and Londoners. I have utter conviction that the Black Londoners featured will in time form important sections of other histories and individual works. They, undoubtedly, are destined to add to the sum total of human knowledge. I would be delighted if *Black Londoners: A History*, by raising awareness, plays a modest contribution in this process.

The theme of making it against the odds and triumph over adversity is a universal human theme, from which all can gain inspiration. Who hasn't had to transcend their circumstances, or at some stage confounded the expectations of others and battled barriers of one kind or another?

The most remarkable thing, and one of the most moving as an author, has been the sheer generosity of spirit shown by the contributors. This book has come well after most of

BLACK
LONDONERS
a history

SUSAN OKOKON

The History Press

This book is dedicated to my mother, Mrs K.A.M. Okokon (SRN, SCM), whose ability to memorise the family tree of a nation has always been a source of inspiration and wonderment to me. Her narrative style has breathed life into the whole notion of history.

I would also like to thank my sisters Elizabeth and Josephine for their generous contributions to this publication, wise counsel and commentary. Always challenging and demanding, you have forced me to be challenging and demanding of myself.

The author and the publishers would like to thank the editors and staff of the following publications without whose cooperation this book would not have been possible.

Caribbean Times incorporating African Times

New Nation

WEST AFRICA

First published 1998
This updated edition first published in 2009

The History Press
The Mill, Brimscombe Port
Stroud, Gloucestershire, GL5 2QG
www.thehistorypress.co.uk

© Susan Okokon, 1998, 2009

The right of Susan Okokon to be identified as the Author
of this work has been asserted in accordance with the
Copyrights, Designs and Patents Act 1988.

British Library Cataloguing in Publication Data.
A catalogue record for this book is available from the British Library.

ISBN 978 0 7524 5375 0

Typesetting and origination by The History Press
Printed in Great Britain

South African gold mine, 1933. South African gold mines featured in the First Pan-African Conference, 23–25 July 1900 in Westminster town hall. The event was aimed at '[taking] steps to influence public opinion on existing proceedings and conditions affecting the Natives in the various parts of the Empire, viz., SOUTH AFRICA, WEST AFRICA and the British WEST INDIES'. (see p.36)

those featured have established themselves through their achievements. They do not need *Black Londoners: A History* to give them fame or to achieve their ambitions. Most had arrived at clear, well-considered conclusions about their life's work and its lessons and were determined to share these, especially with the young. But despite this openness to sharing their aspirations, lessons and achievements, one rather got the impression that many contributors would happily remain anonymous, as long as they could continue their work.

There was also a sense in which, 'it' or their achievement, was bigger than the achiever. The question of vanity played no part, because having produced or created 'it' or achieved their goal, it now somehow hangs outside of them, as its own entity. Recognition alone, like hearing the applause a long time after it counted, was not their motivation but the fact that we need to know they exist for our own sakes, to know ourselves better and to attain a more accurate picture of those who have made history.

This determination to share or communicate to those outside of their various disciplines, comes not from arrogance or self-importance, but has been granted with a humility, in the manner of an experienced climber, aware of a well-known path down a mountainside, while also happy to acknowledge that less well-known pathways exist, beyond their experience too.

Certain themes form a thread running through *Black Londoners: A History*, such as that of contributors' family histories: their sense of place, and their relationship to London and the wider world. A fascinating myriad of answers were frequently solicited from the same question. Certain patterns in answers did emerge, however. One was the sense of 'rootedness' conveyed by most contributors. No-one I encountered lacked a sense of who he or she was and where they came from. Each had interrogated older family members and/or had undertaken conventional historical research to achieve this knowledge of self. This raises certain fundamental questions about achievement 'against the odds' and what it takes, beyond excellence in one's discipline to complete one's journey. Recalling the biblical quote: 'The race is not for the swift, nor the battle for the strong... but for he [she], who abides' (or 'But to those who keep running')[2]. Some races and battles are not just about what they appear to be. It is not a given that talent and 'genius' are automatically recognised or recognised at all. No contributor managed to avoid racism. Ironically, some of the highest achievers had experienced it in its most virulent forms, and in the most rarefied of environments.

The intention of *Black Londoners: A History* has always been to propose a broader definition of what it is to be a Londoner, historically as much as in the twenty-first century. Black people have been born Londoners and arrived in London as part of the global mass movement of people for centuries whether by choice or by coercion. In the future, it will be impossible to write a history of London without reference to London's African and Caribbean heritage. For many histories this vital part of the city's jigsaw, remains a 'structured absence'[3]. Black people are connected to this London and other Londoners of the past, historically, genetically and culturally. To quote Sister Sledge – 'We are family'.

To celebrate and acknowledge Black Londoners should not mean the diminution of other ethnic groups. This would run counter to the progressive spirit of this work. Contributors to *Black Londoners: A History* themselves have been the first ones to assert this point. Indeed, every Black Londoner featured has achieved their ambitions in the context of friends, families and colleagues from other ethnic backgrounds, who have fought alongside them against injustices, collaborated with them, been led by them, taught them, invested in them, employed them, believed in them, championed them, ennobled them, respected them, defended them supported them, promoted them, published them, recognised them, befriended them, loved them – and today share in the triumphs of a Black Londoner.

Notes:

1. America has been the site of intensive reappraisal of their history and the role of Black people within this. This fact is to be applauded but cannot be an excuse to avoid vital work of our own, closer to home.

2. King James Bible, *Ecclesiastes* 9:11.

3. Reference to Toni Morrison (American, Black female Nobel Laureate) quotation from 'Playing in the dark: whiteness and the literary imagination', The William E. Massey, Sr. lectures in the history of American civilization, Toni Morrison, Harvard University Press, 1992.

Peckham Library at night. This innovative design was created by Albert O. Williamson-Taylor/Adams Kara Taylor (see p.92).

INTRODUCTION

This book comprises a collection of brief biographies of Black Londoners. The aim is not to argue a case, but to remind readers of the contributions of Black Londoners in the past and the twenty-first century. This book does not pretend to be comprehensive.

In the nineteenth century, Black Londoners consisted of the sons and daughters of earlier generations of Black people, students, workers from the 'old Empire' or the British colonies in the West Indies, and the soon to be 'new Empires' in Africa, whose annexation was already being planned among the 'European powers'. One group that is often forgotten in our focus on Africa's disempowerment at this time, is that of African kings and queens and their emissaries. Church Missions were another motivating force for Black people who came to London, many of whom were to play an active part in the evangelical movement, such as Sylvester Williams and George Mappike, taking with them the hopes of a community, and acting as their agents in the wider world.

In addition, many Black children were raised in military or naval schools which acted as schools cum orphanages, and technical colleges. Black Londoners also featured among the very poorest in society. In the late nineteenth century, we begin to see attempts of social reformers such as Booth* to define the poor. At this time anthropologists also attempted to classify 'types' among the poor. It is often the case that poor people are described as being a 'race' apart. While some may interpret this to indicate the social scorn heaped upon the poverty stricken, it may also be supposed that at least some of the poor may have African physiological traits.

There is nothing inevitable about history. History consists of those bits of the past that someone had the knowledge, interest, foresight and ability to record for future generations. The telling of the Black history of London, ancient and modern, is more flawed than most historical narratives for several reasons, some personal and individual, others institutional and cultural. The story of Dr George Rice and schoolmistress Mary Lucinda Rice illustrates

---

* Booth, Charles, *Life and Labour of the People in London*, (17 vols), Macmillan and Co., 1902–1903

the problems of continuity in historical record-keeping, even in the case of exceptional individuals. A Black man was clearing a house for the local authority, the contents of which were to be consigned to the local rubbish dump. He came across a discovery as shattering to him as the discovery of a pharaoh's tomb was to the early Egyptologists. He came to the conclusion that what had been classified as 'junk' by the local authority was in fact Black gold. It was a series of papers and artefacts documenting the life of a Black doctor and his family who lived in Woolwich in the 1890s – the Rice family. We know of Dr Rice because his daughter, Miss Mary Lucinda Rice, had recognized the importance of keeping a family archive. The trouble was, she had neither family nor anyone else left to value her own or her family's possessions when she died. But for fate, or the wise stranger sent to clear her house, we would not know anything about Dr Rice or Mary Lucinda Rice.

The story of the Rice family challenges what we might have expected of the life of a Black man and woman in Edwardian Britain. Dr Rice ran a series of hospitals in the north of England and in south London, and was a highly respected man within the upper echelons of the medical profession. His daughter, Lucinda Rice, ran a preparatory school. Their descendants are White people who are extremely proud of their ancestors, especially since they began to find out more through researching their family history some years ago.

Throughout Britain there have probably been thousands of people like Dr Rice. Perhaps not all of them were as accomplished as he was, but their stories are none the less important in telling us about the Black history of the British Isles. Every year hundreds of White British are discovering African ancestry from the waves of immigration centuries ago. Black people must also lay claim to this past. A multicultural community must, by definition, make all its members proud and confident about the achievements of its Black citizens, both nationally and internationally, wherever they are found.

THE NATURE OF 'GREATNESS'

To be recorded by official institutions, an individual or an event must at some stage be deemed to be of particular value to society. The notion of 'greatness' is a highly subjective one, governed by considerations of race, class and gender, and by a person's or event's place within our affections. Despite the enormous fame of Mrs Seacole in the nineteenth century, the deaths of her friends and supporters and her lack of dependants, caused her place in British history to be diminished. Her age was preceded by a period of imperial expansion and control when ideology sought to justify this expansion by diminishing the achievements of racial groups considered 'inferior'.

In this context, the contribution of Africans and their African-British descendants was not valued. It was therefore not surprising that with the growth and expansion of museums in the nineteenth century, the reputation of those such as Mrs Seacole, who was a Jamaican woman of mixed race, gave way to the new heroes and heroines of 'pure European blood', of the British Empire. The status of Mary Seacole as a British heroine has been enhanced by the growth in Britain of a multicultural society which has encouraged Black people to seek the roots of their past, in Britain as well as in Africa and the West Indies.

ONE FAMILY'S STORY

In the modern age, the inclusion within this book of the Moodys, an influential Black family which spanned the twentieth century, gives us new insights into a dynamic range of community and personal survival strategies available before the advent of the mass immigration in the 1950s, and the more recent gestures and safeguards afforded by race relations laws and policies.

Members of the Moody family have been included in several chapters in this book, demonstrating an almost breathtaking and wholly inspiring self-confidence and self-assertion, which, with hindsight, have proved to be among the most powerful weapons in the face of ignorance and prejudice. Theirs is a story which raises issues of the interplay of the politics of class, gender and race.

Cynthia Moody was an early exponent of international television and cinema advertising. Yet this heroine of the modern age is the first to acknowledge the debt owed to her forebears, such as Harold Moody, an uncle, who by confronting injustices on behalf of his family and community as a founder of the League of Coloured Peoples made survival for many Black Londoners tolerable.

THE PATH OF 'PROGRESS'

Researching the biographical narratives of this book, it became clear that progress for Black Londoners is not a linear process in which rights increase with time. An alternative reading would suggest the possibility of progress, privileges and enlightenment coexisting alongside extreme prejudice. Samuel Coleridge-Taylor, composer and musician, recalls a racial assault by a fellow student at the Royal College of Music, London. The same day, Coleridge-Taylor was described by the Principal as among the most gifted students in the College. Assaults on his person were not rare occurrences. One day Coleridge-Taylor would be conducting an élite orchestra, performing his own composition, the next he would be spat at in the streets. His answer was the pursuit of excellence, and to use his privileged position to campaign for the rights of his fellow Black citizens of London and the British Empire.

In the 1940s, Rudolph Dunbar was to take up Coleridge-Taylor's baton as the next Black man to conduct at the Royal Albert Hall. However, despite Dunbar's historic contribution to classical music before and immediately after the Second World War, he was shunned by the musical establishment from the 1950s until his death. Ian Hall, his nephew, himself a conductor and composer, recalls an incident at one post-performance reception at the Royal Albert Hall when Dunbar, then an old man, congratulated a young clarinettist upon his performance. When asked what inspired him to take up the clarinet as a career, the young man replied, 'A book on the clarinet written by a man called Dunbar.' Dunbar said nothing, smiled and moved on. The irony was not lost on Hall, who later commented, 'Dunbar's pupil was able to perform, when the master was destined to be shut out from the world of classical music.' Dunbar was to spend the rest of his life as a journalist and political activist, fighting the system which deprived him of his first love – classical music.

It is an intention of this book to acknowledge the presence of Black Londoners in spaces from which many may have assumed them to have been excluded. Many of these careers do not contradict the fact of racial exclusion but add new understanding to sets of circumstances in which enormous achievement, creativity and enterprise are able to flourish, often like oases in deserts of despair.

An image from *The Manga Bible*, created by Siku (see p. 23).

CHAPTER ONE

THE ARTS, ENTERTAINMENT AND SPORT

A close reading of the biographies of Black Londoners often reveals the complex nature of fame and achievement – nowhere more so than in the realm of the arts and entertainment.

Ronald Moody, for example, became one of Britain's most outstanding postwar sculptors, yet dentistry had originally brought him from Jamaica to England in 1923 to study at King's College, London. Moody was intending to develop a dental practice alongside his brother's medical practice in Peckham. Inspired by Egyptian artefacts at the British Museum, however, Moody felt compelled to sculpt. His life defies narrow categorization; he was a regular exhibitor at the Royal Academy and the Royal Society of Portrait Sculptors, and sat on its governing council from 1950. Yet he was also a member of the Caribbean Artists Movement, based in London from 1967.

Uzo Egonu was an artist, printmaker and art history scholar, who came to Britain at the age of thirteen and later became one of the most internationally recognized Black artists in Europe. A Londoner who lived and worked in Hampstead and Wembley, Egonu received some of the world's major art prizes. He died in 1996, and how many people beyond artistic circles are truly aware of his legacy? Uzo Egonu's story suggests some of the reasons why Black Londoners' historical contributions have often gone unrecognized. He was born in Nigeria and, like so many Black Londoners, his place of origin has made it more difficult for his contribution to his new home to recognized. Also, Uzo Egonu occupies a contested cultural space. He simply does not fit easily into Western notions of the African artist as being 'primitive', untutored and non-intellectual. That he studied both African and Western art history traditions, sought to concentrate upon universal themes, and was received internationally, has rendered Uzo Egonu almost invisible as a Black Londoner.

The career of Elisabeth Welch suggests another kind of invisibility which successful Black Londoners engaged in the arts, entertainment and sport may still face. Historical narratives tend to focus on ancient or relatively recent historical figures. Those who predate our living memory but have not yet been included in historical texts are victims of a kind of cultural amnesia. Elisabeth Welch has been a prominent member of London's theatrical community since the 1930s. She was one of the first Black people to have her own BBC radio series, *Soft Lights and Sweet Music*, which made her a household name in Britain. The illusion of showbiz glamour has been almost too successful in concentrating on her celebrity status at the expense of her status as a Black woman in a highly competitive and commercial enterprise in 1930s Britain.

In Elisabeth Welch's case, as in so many in this chapter on the arts, entertainment and sport, our attention is drawn to the end product or the surface personality, and not to the often very complex social and historical circumstances which led to their emergence. With greater curiosity, and more research, we may come to realize that most of these personalities carry within their stories access to yet more hidden histories of London.

Orlando Martins in *Where No Vultures Fly* (1951). Born in Nigeria in 1899, he settled in London in 1919, earning a living as a porter at Billingsgate fish market, a snake charmer with Lord John Sanger's Circus (Olympia), a night watchman, a kitchen porter, a sailor in the Merchant Navy and a ballet extra at the Lyceum. Martins eventually became the foremost Nigerian actor in Britain, performing on stage, screen, television and radio. He came to prominence through such films as *West of Zanzibar* (1929) and Paul Robeson's *Sanders of the River* (1936), and as Toussaint L'Ouverture at the Westminster Theatre. When British film competed with Hollywood, Orlando featured in *The Four Feathers* (1939) and the technicolour fantasy *The Thief of Baghdad* (1939). He later became associated with films set in Africa, such as *Simba* (1955). Two of Martins's films, *Where No Vultures Fly* (1951) and *Sammy Goes South* (1963), were granted Royal Command Performances. A career on the London stage included *The Heart of the Matter* (1953). In 1954 he starred in *Cry the Beloved Country*, a political protest play about South Africa, in St Martin-in-the-Fields, Trafalgar Square, later starring in the British television version (1958). In 1970 Martins was granted honorary life membership of Equity (the actors' union). He retired to Nigeria in the early 1980s where he died in 1986, receiving a state funeral.

Ronald Moody, one of Britain's outstanding post-Second World War sculptors. Moody was born in Jamaica in 1900 and came to England in 1923 to study dentistry at King's College, London. But he was inspired by Egyptian artefacts at the British Museum and turned to sculpture. He later settled in Paris and exhibited his bronzes and carvings there in 1937. When Germany invaded France in 1940 he fled to England where he worked as a dentist in a public health department and took part in London's civil defence. After the war he was a regular exhibitor at the Royal Academy. In 1963 he was commissioned by the Jamaican Government to produce a sculpture of the Savacou bird of Carib mythology. One of his sculptures now stands in the Department of Culture, Media and Sport, and has been adopted as a logo by the Caribbean Artists' Movement and by the Caribbean University Press. Based in London, in later life he received Jamaica's Musgrave Gold Medal (1978) for contributions to culture, and the Minority Rights Award for contributions to sculpture in Britain. Moody died in 1984. The picture shows him working on the wood carving 'Three Heads' which is now exhibited at the Nehru Memorial Museum in Delhi.

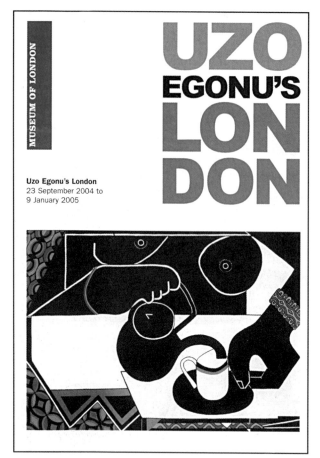

MUSEUM OF LONDON

UZO EGONU'S LONDON

Uzo Egonu's London
23 September 2004 to
9 January 2005

According to UNESCO, **Uzo Egonu**, artist, printmaker and art historian, was one of the foremost artists of African origin in the twentieth century. Arriving in wartime Britain in 1945, at the age of thirteen, Egonu was to make suburban London his home, with studios in Hampstead and South Kenton, Wembley. His art challenges Western myths of the naïve African artists, and credits Africa as the crucible of modernism.

Egonu's art is famous for its large-scale graphic, representational forms. While modernism has become synonymous with Western art forms, we are reminded, through Uzo Egonu's art, of its actual African origins. His early works tended to reflect themes, which included Nigerian folklore and studies of village life. Heavily influenced by the Nigerian Civil war, later works have tended to be more allegorical, questioning the nature of conflict, social issues, philosophical questions of human existence and exploring colour and form within highly graphic and stylised prints and paintings.

Born in the city of Onitsha, Uzo Egonu (1931–96) was considered a child artistic prodigy and was originally taught by African master painters as a student in Nigeria. After winning a major national Nigerian art competition, his father, a progressive chieftain and local administrator, believed that London offered greater opportunities for the development of Egonu's talents, on an international stage. He initially was sent to study art at Little Snoring, Norfolk. Egonu went on to study at Camberwell School of Art in South London in the 1950s, and was later to embark upon a successful international career, with the competition, which he won as a child, becoming the first of many successes at art competitions, throughout his life.

Egonu's major art prizes have included being awarded: Bronze Medal, 'Les Arts en Europe', Brussels, 1971; Cup of the City of Caserta, 'Italia 2000', Naples, Italy, 1972; UNESCO Prize, Unesco International Poster Competition, Paris, 1976; Purchase Prize, 13th International Biennial of Graphic Art, Ljubljana, (former) Yugoslavia, 1979; Honorary Counsellor (for life), International Association of Art Unesco, Paris, 1983; Medal, 10th International Print Biennale, Cracow, Poland, 1984.

Egonu's art has been collected by the Victoria and Albert Museum, has been displayed at the Museum of London, Norwich City Gallery, Bradford City Art Gallery and is on display in museums and art galleries across the world, including FBA Galleries, London 1963; National Museum of Wales, Cardiff, 1965; City Art Gallery, Bristol, 1968; Kresge Art Gallery, Michigan State University, Michigan, USA, 1974; Three Dimension Gallery, Berkley, California, USA, 1975; FESTAC, Lagos, Nigeria, 1977; Museum of Modern Art, Raijeka (former Yugoslavia) 1978; Imabashi Gallery, Kyoto, Japan, 1978; Utubo Gallery, Osaka, Japan, 1979 and many, many more.

The esteem with which Egonu was regarded internationally was reflected in his appointment by UNESCO as Honorary Counsellor for life in 1983. He was one of only twenty-one other artists of the twentieth century to be so honoured; other Honarary Counsellors included: Picasso, Matisse and Cézanne. Egonu studied European and Nigerian art history and observed that Nigeria's Nok civilization of the ninth century BC was regarded as 'classical' until Europeans discovered it had been created by Africans and not the ancient Greeks; then it was redefined as 'primitive'. In this instance, and throughout his life, Uzo Egonu fought against restrictive categorization of artists of African origin within modern art. Egonu died in 1996. In 2005–06 the Museum of London in association with Minority Contractors in Europe mounted an exhibition of Egonu's paintings and prints, 'Uzo Egonu's London', curated by Susan Okokon.

Isaac Julien describes himself as an artist whose medium is video installations. He is also a filmmaker whose films have included seminal works such as *Looking for Langston* (1989). *Paradise Omeros* (2002), like *Looking for Langston*, was a British-based production. Julien has also exhibited a strong enthusiasm for international projects, such as Baltimore, on which he worked with the late revered Black film pioneer Melvin Van Peebles (father of the famous actor Mario Van Peebles).

Isaac Julien's work has encompassed the political in films such as *Franz Fanon* (1996), and *Territories* (1983), representing significant periods in British history, which dealt for instance with the question of police brutality. *Looking for Langston* (1989) received national and international recognition, and represents a pivotal moment in our national film culture, in which Black British art and film emerged with a new, precise voice and cultural interrogation. Julien was interested in film as a stylistic device, utilising Black and White photography and cinema to comment upon Black gay desire.

Looking for Langston (1989) was recognised as an avant-garde documentary on the cultural watershed that was the period of the Harlem Renaissance (1920–1930s), with Julien, in turn, producing, what Gilroy refers to as a

'Black-Atlantic aesthetic'. Shot in London, *Looking for Langston* created a dialogue or conversation, between Black British and Black American arts. *Looking for Langston* was very much a Black British take on American culture. It subsequently generated enormous interest internationally, showing at the most prestigious festivals.

Julien's international reputation, beyond filmmaking, as an established video installation artist, was demonstrated by an invitation to participate in '40 Years of Video Art' at the Pompidou Centre, Paris (2005). This exhibition has since toured internationally, exhibiting in Taipei, Miami and Sydney, and at the Museum of Contemporary Art, Paris. Additionally, 2006 saw the Pompidou Centre host an important Isaac Julien solo exhibition.

Born in Bow, East London in 1960, Julien attended Dameford School for Boys, Bethnal Green, where he became interested in youth activism, inspired by Sheila Rowbotham, and Omeros River Press. Omeros gave support to working class filmmakers. Julien was also involved in the Socialist Youth Organisation, the Youth Section of the Workers Revolutionary Party (with which Vanessa Redgrave was involved), the International Marxist Group and Socialist Challenge.

In the 1980s Julien participated in the gay and lesbian project, Framed Youth, through which he made the film, *Revenge of the Teenage Parents*. This film went on to win a prestigious Grierson Award in 1983 (an award commemorating Paul Grierson, 'the father of documentary filmmaking').

Isaac Julien established Sankofa film production company after leaving the Black Audio Film Collective, because he wanted 'To articulate being gay through being Black'. His other aims included a desire to organise around the Brixton Riots, 1981 and 1983.

Local affinities remain with East London, which has experienced a cultural explosion in recent years and where Julien's representatives, the Victoria Miro Gallery, are located. Julien's other London affinities include Bloomsbury, with which he has maintained a connection since the 1980s. Julien studied at St Martin's school of Art (1980–84), and at one stage shared a home with David Bailey and Cheryl Smythe.

Isaac Julien's grandfather was the earliest member of the family to join the established St Lucian community in Bow and Tower Hamlets, in the 1950s, enabling the later settlement of Julien's mother and father, who were a matron in geriatric care and a hospital porter respectively. Julien's grandfather was the first to leave London, for greater entrepreneurial opportunities in Brooklyn, New York, acquiring a string of 'brown-stone' houses. Julien revisits this history of the aspirations of West Indian immigrants during the 1950s, in his film *Paradise Omeros* (2002), which he made in collaboration with the Nobel Laureate, Derek Walcott.

Julien was nominated for the Turner Prize in 2001 for his film *The Long Road to Mazatlan* (1999). Earlier works include *Frantz Fanon: Black Skin, White Mask* (1996), and *Young Soul Rebels* (1991), which was awarded the Semaine de la Critique Prize at the Cannes Film Festival the same year, as well as the acclaimed poetic documentary *Looking for Langston* (1989). With a career which ranges from narrative feature film to video art, from gallery installation to television documentary, Isaac Julien has not only attracted critical attention from leading international arts organisations, but continues to be featured on the British Art History, Film, Media and Cultural Studies syllabus of the National Curriculum, and on undergraduate and postgraduate degree courses. Julien is a well-respected academic and lectures at Harvard University, Whitney Museum of American Arts, University of Arts, Hamburg and the Guggenheim Museum, New York. He has also served on the Jury of BAFTA and the Berlin, Rotterdam and Sundance Film Festivals, as well as film festivals in Britain, Germany, the Netherlands and the USA.

Julien has recently worked on a national heritage initiative on Derek Jarman in association with the Serpentine Gallery, the Jarman Estate and the British Film Institute. He also directed a documentary about Jarman, starring Tilda Swinton, in 2008. Production of an ambitious film project *Small Boats (Better Life)* was completed in 2007, and premiered at Sadler's Wells, London in collaboration with award-winning choreographer Russell Maliphant. The production travelled to New York as part of the Performance Triennial at the Brooklyn Academy of Music (BAM).

The Isaac Julien Archive and Collection, Archive Futura, operates as an unincorporated, not-for-profit organisation and is currently seeking status as an educational charity for the public benefit.

Christopher Ofili is one of Britain's leading young artists. He was not only the first Black artist to win the Turner Prize (1998), but also the first painter in twenty years to win this prestigious art award. Ofili's major works have included the controversial and sensational: *No Woman No Cry* (1998), *Captain Shit and the Legend of the Black Stars* (1998) and *The Upper Room* (2002). Ofili also served as Trustee of Britain's Tate Gallery for five years (2000–05).

Chris Ofili states that his major achievement is, 'Being able to perform along a pathway which is his own, notwithstanding the support which he has had along the way'. This artist has also been able to experiment with ideas that are important to him and others. This fact has had greater significance to Ofili than awards: 'awards don't define a person more than their achievement.' When he won the Turner Prize he was excited by the recognition, but more so because it enabled a wider audience to know about his work: 'Winning the Turner Prize was one reason why a certain picture, which the general public, not necessarily an art public, could engage'.

The painting which won the Turner Prize, *No Woman No Cry*, was inspired by Doreen Lawrence and it brought a renewed attention to the Stephen Lawrence case: 'It was about the suffering and sorrow that Doreen has gone through'. Ofili felt that, his work, 'could address the public at a higher level than it had done before. This was exciting!'

Of his fame, Ofili states, 'You need to separate a public personae from a private personae. What you have to accept is that you are a public person, and an artist.'

Christopher Ofili was born in Manchester in 1968 to Nigerian parents, who arrived in England in the early 1960s. Both parents worked at McVities biscuit factory for over thirty years. Ofili's parents pushed the importance of education, and he and his siblings grew up with a strong sense that they needed to be ambitious in order to survive: 'If you are young and Black and want progress, there are not many doors open to you, unless you are well equipped'.

At the age of twenty Chris Ofili settled in London, originally to do a BA Degree at Chelsea Art College (1988). A masters was to follow, at the Royal College of Art (1993). Ofili's achievements as Trustee of the Tate have included the review of diverse collections, the development of scholarships in association with the Arts Council, and campaigning to reflect changing audience diversity within Tate exhibitions. To the surprise of many, Chris Ofili has been the creative force behind the Icebox organization, and the Freeness Project. This is a platform for unsigned musical artists across the UK, of Black, Chinese and Asian decent.

Ofili, states, 'As an artist, as an undying principal, freedom is important. Personal freedom, and creative freedom'. Ofili's commitment to the Freeness project is a reflection on how musical expression has always influenced his work.

Chris Ofili has recently left London to live in Port of Spain, Trinidad, where he continues to work on his art, returning occasionally to London to oversee the Freeness Project. Of the future, Ofili intends to reap the rewards of his labour and 'To continue to lay the foundations'. 'It is useful to one's intellectual freedom to move out of one's comfort zone. London can be sometimes all consuming'. He says humorously, 'In Trinidad they call me Englishman!'

Born **Ajinbayo Akinsiku** in Leicester in 1965, this graphic novelist is known to millions throughout the world simply as, **Siku**: the artist behind Judge Dredd, in the cult comic 2000 *AD*.

The Akinsiku family moved to London in 1966, with their young son Siku growing up enthralled by cartoons. The family lived in a basement flat in Notting Hill Gate: 'Looking through the windows I saw feet walking past not faces'. Hours spent playing cowboys alone, surrounded by imaginary Indians, helped to hone Siku's sense of imaginative drama: 'I decided that I would be an artist at three years old!'

Watching British television as a child his influences were *Batman*, *Superman*, the *Twilight Zone*, *Film Noire*, *Dr Who*, 1970s comics and eventually graphic artists such as Adam Neil, Boris Vallego and Frank Frazetta: 'I wanted to draw and conceptualise things. I drew all the time. My parents destroyed my drawings and teachers told me off for drawing.'

The eldest of four children, Siku was discouraged from the world of art by a mother who wanted him to be a doctor and a father who wanted him to become an engineer. 'What are you going to eat as an artist? Are you going to beg?' His parents complained. Ironically, not only did Siku become a graphic novelist, but also one of his brothers became Art Director of Nickelodeon UK. Of her mistaken earlier attitude to her son's creativity, Siku's mother (pictured above) quotes the Yoruba saying, 'Who knows tomorrow?'

Siku's mother and father, originally from Nigeria, decided to move their family back to post-war Nigeria (Following the Nigeria-Biafra war in 1971) to help with the nation's reconstruction. His mother was a secretary and his father was a qualified engineer, with an American company called Wayne. Siku left London for a Nigerian Boarding School, aged six. His memories of this time are of extreme unhappiness. Siku paints a picture of himself as a young Londoner, 'like a fish out of water', transported to Nigeria, struggling to catch up with the curriculum and the language barrier, since he only spoke English. 'Nigerian Schools were far more advanced than the schools in Britain. For example, they were way ahead of us in their teaching of mathematics, and in their attitude.' Eventually, Siku was moved to a private school on the outskirts of the city, still largely under construction, at which he was able to settle. Siku recalls the sheer enormity of the school buildings, covering approximately fifteen football pitches: 'It was built when Nigeria was still rich from its oil'.

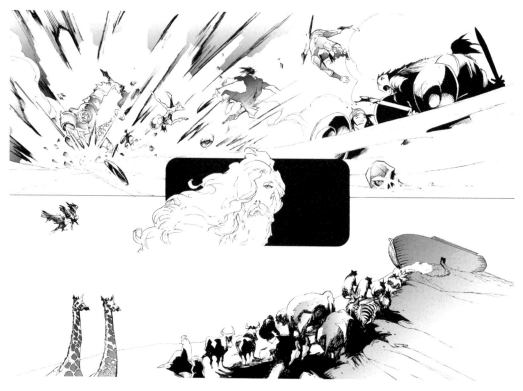

Things were looking up: Siku recalls the beginning of a Nigerian childhood adventure, when he was allowed enormous freedom, living next door to the King of Ondo and permitted to play in the king's statued grounds. 'I experienced magical times going back to Ondo, watching sunsets from its hills of red soil, watching aluminium roofs reflecting this red glow.' Both his mother and father were originally from Ondo, and Siku had the privilege of meeting his grandfather, a man who achieved great wealth through establishing the Akinsulire Memorial Hotel (the first two-storey building in the town, which still exists to this day), and a fleet of buses and cars.

As his education progressed, so did his enthusiasm for art: 'My teacher Mr Aina, encouraged me to complete a GCSE in art, and I decided to do so secretly.' This was followed by a degree in graphic design, at Yabba College of Technology, with Siku returning to England at the age of twenty-two to work as a visualiser for an advertising agency.

Siku would eventually go on to be the graphic artist behind Judge Dredd, in the cult magazine classic 2000 AD (1991–2001), during one of its most influential phases. This was followed by Siku's involvement in the computer games industry. Here, he was responsible for the development of innovative tools, which have simplified the creation of new computer games, halving the time of game development.

Siku formed his own computer company, Midax, and was responsible for testing prototypes for international games companies, such as Soft Image (France), and Numerical Image (USA). Popular computer game formats created by Siku, include 'Evil Genius', the James Bond spoof game.

In 2004 Siku decided to study for a theology degree (2004–2007), at the London School of Theology. This decision was to influence his publication of the series of six versions of *The Manga Bible*, published by Hodder and Stoughton (pictured above). It was hailed as a completely new interpretation: 'It will convey the shock and freshness of the Bible in a unique way.' (The Archbishop of Canterbury Most Rev. Rowan Williams).

In 2008 Siku expressed a heartfelt desire to travel to Darfur to complete 'The most important project of my life' – a graphic narrative of the situation in Darfur, to create awareness and stimulate change.

Dr Augustus (Gus) Casely Hayford has demonstrated outstanding leadership and innovation within some of Britain's major arts and cultural institutions. An art historian and curator, Dr Augustus Casely Hayford has served as Director of INIVA (The Institute of International Visual Arts), been elected to the Tate Britain Council (2004), and served as Executive Director of Arts Strategy for the Arts Council of England (2007). A Special Advisor to the Heritage Lottery Fund (2004), Dr Casely Hayford has worked with the British Museum (2002 onwards) and has been an Art Commissioner on the Commission on African & Asian Heritage, GLA (Greater London Authority) (2003).

Born in Tooting in 1964, he was raised in Hampstead to a Ghanaian father and a mother from Sierra Leone. Gus Casely Hayford's father came to Britain in 1954, working in insurance and later joining the Civil Service. Casely Hayford studied at the Central School of Art and gained a PhD in African History from the School of Oriental and African Studies, London University.

The Casely Hayford family history has had a profound impact upon the politics of Ghana. As a Pan-Africanist politician, lawyer and journalist Augustus' ancestor J.E. Casely Hayford successfully campaigned for African conservation and human rights and formed West Africa's first nationalist movement, the National Congress of British West Africa, in 1919. Gus Casely Hayford, through his own research efforts, has been able to trace his family's links with Europe to the sixteenth century.

Gus Casely Hayford was himself to make history, as initiator and director of the year-long Africa 2005: one of the largest and most successful seasons of African art and cultural programming which Britain has ever seen. Casely Hayford took the lead in forging partnerships with over 150 leading arts organizations in the UK, including the BBC, which scheduled Africa '05 television and radio programming throughout 2005.

Casely Hayford's Africa '05 experience led to his expertise being sought as panelist for a major conference on a World Cultural Festival in 2012, University of East London, Docklands (June 2008), to consider the opportunities for the arts and cultural industries, that the 2012 Olympic Games and Paralympic Games could bring.

Augustus has also written extensively for academic journals and has lectured at Sotheby's Institute, as well as at Goldsmiths, Birkbeck, City University and University of Westminster. He has been a Clore Fellow, a Heritage Lottery Fund Special Adviser and a member of the National Museums Directors' Committee.

Today, as Joint CEO of Zamyn, Dr Casely Hayford has been commissioned to develop the future audience vision for the Tate family of galleries – its website and broadcasting arm. He is also currently writing a digital publication for Channel 4 that will provide the educational web context for the Big Art Project television series: the most ambitious arts programme ever commissioned by Channel 4 (2008–09).

Born in British Honduras, **Nadia Cattouse** was to become one of the earliest Black actresses to act in a BBC drama, and became a pioneer of radio, cabaret, folk music, calypso and religious programming in the UK.

From an early age her ambitions were to pull her in two directions: teaching and entertainment. Cattouse's second greatest influence was her mother (one of thirteen children), who was a teacher. Nadia Cattouse originally undertook teacher training, under the Pupil-Teacher system in the West Indies; following study at Glasgow University (1946), Cattouse was eventually to achieve her teaching ambitions, returning to Belize (1949) to become headmistress of Galanjug Mission Infant School. Cattouse was brought up with a strong sense of Belize ecological heritage, influenced by her uncle, who later in his life became known internationally for his ecological work as 'The Mahogany Man'. His mission was to re-forest Belize with the Mahogany tree. By the time he died aged ninety-seven in 2003 he had re-planted 30,000 trees.

Cattouse used to travel to London on leave from Scotland during the Second World War. In 1951 she returned to London to study Social Anthropology at the London School of Economics (LSE). While in her second year, Cattouse was approached by the Colonial Office to become a Welfare Liaison Officer, to meet the arriving West Indian Migrants, during the start of Britain's historical mass immigration from the West Indians.

Fate was to conspire to finally lure Cattouse away from her course at LSE when she was approached, in the middle of her third year, to join a Variety Show, the 'Disc Doubles' (1955), featuring tribute performances of the music of popular acts, such as the Platters and Lena Horne. In 1958 Nadia Cattouse was invited to perform in Paul Robeson's 'Thank You Concert', for his supporters, including Claudia Jones, and her West Indian Gazette and, Britain's most respected actress of the day, Dame Sybil Thorndike.

By the mid 1950s Nadia Cattouse had 'got the call from the BBC', and was invited to perform in a radio folk play, *My People, Your People* by Cy Grant. She went on to perform on one of the BBC's first drama documentaries addressing the harsh realities of mass immigration, *A Man From the Sun* (1956). One of the earliest dramatisation by a Black British actress, it was transmitted live to the nation. This performance increased Cattouse's public profile, and she went on to star in *Dickson of Dock Green* (1974) and *Laurence Olivier Presents: Cat on a Hot Tin Roof* (1976). Cattouse was to instigate a 'cultural revolution' at the BBC, introducing a West Indian folk choir. Ewan MacColl, one of the leaders of the British folk revival of the 1950s and '60s, invited Cattouse to join the folk club circuit in the early 1960s. Her skills as an all-round entertainer, led to her introducing the popular radio programme *Women's Hour*, for a week in 1961. Cattouse was to feature on national TV 'institutions', such as the News Year's Eve celebration, *Hootenanny for the Place*. Cattouse at her height of popularity was also to sing at the Royal Albert Hall.

As British TV of the late twentieth century began to reflect the diversity of the nation, Cattouse played her part by performing in a number of groundbreaking drama series, such as *Between These Walls* (1975), a gritty modern drama set in a women's prison, and *Angels* (1975), a hospital drama. *Halleluiah* was another pioneering series, which occupied the 'God spot', or religious programming of BBC television. Cattouse believes that this series anticipated what was to become known as ecumenicalism, in its insistence on the bringing together of different denominations and faith communities. It also introduced African Caribbean musical styles and hymn repertoire into British religious programming.

Also, in an era of protest and counter-culture, television began to change its staid image, and Cattouse recalls being asked to sing Bob Dylan and other songs emerging from the various protest movements in the USA, including *Freedom Road* (1964), which spawned a soundtrack recording. Cattouse became involved in the British Anti-Apartheid Movement, contributing her time and talents to fundraising concerts. She recalls rallies at Trafalgar Square, supported by Vanessa Redgrave and Harold Wilson. Cattouse gave similar support to Christian Aid. Cattouse has been a prolific songwriter, and was commissioned to write songs for the Church Missionary Society; one song which became popular was 'Long Time Boy' (1962).

The 1990s saw Cattouse's gradual withdrawal from public performance, however she continued to maintain a commitment to community activism and public service e.g. serving on the British Commonwealth Ex-Services League for fourteen years, and the Central Religious Advisory Committee for the BBC and ITV.

The seamstress **Esther Bruce**, with her stepmother and father. Esther Bruce created gowns for many famous women; Elisabeth Welch is wearing one of her creations in the iconic photograph on p.28. Esther was born in Fulham in 1912 to a Scottish mother, Edith Brooks, and a Guyanan father, Joseph Bruce. After the death of her mother, she was taught to sew by her stepmother, Jeanie Edwards, who had emigrated to England from British Guyana. After leaving school at the age of fifteen, Esther Bruce worked for the dressmaker Madam Polly and Barkers of Kensington, being sacked from the latter in 1931 because of her colour.

From 1935 to 1941 **Esther Bruce** worked for Mary Taylor in Chelsea, dressmaker to the rich and famous. Her father Joseph died in London during the Blitz and Esther moved in with neighbour and family friend Granny Johnson, the matriarch of Dieppe Street. In 1941 Esther began war work in the linen room at the Brompton Hospital, where she was to stay for fourteen years, leaving in 1956 to make curtains in Fulham. She retired in 1972, but boredom brought her out of retirement to work for another curtain manufacturer in Battersea. Poor eyesight forced her to retire finally at seventy-four. Esther Bruce died in 1994, having published her autobiography, *Aunt Esther's Story*, three years earlier.

Elisabeth Welch was a prominent member of London's theatrical community since the 1930s, as both a singer and actress in radio, film, television and theatre. In 1936 she starred with Paul Robeson in the film *Song of Freedom*. In the same year, she was filmed singing live at Alexandra Palace and became one of the first British television stars. Born in New York in 1904, maternal encouragement led Welch to join the Europe-bound Americans of the 1920s. In the craze for musical revues, Elisabeth Welch joined Florence Mill's Blackbirds in 1928 in Paris.

Her London debut was at the Leicester Square Theatre, in 1933, in *Dark Doings*, introducing the song 'Stormy Weather'. Elisabeth Welch was one of the first Black people to have her own BBC radio series, *Soft Lights and Sweet Music*, as early as 1934, which made her a household name in Britain. Welch performed at some of the most prestigious theatrical venues in London and appeared in two Royal Variety performances (1979 and 1985).

Welch aged well, and upon her return to New York in 1980 after a 50-year absence stunned and delighted audiences and critics alike with her acting and singing talents. Age had failed to dim the light of this great star, who was a living link to the jazz age and the greats of British and American musical theatre.

Welch was to make a dramatic appearance in director Derek Jarman's 1980 version of Shakespeare's *The Tempest*. This 'comeback' was followed by Welch's appearance in *Black Broadway* (1980), the Broadway show celebrating the Harlem Renaissance, starring some of its last remaining performers. Despite being mugged and beaten unconscious in 1985, at the age of eighty-one, the show literally went on the next day for Welch.

Appearances in *Jerome Goes to Hollywood* (1985), Donmar Warehouse, London, won Welch a Laurence Olivier award. She participated in 'Jerome Kern: A Centennial Celebration' in Los Angeles (1985), and in *Jerome Kern Goes to Hollywood*, transferring to Broadway (1986), for which she received a Tony nomination. *Time to Start Living* (1986), her one woman show, at New York's Lucille Lortel Theatre, won Elisabeth Welch an OBIE (Off-Broadway Theatre Award) and a special award from the Outer Critics' Circle 'for making old song favourites sound young, fresh and vital'.

A documentary film was made about Elisabeth Welch for Channel 4 – *Keeping Love Alive*, described as a 'self-portrait in words and songs' (1987). Elisabeth Welch's long list of credits for television drama culminated in a Variety Club of Great Britain Award for services to British Entertainment in 1988.

An Australian Tour (1988) was followed by a recital at Weill Hall, at Carnegie Hall, New York (1989). Elisabeth Welch's last encore, her final professional appearance in 1996, was a Channel 4 documentary called *Black Divas*. It was fitting that Elisabeth Welch should choose to sing one of her earliest hits, and her signature tune, 'Stormy Weather', for her professional farewell. She died aged ninety-nine in 2003.

Earl Cameron is a British actor of screen, stage, television and radio. Earl Cameron broke through the glass ceiling of British cinema to play leading roles in the 1950s. Until then, Black actors had largely been consigned to menial parts, stereotypical roles, and crowd scenes. As a leading man he was given the 'Big Poster' treatment, with his handsome image being utilised by the film industry's publicity machine. Earl Cameron played a leading role as a London doctor in *Sapphire* (1959), a ground-breaking detective film dealing with racial attitudes in Britain, and including some of the leading Black and White British actors and actresses of the 1950s. *Sapphire* was a critical and box office success in both the UK and America. Earl Cameron was born in Bermuda in 1925. He joined the British Merchant Navy and came to London to live in 1939. His cinema debut, also considered a classic, was *Pool of London* (1950).

Cameron's other films have included Graham Greene's *Heart of the Matter* (1953), *Simba* (1955), *Accused* (1957), *Flame in the Streets* (1961) (pictured above), *Term of Trial* (1962), *Thunderball* (1965), *Battle Beneath the Earth* (1968) and *The Revolutionary* (1979). Cameron's performances have spanned all film genres from action to science fiction to social realism, and he has played opposite noted international actors, such as Sidney Poitier and Laurence Olivier. His work in several popular television series, such as *Dixon of Dock Green*, *Emergency Ward 10* and *Danger Man* did much to increase the visibility of Black actors on British television. Cameron's later film roles included *The Message* (1976) the story of the Prophet Muhammad, *Cuba* (US, 1979) and *The Great Kandinski* (1995). His later TV appearances included *Lovejoy* (1995). During the 1990s, Cameron retired, moving to the Solomon Islands as a member of the Baha'i community.

This retirement was short-lived however, with Cameron returning to film and television, including starring in popular TV drama series in Britain and America, such as *Eastenders* (2001) *Babyfather* (USA 2001–02), *Final Cut*, (2003) *Waking the Dead* (2003), *Dalziel and Pascoe* (2006), and *Casualty* (2008).

Recent film roles, suggest a belated appreciation of Cameron's grounding as a mature classical actor. In the horror film *Revelation* (2002), Cameron played a Cardinal central to the film's apocalyptic plot; in the *Interpreter* (2005) Cameron had a major role starring opposite Nicole Kidman as fictional dictator Edward Zuwanie. He also appeared as an empathetic portrait painter to the queen, who was played by Helen Mirren in *The Queen* (2006), in which Cameron dominates the film's opening sequences establishing its sympathies.

Recalling his tough early years in Britain, Cameron states: 'At that time [1939] it was almost impossible for a Black person to get a job,' he said. 'I spent three days without food. I even contemplated suicide. London hit me hard.'

As he approached his ninetieth decade, reviewers universally praised Cameron for his role as Edward Zuwanie in *The Interpreter*. *The Baltimore Sun* stated: 'Earl Cameron is magnificent as the slimy old fraud of a dictator...' *Rolling Stone* described Cameron's appearance as 'subtle and menacing', whilst Philip French in the *Observer* referred to 'that fine Caribbean actor Earl Cameron.'

Rudolph Walker, actor of stage and television, was born in Trinidad in 1940. Walker arrived in London in 1960, where he worked as a compositor in the printing trade by day, while at night he studied drama at the City Lit (City Literary Institute).

After a series of small parts in TV, film and theatre, Walker's big break came with the TV comedy *Love Thy Neighbour*, which ran for five years and earned him the TV Personality of the Year Award from the Variety Club of Great Britain in 1972. One of Britain's most popular television comedies, *Love Thy Neighbour* dealt with a Black family's encounter with racism in a White suburb. It used comedy to look at racism in modern Britain, which until then had only been dealt with in highbrow drama or worthy documentary, if at all.

Walker became a beloved character, playing Police Constable Frank Gladstone in the BBC TV comedy *The Thin Blue Line* (1995–96). Rudolph Walker has also enjoyed a successful West End stage career, with leading roles in *The Tempest* and *Othello*. In 1992 Walker was presented with the Scarlet Ibis Award for 'Outstanding and Meritorious Service' by the Trinidad and Tobago High Commission.

In 1998 Walker stared in *The Iceman Cometh* at the Old Vic Theatre. In recent years, Walker has become known to a whole new generation for his role as Patrick Trueman in *Eastenders*, first appearing on one of Britain's most popular soap operas in 2001 and continuing until the present day. To mark his forty-second year on stage and television, Rudolph Walker wrote his autobiography in autumn 2008.

Nina Baden-Semper, actress of television, stage and film, was born in Le Brea, Trinidad, and came to Britain in 1965 to study nursing at the Hammersmith Hospital, where she became an SRN and SCM (State Registered Nurse and Health Visitor). Baden-Semper and her co-star Rudolph Walker in the popular comedy, *Love Thy Neighbour*, were the first Black actors to star in a major British television series.

Baden-Semper became a style and cultural icon in the 1970s, as the embodiment of the emerging American-influenced ideology of 'Black is Beautiful', which sought to turn on its head, the hitherto unchallenged dominance of Western aesthetics in popular culture. Until then, beautiful women on television were almost exclusively White Europeans. In 1973 Baden-Semper's feisty female character, Babreen, earned her an ITV Joint Television Personality Award by the Variety Club of Great Britain and Outstanding Female Personality of the Year PYE TV Award. She appeared on *This Is Your Life* (1975) and was presented with the Scarlet Ibis Award for 'Outstanding and Meritorious Service' by the Trinidad and Tobago Government (1990).

In 1996 Nina Baden Semper made a dramatic comeback, starring as Sister Rose Peters, matriarch of the Black British TV comedy drama *Brothers and Sisters*, set within a northern church community. This reappearance was followed by the film *Rage* (1999), and appearances in *Crossroads* (2002) and *Casualty* (2008).

Patricia Cumper is the current Artistic Director of Talawa Theatre, one of the oldest surviving Black-led theatre companies in London. Cumper is convinced of the continuing need for a Black theatre, and asserts that without the existence of Talawa, some of the leading actors in British theatre, film and television would never have emerged. Talawa's illustrious alumni include: Jane Binta-Breeze, the late Norman Beaton, Don Warrington, Cathy Tyson, Dianne Parish, Rudolph Walker and Kwame Kwei Armah.

Patricia Cumper has been writing theatre scripts for twenty-eight years, and says of her appointment that it is unusual for a writer to become an artistic director. However, Cumper has worked with Talawa over decades as writer, trainer 'and all-round "dogs-body"', with a genuine commitment to supporting fellow writers and producers in the mounting of productions.

Born in Kingston, Jamaica in 1954 to an English father and Jamaican mother (pictured below), who met while both studying at Cambridge University in 1947, Patricia Cumper followed in her parents' footsteps, coming to Britain to study at Cambridge in the 1980s.

Prior to establishing herself as a writer for theatre in the UK, Cumper had pioneered 'outside' or 'open-air' theatre, at the University of the West Indies, mounting productions with writers such as the Nobel Peace Prize winner, Derek Walcott.

Cumper cites her mother as the leading lawyer responsible for the establishment of Family Courts in Jamaica, and the re-drafting of the Bastardy Acts. Both legal watersheds were to transform the life chances of 'outside' children or children born outside marriage, and to reduce the unfavourable legal and economic distinctions between 'inside' and 'outside' children.

Cumper was raised with a strong awareness of family history, and remembers her grandfather who was African-Indian and grandmother who was Scottish-African-Caribb ('Caribbs' were the original Amerindian inhabitants of much of the West Indies). She also affectionately recalls tales of her grandfather, who used to follow the West Indian cricket team to London in the 1930s.

Film-maker **Menelik Shabazz** is shown here working on the television documentary *Breaking Point* in 1978. Shabazz was born in 1954 in St John, Barbados, and has lived in London since the age of five. He attended the London International Film School (1974–76) and has worked as an independent filmmaker since. In 1980 with his first feature-length film *Burning an Illusion*, which he both wrote and directed, Shabazz forged new traditions in British Black filmmaking, which extended the vocabulary of film drama for all of Britain's diverse communities. *Burning an Illusion* attempted to capture the Black urban experience and was a tale of the pressure endured by the young British-born Black community. He has since completed many other projects including *Catch a Fire*, a drama documentary made for the BBC and a film on the 400-year African liberation struggle, *Time and Judgement* (1988).

Shabazz, frustrated by the lack of showcasing opportunities for Black films and filmmakers, established the *Black Filmmaker* magazine (1998), and the BFM International Film Festival (1999). In 2008, the tenth anniversary, the BFM International Film Festival was held at the edgy and prestigious ICA (Institute of Contemporary Arts), the Mall, London.

Cassie McFarlane and Victor Romero Evans in *Burning an Illusion*, 1981.

Cynthia Moody directing an advertisement for Beecham's, 1964–65. Cynthia Moody's career charts the early movement of Black British women as filmmakers. She founded her own production and post-production companies. Cynthia Moody has also been an early exponent of international TV and film advertising. Born in 1923, Moody trained at the Shell Film Unit and was a cine operator in the WRNS during the Second World War. After the war, Cynthia Moody trained as a film editor, dialogue writer and dubbing editor, and went on to produce films for British Films Ltd, the Central Office for Information and the Children's Film Foundation; she also worked with Jacques Tati in Paris on *Monsieur Hulot's Holiday*. Moody's work has won many awards. Cynthia Moody is now the curator of the Ronald Moody Archive in Bristol.

The **Ital Lions** (Brinsley Forde, Brian Bovell, Victor Romero Evans, Trevor Laird and David N. Haynes) with Ronnie (Karl Howman, centre) in *Babylon*. *Babylon*, a film made by Franco Rosso in 1980, marked the coming of age of Black London youth and was a milestone in their cultural resistance against social injustice. The film describes the experiences of a young Londoner torn between the two worlds of low-paid employment as a mechanic and evening work as a DJ improvising lyrics over reggae soundtracks at a night-club. The counter-culture of the latter is portrayed as both an escape from the ghetto and a coming to terms with an

emergent Black self-identity. The film's soundtrack featured some of the finest exponents of London's reggae scene, and challenged the narrow perception of this music. Reggae stars also took leading acting roles, such as the members of the group Aswad. *Babylon* today stands as a social document of Black London youth and culture in the 1980s, commenting as it does on the crumbling inner city, police harassment and contemporary music and dance.

Brinsley Forde, actor and singer with leading reggae band **Aswad**. He was a child star of the 1960s children's television series, *The Double Deckers*.

Samuel Coleridge-Taylor (pictured on previous page) was the composer of the English choral orchestral work *Hiawatha's Wedding Feast*. Sales of sheet music show that this was the most popular choral orchestral piece between 1898 and 1912. Coleridge-Taylor was considered by Edward Elgar, as well as by Sir George Grove, his Principal at the Royal College of Music, to be one of the most outstanding British musicians and composers of his generation. Born in Holborn in 1875, Coleridge-Taylor moved to Croydon, where he was an early supporter of Pan-Africanism, a London-born movement to secure civil and political rights for Africans throughout the world. Coleridge-Taylor and John Archer (see p.112) were voted onto the Executive Committee of the Pan-Africanist Association at the Pan-Africanist Conference, which they helped to organize. The Conference was held at Westminster Town Hall in 1900. Coleridge-Taylor's popularity as a musician led to an invitation to the White House by President Theodore Roosevelt and to his being championed by America's Black community. He became Professor of Composition at the Trinity College of Music in 1903 and at the Guildhall School of Music, London in 1910.

Although his legacy remains with us today, sadly Samuel Coleridge-Taylor was to die young, at the age of thirty-seven, from double pneumonia. One wreath at his funeral was in the shape of the African continent and was inscribed, 'From the sons and daughters of West Africa at present residing in England'. On his death, Hubert Parry, Principal of the Royal College of Music wrote of Coleridge-Taylor:

> There will be thousands … who will feel a sense of saddening loss when … they miss the arresting face in which gentleness, humour, and modesty were so strangely combined with authoritative decision when matters of art were in question. ('A Tribute from Sir Hubert Parry', *Musical Times*, LIII (1912), 638)

Arguably, Coleridge-Taylor's authoritative decision-making saw him championing the interests of Black people in Britain and internationally too, by word and action through his activism, at the height of the imperial era. In the first issue of the London-based journal, *The African Times and Orient Review* in 1912, Coleridge-Taylor asserted that White Europeans were largely interested in Black peoples for economic reasons and the small number who took a more concerned interest, rarely acted upon this concern.

> One accomplished fact carries far more weight than a thousand aims and desires, regrettable though it may be. It is imperative that this venture (the journal) be supported by the coloured people themselves, so that it shall be absolutely independent of the whites as regards circulation. (*The African Times and Orient Review* 1/1, July 1912)

Married to Jesse, a White, English fellow student at the Royal College of Music in 1899, Coleridge-Taylor was to be succeeded by his wife, a son Hiawatha (who later became a conductor) and a daughter Avril (who became a composer and conductor).

> There is an appalling amount of ignorance amongst English people regarding the Negro and his doings… Personally, I consider myself an equal of any white man who ever lived, and no one could change me in that respect; on the other hand, no man reverences worth more than I, irrespective of colour and creed. Really great people always see the best in others; it is the little man who looks for the worst – and finds it.

> … It was an arrogant 'little' white man who dared to say to the great Dumas, '… And I hear you actually have Negro blood in you!' To which Dumas responded, 'Yes…My father was a Mulatto, his father a Negro, and his father a monkey. My ancestry begins where yours ends'

(Extracts from: *Croydon Guardian and Surrey County Gazette*, No. 2, 243 (10 Feb 1912, No. 2, 245; 24 February 1912, No. 2, 246; 2 March 1912. 8 (from Duse Mohamed Ali) 12 Letter) and (*Staying Power: The History of Black people in Britain*, Peter Fryer, Pluto Press 1984)

Born in British Guyana in 1907, **Rudolph Dunbar** was trained at the Institute of Musical Art, Juliard School, New York (1919). Coming to Europe in 1928, Dunbar studied journalism and music at the University of Paris and Conservatory of Music; he also attended conservatories in Leipzig and Vienna to study conducting, composition and the clarinet.

In 1936 **Rudolph Dunbar** was commissioned to act as roving reporter for the Associated Negro Press to cover the Italian invasion of Ethiopia. On 26 April 1942, Dunbar led the London Philharmonic Orchestra, at the Royal Albert Hall, to raise funds for persons of African descent in the Allied fighting forces. He was appointed as an accredited war correspondent in the Second World War and achieved the distinction of covering the Normandy invasion, the liberation of Paris and the fall of Berlin. He is shown here with Lady Pitt.

Dunbar conducted classical concerts in both Paris and Berlin, the orchestras of the Paris Conservatoire, the National Symphony of Paris and the Berlin Philharmonic Orchestra. But London had always been the base for his international career. In his early career he led a series of jazz orchestras, with residencies at several London restaurants, such as the Cossack, to finance his classical studies. In the mid-1920s he accompanied performers such as Florence Mills and Josephine Baker on their European tours. He formed his own clarinet school and wrote the first ever treatise on the clarinet in 1939; his training manuals for the clarinet became classics for aspiring clarinet players. Rudolph Dunbar died in 1988.

Professor Ian Hall, born in Guyana in 1940, has become a leading light in church and classical music in London since the 1960s, when he became Assistant Organist at St Martin-in-the-Fields and Deputy Organist and Chorister at Southwark Cathedral. He was appointed Director of Music to the Inner London Education Authority (ILEA) in 1966, and later Conductor and Director of Music both of London University Church of Christ the King and of the University of London Choir.

Professor Ian Hall also happens to be the nephew of the Black British conductor Rudolph Dunbar (see p.37–8). In 1970 Hall founded the Bloomsbury International Society for the Propagation of Racial Harmony Through Music, which grew out of a multicultural festival to celebrate United Nations Human Rights Day. In 1982 Hall was appointed Special Consultant to the United Nations Centre Against Apartheid. In 1996 Hall conducted his own work, *Vivat Pax*, in New York before assembled world leaders, as part of the United Nations' fiftieth anniversary celebrations. In 1997 Professor Hall was appointed Master of Ceremonies for the Commonwealth Summit in Edinburgh.

For Professor Hall's distinguished contribution to sacred music internationally, two honorary degrees have been conferred. He was also invited to become an Honorary Professor of the University of Sierra Leone (1996) and the University of Ghana (1997).

An exuberant personality, and charismatic speaker, His Excellency Professor Ian Hall was appointed Ambassador-at-Large of the World Association of Non-Governmental Organizations in 2000. He has coined the phrase 'cultural politician'; to more clearly define his role in his cultural extravaganzas, which go beyond that of artistic director. These events bring together international audiences of children, faith groups, diplomats or the general public to campaign for peace and unity or to mark global humanitarian watersheds. Hall's concerts and cultural productions have thus earned him the personal support and appreciation of the royal family and heads of state.

Tunde Jegede, composer and musician of classical African and Western music, was born in 1972. Jegede began studying the kora, the African harp-lute, when he was six; when he was seven he joined the Purcell School of Music in London, and in 1980 took up a musical apprenticeship in the Gambia, a first for a British musician. On his return he joined the Guildhall School of Music and Drama; before he left in 1992, he was at the heart of a musical and cultural revolution that re-evaluated the African classical music tradition.

Tunde Jegede has traced the African roots of Western classical music to the Moorish invasion of Spain and the *rebab* (or *rebec*), from which the modern violin has evolved. Jegede formed the African Classical Music Ensemble in 1991; he has also written and performed music for dance companies, theatre and film, and written several books about African music. His work continues to ensure that African musical traditions find expression in the West.

Tunde Jegede was the composer on the BBC TV documentary, *Africa I Remember* (1995), and performed this work in collaboration with the London Sinfonietta, conducted by Markus Stenz. Appointed Innovations Composer for the Eastern Orchestral Board, Jegede was to work with some of the UK's leading orchestras, such as The Royal Philharmonic Orchestra, The Philharmonia, Britten Sinfonia, Viva Sinfonia, The London Mozart Players and The Bournemouth Symphony Orchestra.

Tunde Jegede's talents as a composer have been highly sought after, and he has been commissioned to write a percussion concerto for Evelyn Glennie and double orchestra, an oratorio for the City of Milton Keynes and a string quartet for the Brodsky Quartet, as a part of their 'Beethoven Op18' recording. This piece was eventually released on the Vanguard label and is still being performed by the Brodsky Quartet worldwide.

In 2002, Jegede launched his own company ACM Productions, aimed at 'Accessible quality productions across a small spectrum of genres, namely: Urban, Pop, Classical and Jazz'.

The singer-songwriter **Gabrielle** served her apprenticeship on the London nightclub circuit, singing cover versions of Motown classics. Her anthem 'Dreams' came out of this period, and describes her dejection at the elusiveness of professional success. This song however, made chart history by going straight in at number two, the highest entry for a debut artist at the time. Her debut album *Find Your Way*, sold one million copies when it was released in 1993. Her second album, *Gabrielle*, was released in 1995. It included the hit single 'Give Me a Little More Time', and led to a new creative direction in producing for the Boilerhouse Boys.

Gabrielle won a Brit Award for British Breakthrough Act (1994), and for Best British Female (1997). 'Give Me A Little More Time' and 'If You Ever' — a duet with East 17, followed. Personal problems meant a creative retreat for Gabrielle until she re-emerged in 2000 with the sampling of Bob Dylan's 'Knockin' on Heaven's Door', and 'RISE', which was to become Gabrielle's second number one in 2000. The song 'Out of Reach', reached an international audience when it was used as the soundtrack to *Bridget Jones' Diary*, charting at number four in the UK.

In 2001 the Greatest Hits Album *Dreams Can Come True* – Vol 1, was certified 4X Platinum, and became the UK's fifth biggest selling hit of 2001. This was followed by the album *Play to Win* (2004), the single *Why* (2007) and the album *Always* (2007). Gabrielle headlined at the 'Zermatt Unplugged' festival, Zurich, Switzerland, in April 2008 along with Alanis Morrisette, and at Birmingham Pride, 2008.

Gabrielle's achievements have not been limited to popular success; she has also won critical acclaim within the music industry, winning the prestigious Ivor Novello Award for Best Song Collection (2008).

British MC/Rap artist and music producer **Dizzee Rascal**, born **Dylan Mills**, launched his own recording label at sixteen, and signed a major record deal at the age of eighteen. His first album went gold, and has since been defined as a 'classic', and his third album, *Maths + English*, has been heralded by *The Guardian* as, 'The best British Rap album ever', selling 80,000 copies in its first two months.

To date, Dizzee Rascal has had over thirteen singles in the UK Charts and four albums; *Boy in Da Corner* (2003), *Showtime* (2004), *Maths + English* (2007) and *Tongue 'n' Cheek* (2009), as well as numerous collaborations with other recording artists. His first major success was the top thirty hit single 'I Luv U', about accidental teenage pregnancy, from the album *Boy in Da Corner* (2003). It was through *Boy in Da Corner* (2003) that Dizzee Rascal was to reach critical acclaim, and make music history, by being at aged nineteen the youngest person to win the prestigious Mercury Prize for Best Album, and only the second rapper (the first being Ms Dynamite in 2002).

Any suggestions that his Mercury Prize represented a fluke were quashed by his second Mercury Prize nomination in 2007. He was among twelve artists nominated for his album *Maths + English*. That the Mercury Prize is given to what are considered to be Britain's best albums of the year, indicates profound recognition by the music industry of Dylan Mill's songwriting abilities, producing and performing talents, which transcend musical genres.

Dylan Mills regards these as his greatest achievements to date, in addition to the launching of his own record label XL Recordings: 'XL Recordings will promote the work of artists, from similar deprived backgrounds to me'. The Newham Generals were the first act from the XL Studio stable to be launched:

> I am more able to help others, and speak their language, which is raw, straight up, not necessarily anti-pop, but real. The musical styles produced by the XL stable will be similar to my own.

As part of Band Aid 20, in 2004, Dizzee Rascal was the only artist permitted to add new lyrics, in the form of a rap, to the original song 'Do they Know It's Christmas?': 'Spare a thought this yuletide for the deprived, if the table was turned would you survive?' and 'You ain't gotta feel guilt just selfless, give a little help to the helpless.' Dylan's own words on his success: 'I am happy be pursuing my dream, and to have made it out of my own situation, and be in a position to help my family'.

Dylan Mills was born in Benin City, Nigeria in 1984, to a Ghanaian mother and a Nigerian father. 'My father worked for the Mint, but died by the time I was two years old'. Dylan's mother brought him to London in 1984, while he was a babe in arms, to start a new life. 'It was just the two of us, and my mother worked several jobs to support us'. Dylan remembers his mother as a student, 'I remember her trying to study. She studied Law.' However, the reality of a small child to support motivated Dylan's mother to earn money as a waitress, buying clothes wholesale to sell locally, and becoming an Avon and a Tupperware lady.

It was this entrepreneurial spirit, which Dylan claims to have most influenced him. 'My mother was always working'. Dylan delivered and sold clothes for his mother, and helped to process and deliver her orders for clients for Avon and Tupperware.

Dylan has strong associations and attachments to North, South and East London. His earliest memories are of Ilford and Forest Gate, which were his first homes. East London is associated with Dylan's first and last experiences of formal education. It was in Bow, East London, where he has lived longest, and in which he attended his first school.

Dylan associates North London with his later school career, in which he attended the famous Anna Scher, described as, 'Britain's least conventional theatre school', for six months, sharing a class with James Alexandrou, aka Martin Fowler from *Eastenders*. It was from North London that Dylan Mills was to launch a successful career as a DJ on pirate radio stations including Heat FM, Rise FM, Flava FM and Eclipse FM in 1999–2000.

South London has two contrasting associations for the artist. The first is religious, and the second is music industry-based. Dylan Mills came from a very religious background: 'We didn't just go to church every Sunday, but sometimes went up to four times a week. Our church was based at Brixton, Town Hall, and South London, led by Bishop Hempel. So Brixton has strong memories for me'. It was also in Greenwich and Bermondsey, South London, where Dylan first went into the studio, including Atomic Studios, where he made his first album in 2000.

Dylan Mills has always maintained a complex relationship with schools. A gifted child, Dylan's mother sent him to the private Ryde College where he took his IT exams early at the age of fifteen. However, Dylan was expelled from four schools: Langdon Park, Poplar; Blessed John Roach; St Paul's Way, Bow; Anna Scher, Islington. Yet, Mills describes school as 'a refuge', keeping him on the straight and narrow. Why was this gifted and exceptional pupil thrown out of four schools, despite claiming that he actually enjoyed some aspects of school? Dylan replies, 'It is only recently that I have been able to make sense of things. As a young child, I was emotionally and physically abused by a child minder. There were a whole group of us, and we were treated like animals. They regularly beat us up'. Painfully aware of his mother's need to work to support the family, Dylan protected his mother from this knowledge, and never told her what was happening until much later.

During his early childhood, Dylan describes his schools. 'School was like an escape. They were a safe place to have tantrums, and to express the anger I felt. Throughout school I fought a lot'. Looking back at it now, and analysing the situation, Dylan believes that he tried to establish an identity inside and outside school, through violence. Being raised by a single mother only added to the need to build up a strong masculine identity. Despite all of this, Dylan's mother always believed in her son's unique abilities and academic potential, arranging private tuition, and independent intelligence testing.

Today, Dylan finds himself acting as a masculine role model to his young cousin. With almost paternal frustration he says, 'His expressions and attitude remind me of my younger self. I talk to him and get him to leave the road thing alone. It's different now. It's more dangerous with more guns on the street and killings'. When asked how he reaches his young cousin, Dylan replies, 'I talk to him, beat him up – play fight, challenge him, show him I care.' This big brother role is extended by Dizzee to his XL Recording Label, which exists to give support to talented artists who may be seen by conventional recording studios as too risky to support, because of their social problems and deprived backgrounds.

Dylan Mills' love of music led him to form a band at school, which practised for two major performances a year. School also enabled Dylan to learn how to programme computers, his second great interest. While at school, a passion was to begin for jungle, drum and base DJing. By fifteen, Dylan had his own DJ pirate radio session 1–3am, getting up later that morning to do a full day at school. When asked what motivated him to go to school after DJing through the night, Dylan replies, 'Wagging school was boring.'

Redbridge College was a turning point in Dylan's decision about his future career path. After enrolling, he began to ask himself, 'Why am I here?' By this time it had become apparent to him that he was already quite famous among fellow students as a DJ, using raves to spread the music. The release of his famous hit 'I Luv U', eventually reached number twenty-nine in the UK chart, followed by 'Fix Up, Look Sharp' which went to number seventeen in August 2003.

Dylan concluded that if the object of college was to establish a career, he no longer needed to be there. The same year he left college, and signed his first recording contract. 'Although I left Redbridge I really enjoyed student life. I had never met such a wide range of people before, and they were great. I was quite popular, and quite well known. I still bump into my old friends from Redbridge from time to time'. And the rest, as they say, is history...

Baron Leary Constantine of Maraval with the Trinidadian premier Sir Eric Williams, 1962. Leary Nicholas Constantine was born on a cocoa estate in Trinidad in 1901. He came to London in 1923 and became a phenomenal cricketing success as a batsman, fast bowler and fielder. In 1928 he took 100 wickets and scored 1,000 runs, and was invited to settle in Britain. In the 1930s he became a spokesperson for the Black community, negotiating with employers and the trade unions to place Black workers in industry during the Second World War. As captain of the West Indies cricket team against England at Lords in 1943 he sued the manageress of the Imperial Hotel, Russell Square, for breach of contract in refusing accommodation to Constantine and his family because of their colour. He was awarded an MBE in 1945, and went on to serve as Minister of Transport and as the Trinidad and Tobago High Commissioner to Great Britain. Knighted in 1962, Constantine was made a life peer in 1969. He died in 1971.

Harold Ernest Moody as Mayor of Auckland, New Zealand. Moody was born in Peckham in 1915, the son of the Black community leader and Congregationalist minister Harold Moody (see p.65). He qualified as a doctor in 1941, serving as a commissioned officer and army doctor on troop ships in many theatres of war, and then in India, before returning to the family practice in Peckham. In 1948 he represented Britain in the shot-put and discus at the Olympic Games, held at Wembley Stadium. He went on the win gold medals for these events at the 1950 Empire Games. He settled in New Zealand in 1951, where he became a popular and active member of the Auckland community, serving as mayor from 1967 to 1971. He died in 1986.

Ian Wright, who was awarded the MBE in 2000 for his footballing achievements, was born in in Brockley, Woolwich, South London in 1963, the third son of Jamaican immigrants Herbert and Nesta.

Having left school at sixteen, Ian Wright trained as a bricklayer and plasterer. Wright started out in non-league football and was rejected by many football clubs, before he was spotted by a talent scout and got his first break – a contract with Crystal Palace. He then spent seven years at Arsenal before moving on to West Ham, Nottingham Forest, Celtic and Burnley, picking up England honours on the way.

During an outstanding footballing carer, Ian Wright achieved thirty-one caps for England, and has gone down in sporting history as Arsenal's leading goalscorer of all time, netting 184 times in 285 appearances between 1991 and 1998. This last achivement has more recently been overtaken by Thierry Henry.

When Ian Wright retired from football in 2000, he embarked upon a career in the media and entertainment industry. Even when assessed in their entirety by a non-footballing audience, Ian Wright's achievements in a ten-year media career have been truly astonishing. His second career has spanned documentaries, game shows, sport, reality TV and TV specials. Wright's entrée into the media and entertainment industry was initially as a presenter on *Friday Night's All Wright* (1998–2000). This was later followed by *Friends Like These* (2001) and *Guinness World Records* for LWT (1999), and three one-off Saturday specials. Ian Wright has also worked for BBC 2, acting as a team captain on *They Think It's All Over* (2004–06). In 2007 Wright was signed to the national radio station TalkSport. In the reality-travel show *Wright Across America*, he fulfilled his lifelong ambition, travelling coast-to-coast across America on a Harley-Davidson (2005).

Wright has worked for the BBC on sports programmes such as *Match of the Day* (2000–08) including World Cup specials (2006) providing expert analysis. Upon his resignation as BBC sports pundit for *Match Of The Day* Wright made news for criticising the programme for using him as a 'comedy jester'.

Recent years have seen Wright venture into reality TV with a social conscience – raising awareness and providing challenging strategies for the national chilhood obesity crisis with the programme *Unfit Kids* (2006). Wright is also patron of the African-Caribbean Leukaemia Trust. Today, Ian Wright continues to be a popular TV presenter, hosting *Gladiators* on Sky One with Kirsty Gallacher.

Ian Wright's footballing legacy is continued not only though the achievements of his own career, but also through his children, four of whom are making a name for themselves in football. Currently playing for Manchester City and England is his son Shaun Wright-Phillips, while Bradley Shaun Wright-Phillips plays for Southampton. The Wright footballing empire further extends to Blackpool's Jermaine Shaun Wright and Reading's Brett Wright, a reserve team player.

Originally taking up taekwondo as a means of relieving the stress of academic study, **Albert O. Williamson-Taylor** began to appreciate this sport as a means of psychological survival. Later, Taekwondo was to provide his first successful business model as a sport impresario and an entrepreneur. Albert O. Williamson-Taylor went on to become one of Britain's most senior Black civil engineers and in 1995 he co-founded the engineering practice of Adams Kara Taylor (see pp.90–92).

Williamson-Taylor's experiences at Bradford University reflect a time of great struggle. However good times and positive memories can also be gleaned. It was at Bradford that Williamson-Taylor discovered the martial arts, which were to have a profound impact upon his life for the next twenty years or more.

Like many 'freshers', upon enrolling at university, the young Albert was encouraged to sign-up to a host of extra-mural activities, which form the backbone of university life. When he put his name down for Taekwondo, Williamson-Taylor never realised what its true impact would be. He would eventually become an international sportsman, achieving a 5th Dan Black Belt.

Moreover, Taekwondo was to exert a new discipline on his life, and offer much-needed energy and fortification, necessary to deal with troubled times. Ultimately, Taekwondo was also to fuel his entrepreneurial spirit.

Albert went from member to president of Bradford University's Taekwondo Club, in the blink of an eye, winning the 'College Colours' three years in a row, and increasing club membership to 130, making it the biggest club at the university.

Albert made the bold decision to pursue martial arts in parallel to his professional career as an engineer: 'One provided confidence for the other, giving me the opportunity to think, to become calm and confident'. This successful combination was to result in Williamson-Taylor becoming both English and British Champion on two occasions, 1985–86, and 1991–92.

By 1986, Williamson-Taylor had returned to London, establishing London and Regional Taekwondo Martial Arts Clubs, and joining the prestigious engineering consultancy of Pryce & Myers. For two and a half years, he ran one of London's biggest development projects at the time: the Lotts Road Development, Chelsea.

Today, many of Albert Williamson-Taylor's original Taekwondo clubs continue to thrive. For example, the original North London Taekwondo (NLTKD), was formed by him in the 1980s, and still acknowledges Albert Williamson-Taylor, 5th Dan and original founder, in the introduction to its website. They comment: 'The original NLTKD has produced some of the best Taekwondo students particularly in the art of sparring in the country. This is no mystery as Mr Williamson-Taylor is a very proficient fighter in his own right and passionate about the sport'.

Lennox Claudius Lewis (on the right), considered by many as the greatest boxer of his generation, and one of Britain's most successful sportsmen, was born in West Ham, East London in 1965. He is the first Briton to hold a World Heavyweight Championship title since Bob Fitzsimmons 100 years previously. Yet, in 1988 when Lennox Lewis won the Olympic Super-heavyweight title, in Seoul, against Riddick Bowe, he was wearing the Canadian vest of his adopted home. When South London pub owner Frank Malone heard that he was a Londoner by birth, he set about the task of reclaiming this sportsman and chess player for Britain.

With an estimated fortune of £75m million, Lewis has been described as one of the richest sportsmen in Europe, a description he rejects, preferring to live a relatively modest lifestyle. One important charitable commitment has been The Lennox Lewis College in East London (a private secondary school for disadvantaged children of African-Caribbean origin).

Lewis won the WBC title in 1992, lost it in 1994, and won it back in 1997. He is pictured here with Ian Wright (on the left). In 1998 Lennox Lewis won a gold medal in the 1998 Olympics, and went on to become the WBC World boxing champion, defending his title three times and defeating Frank Bruno en route.

His achievements were recognised by the world of sport, when in 1999 Lennox Lewis won the BBC Sports Personality of the Year Award, and the acknowledgement of the nation, with the award of an MBE (1999). In June 2002, in what was was one of the most hotly anticipated heavyweight fights in years, Lewis beat 'Iron' Mike Tyson in a fight which consolidated Lewis' title as the best heavyweight boxer in the world.

The Lewis-Tyson fight at that time was the highest-grossing event in pay-per-view history, generating $106.9 million from 1.95 million buys in the USA alone. The fight yielded a crowd of 15,327, even though tickets were priced as highly as $2,400 at the Memphis venue. In 2002 Lewis' achievement was recognised by two nations, who were proud to call him citizen: Canada, his county of adoption and Britain, his country of birth, awarding him the CM, The Order of Canada, the highest civilian honor, and CBE (Commander of the British Empire), respectively.

Together with Muhammad Ali and Evander Holyfield, Lewis is one of three boxers in history to have won the heavyweight title on three separate occasions: WBC World Heavyweight Champion, 1992–94; WBC World Heavyweight Champion, 1997–2001; and WBC World Heavyweight Champion, 2001–04.

After taking a year's sabbatical, Lewis returned to the boxing ring for the last time to fight Vitali Klictshko, in 2003, beating him in the sixth round. During his career he scored more headlines than any other British boxer of his time, before retiring on 6 February 2004.

Lewis and his partner Violet Chang's (a New Yorker of Jamaican origin) son Landon was born in 2004. They were married in 2005. Now looking towards a career in film, Lewis spends his time taking acting classes and looking after his son. In 2001 Lewis appeared in a brief scene in *Ocean's Eleven*, and in 2005 he appeared in the film *Johnny Was*, with a more substantial role, playing the owner of a pirate radio station.

CHAPTER TWO

MILITARY

In 1775, Virginia's Royal Governor, Lord Dunmore, promised to 'arm my own negroes and receive all others that shall come to me who I shall call free'. This was the promise which encouraged thousands of Black loyalists, who consisted of both those who had been enslaved and freemen, to join the British side in the American War of Independence. When the British retreated, they evacuated 14,000 Black soldiers from Savannah, Charleston and New York, many of whom came to England, swelling the Black population of London. While some were able to continue their trades, for example as cookshop owners and shoemakers, the vast majority joined the London poor as beggars and street musicians, being deprived even of army back pay and compensation for war injuries, and denied work due to prejudice.

The Navy had also been a regular employer of Black Londoners and their relatives, many of whom settled in parts of the capital with naval or military connections. Since the fifteenth century, London ships had set sail for Africa for the purposes of trade, a policy officially sanctioned by the creation of Royal Charter companies, such as the Royal Africa Company (1670). Later the British slave trade and West African commodities funded the building of a modern Navy, and the emergence of British naval might. The Navy ensured the passage of African peoples and cargo, and the Army facilitated conquest of their territory and the maintenance of imperial control.

English regiments regularly served in the West Indies from the seventeenth century onwards, often returning to London with West Indian soldiers, servants, slaves and musicians. With the abolition of the slave trade in 1807, London became the home of thousands of Black people. By this time it had long-established direct links with ports throughout Africa and the West Indies.

This relationship between the major port of London and Africa and the West Indies was to continue with the trade in commodities, which replaced the slave trade. Thus it was that many descendants of the enslaved Africans who peopled the factory islands of West Indies, and descendants of free Africans involved in trade, diplomacy and study, docked in London's ports as soldiers, sailors and adventurers. By the time of the First and Second World Wars, the link between metropolitan London and the Empire ensured the free flow of human capital from the Empire to London.

During the Second World War women were to serve in a broader capacity than in previous generations, as military nurses and doctors, in the ATS, the WAAF and the Red Cross, and to work in munitions factories. Colonel Christine Moody had the distinction of becoming one of the first Black women officers in the British Army in 1940, going on to become a pioneer in the early years of the United Nations World Health Organization, on regional health projects in West Africa and the Caribbean.

Many African and Caribbean men and women came to London on active service in the Army, Navy and Air Force. Many met and married Black Londoners from families that had settled under previous waves of immigration. And many who came to London in the postwar wave of immigration had previously come to London as servicemen and women and war-workers.

Despite the historical links of Black Londoners to the armed services, the experience of people like Richard Sykes, Britain's first Black Guardsman, demonstrates that little has changed in their discriminatory treatment. Despite a well-publicized arrival, his military career was ended by a campaign of racial harassment.

Donald Adolphus Brown, sailor. Brown was born in 1874 at Woolwich to an English woman and a Jamaican petty officer in the Royal Navy. He was one of the many Black children educated at the Royal Hospital School in the nineteenth century; he then served as a sailor in the Merchant Navy, before becoming foreman at Woolwich Arsenal. He was awarded the Edward Medal for bravery in 1921 after he put out a fire in an explosives store at great risk to his life. Brown married the noted Suffragette Eliza Adelaide Knight. He died in 1949.

West India Regiment, *c.* 1919. Rules on alien enlistment are revealing about the perception of Black people as falling into a unique category, neither alien nor British. Black people were quite simply regarded as an 'exception'. While the proportion of aliens within a regiment was not supposed to exceed one in fifty, this rule was not applied in relation to Black men and women. Without this exception, the British Army in Africa and the Caribbean could not have maintained the Empire.

This photograph shows the British West India Regiment. Many of these men were later to become disillusioned with London, where they stopped on the way home, by a spate of anti-Black riots which took place in the capital. The rioting was in response to the increased Black presence due to military demobilization of African and West Indian troops after the war. Black troops were also denied participation in the victory celebrations, referred to as the Peace March, on 19 July 1919. Riots took place in Stepney, Limehouse and West India Dock Road with assaults on Black Londoners and soldiers and damage to their property.

The history of colonial troops in British Army began long before the beginning of the Second World War. The coronation of Edward VII in 1902 provided a unique opportunity for a show of imperial military strength. In June, therefore, Alexandra Palace was turned into a barracks and the grounds into a tented camp for 2,500 colonial troops. Because the coronation was delayed due to Edward's illness, the troops stayed for the entire summer. The trustees of the palace capitalized on the camp as a tourist attraction by organizing a review by the Duke of Connaught and by inviting the troops to attend the London Coronation Cup race meeting in July. On August Bank Holiday over 100,000 Londoners flocked to Alexandra Palace to view the spectacle of troops from every colonial regiment from the West Indies to the Sudan. The aim was to demonstrate living proof of the reach of Empire. The late Dr Bernie Grant, the Black MP for Tottenham, eventually became a trustee of Alexandra Palace.

Constance Goodridge-Mark (*left*) on her way to work, Jamaica, 1944 and (*right*) in the 1980s. Born Constance McDonald in Kingston, Jamaica in 1923, she joined the British Army in 1943, serving in the ATS, the Women's Royal Army Corps and Queen Alexandra's Royal Army Nursing Corps before becoming senior medical secretary in the Royal Army Medical Corps for ten years, working in the North Caribbean. When Marks joined the West Indian Ex-Servicemen's Association, she was instrumental in extending its name to the West Indian Ex-Servicemen & Women's Association, to commemorate the contributions of West Indian women who served in the armed services. Constance Goodridge-Mark regularly marched in the annual Remembrance Day parade at the Cenotaph, while she she retained her mobility.

Connie Mark had joined her husband, a professional cricketer, in Shepherds Bush (London), from Jamaica in 1954, and became medical secretary to some of London's most distinguished specialists, including Sir John Peel, the Queen's gynaecologist. Goodridge-Mark became project officer for the British Council for Aid to Refugees in the 1980s, being responsible for the settlement of the Vietnam 'Boat People' in Britain.

Connie Mark also played a leading role in several national and local organizations, such as the Commission for Racial Equality, and founded several organizations of her own, including the Friends of Mary Seacole Memorial Association (1986). She was awarded the British Empire Medal for services to the community in 1992 and was awarded an MBE on the Queen's honours list in 2001. Shortly after her death in June 2007, Mark received the posthumous honour of a commemorative blue plaque at Mary Seacole House in Hammersmith where she had been a resident, installed by the Nubian Jak Community Trust, in association with Care UK and the London Borough of Hammersmith & Fulham.

Connie Mark had became well known as a popular face on British television and voice on local radio. Appearances on BBC TV's *Video Nation* reached an audience of millions, with her pithy and humourous historical corrective film shorts. Delivered with clear Jamaican vowels and an emphatic manner and charm, Marks, like an impatient headmistress, told a Great British public that it was either ill-informed or misinformed about Mary Seacole; the Caribbean and its Second World War contributions; the arrival of mass imigration from Africa and the Caribbean in post-war Britain; the British in the Caribbean and Caribbean culture in general. The *Video Nation* project (1993–2001) originally created by the BBC's Community Programme Unit, had invited fifty people throughout the UK to record different aspects of their lives over a year. Connie Mark, as a contributor, had been given camcorder training and some editorial rights over material which she recorded for this broadcast project. At its height, *Video Nation* film shorts were shown prominently, before *Newsnight* on BBC2. Connie Mark's *Video Nation* shorts now form an important part of this national video archive, appearing on special occasions, and may be said to have anticipated and influenced the trend in blogging.

King George VI and Queen Elizabeth, with Flight Lieutenant De Souza from Jamaica and the Princesses Elizabeth and Margaret, inspecting a parade of **West Indians on VE Day**, May 1945.

Colonel Charles Arundel Moody. Born in Peckham in 1917, Moody became the first Black officer to join the British Army in the Second World War when he joined the Queen's Own Royal West Kent Regiment in 1940. His father, Dr Harold Moody (see p.65), who was President of the League of Coloured Peoples, had protested to the Colonial Secretary about the 'colour bar' (accepted discriminatory practice) in the armed services; as a result the government relaxed the rules regarding voluntary enlistment and emergency commissions. Charles Moody served in the infantry and the artillery in England and Africa, then in Italy and finally in Egypt, where he became a Major in 1945. At the end of the war he returned to Jamaica with B Company of the Caribbean Regiment, settling there for the next forty years. Moody became a Colonel in 1961, and was awarded an OBE in 1966 as the first commanding officer of the Jamaican Territorial Army.

Left: **Group Captain Osborne, OBE**. Osborne was a Coastal Command navigator before becoming a member of the Anglo-German Technical Commission, engaged in the training and re-supply of the German Air Force. He was also responsible for introducing the RAF's computerized supply system into the main depots. In 1969 he was awarded an OBE for his work in maintenance command.

Below: During the Second World War Black servicemen and women were often distributed throughout the country, on different bases and in different branches of the armed services, which led to the isolation of servicemen when they retired. To rectify this situation, Allan Kelly, Hector Watson and Arnaud Horner founded the **West Indian Ex-Servicemen's (and Women's) Association** in 1971, which provided a single venue for Black people who had served in the forces to socialize and share experiences and later to educate the community at large on the historical role of West Indian servicemen and women. This is the earliest available photograph of the founders of the association taken in 1971. Left to right: Anthony Goddard, Michael Armand, Mr Adam, Allan Kelly, Mr Clarke, Neil Flanigan.

Above: Officers and members of the **West Indian Ex-Servicemen's (and Women's) Association** in their Clapham premises. Front, left to right: R. Webb, N. Flanigan, S. King (Mayor of Southwark), Hector Watson, L. Phillpotts. Back, left to right: V. Hunte, Mr Bravo, A. Armstrong, Mr Aiken. One of the more recent highlights of the organization's history was when the Governor-General of Jamaica and the President of Trinidad and Tobago, together with distinguished politicians and high commissioners from all over the Caribbean, joined the association in commemorating the fiftieth anniversary of VJ Day.

Left: **Allan Kelly**. Born in 1918, Kelly joined the RAF in Jamaica and came to Britain in 1944.

After the war **Allan Kelly** became a civil servant, retiring in 1984 after forty years' continuous government service. He is pictured on the left of the photograph above, which was taken in 1997 at the passing out parade for Jamaican servicemen at Sandhurst, with His Excellency Mr Haven, Jamaican High Commissioner to London, and Mr Watson, co-founder of the West Indian Ex-Servicemen's (and Women's) Association. A tireless community activist, he was a leading patron and founder-member of a host of organizations, including the West Indian Ex-Servicemen's (and Women's) Association and Paddington Churches Housing Association, one of the largest housing associations in London. He was Ward Secretary and Ward Vice-Chairman of the Conservative Party and served on various other committees, including the Notting Hill Carnival Police Committee and the Central London branch of the Royal Air Force Association. He has the distinction of having a block of flats in Westbourne Park named after him. Allan Kelly died in 1998 and his funeral service is pictured below.

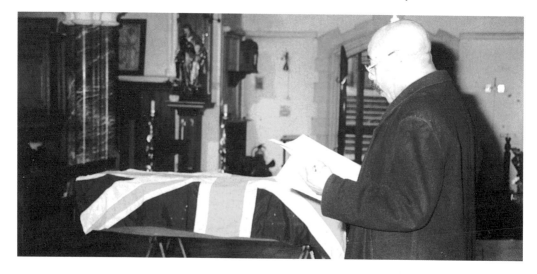

Hector Watson with his wife Edithna, 1970s. Born in 1924 in St Catherine, Jamaica, Watson joined the RAF in Jamaica in 1943 and was sent to Britain in the same year. As well as serving in Bomber Command, he became part of the secret convoy of lorry drivers who drove radar equipment to and from factories concealed in the Welsh mountains. In 1960 he established Flywheel and Co., Lambeth Hill, one of the first Black-owned haulage transport companies in Britain. Flywheel and Co. brought coal from the Midlands to powerhouses in London on 5 ton lorries, using techniques later incorporated into all haulage transport design. Watson's technical expertise was later sought by the Transport Section of the Home Office, where he oversaw the roadworthiness of diplomatic cars for UK and overseas service. Watson was a founder member of the West Indian Ex-Servicemen's (and Women's) Association and President of the Royal British Legion, Brixton and Stockwell. He received an award for services to the community from the Jamaican High Commission.

Neil Flanigan in RAF uniform. Born in Jamaica in 1924, Flanigan joined the RAF during the Second World War and came to Britain in 1944. After the war he worked for many years as an engineer for major British airlines, but in 1985 he retrained as an accountant. He has been involved in many community committees and projects, including serving for eleven years on the Police Consultative Committee, Lambeth. He has also been an active member and officer of the West Indian Ex-Servicemen's (and Women's) Association. In 1993 Flanigan became an Independent Person under the Children's Act for the County of Hampshire, and two years later was made a member of the Independent Persons Committee for Lambeth; in the 1990s he has also sat on a host of committees for the High Commission of Jamaica.

Laurie Phillpotts has been information officer and archivist to the West Indian Ex-Servicemen and Women's Association (W.I.S.A.). In this capacity, he has developed the educational resources for W.I.S.A. that relate to the West Indian and African contribution to war and peacetime.

Laurie Phillpotts has contributed to many exhibitions, including 'Living Memory' (1987), which was shown at the Gunnersbury Park Museum and County Hall.

After serving as a British soldier in the Second World War, Phillpotts returned home to Jamaica for a brief while, only to return to London in 1959. Having married a White English bride during the war, the couple were to face many challenges in a 'mixed marriage' lasting nearly seventy years.

In the documentary, *Jazz Empire* (2005, History ONIKS Educational Resources) Phillpotts recalls the war as a frightening but exciting time as a young man. He remembers that many West Indian soldiers outrageously customised their uniforms, with extra pleats and non-standard detailing. Phillpotts humorously recalls that often curious locals would ask, quite seriously, 'So what army do you belong to?' A printer by trade, Phillpotts was to enter a highly unionised and anti-immigrant Fleet Street, working on national newspapers.

As a community activist, Laurie Phillpotts, was a committed 'committee man', through his civic involvement, supporting newly arrived communities from the West Indies after the war. Phillpotts recalls with sadness how he saw an overnight transformation. West Indians, such as himself, who had been welcomed by the British in pubs and clubs during the war were to be excluded from the same venues after the war. In response Black Londoners formed their own clubs, making the post-war period a heyday for the growth in Black entertainment and club ownership, and the pre-eminence of artists such as Nadia Cattouse (see p.26), who were to become celebrities. Today, Laurie Phillpotts laments the demise of African and Caribbean-owned clubs at the heart of London's West End, which, at one time, attracted celebrities from all over the world.

Richard Sykes, Britain's first Black guardsman, at his passing out parade, Pirbright, Surrey, 1987. In 1997 a campaign was launched by the Ministry of Defence to recruit Black Londoners to the armed services. Despite the historical links of Black Londoners to the armed services, the experience of people like Richard Sykes, who left the service due to racial harassment, demonstrate that little has changed in discriminatory treatment of Black people in the military. Modern Black Londoners are less prepared to tolerate racial harassment, wherever they may be employed.

By the year 1943, **Nadia Cattouse** had already embarked upon a career as a teacher, when it was announced on the radio that women would be able to join the British Women's Army or the ATS (the Auxiliary Territorial Service). Cattouse became a member of the first group of six West Indian women to join the ATS, arriving in Britain in 1943.

Cattouse arrived in the North of Scotland for her army basic training, on the *Queen Mary*, which she had boarded in New York. Cattouse eventually proved to be such a good soldier that she was invited to stay on as a part-time drill instructor after the war, which she agreed to for a time. During the Second World War Cattouse joined the Signal Corps in the ATS. This was vital top-secret work, involving Morse code, radio transmissions, telephone and telegraphy.

Apart from spending some of her leave in London, Cattouse spent some of her leave from the army in Glasgow, with a Trinidadian doctor and his family. After the war, Cattouse was to return to lodge with them, spending a year at Glasgow University, with the intention of returning to teaching. Glasgow University had a very active International Students Club, and it was here that Nadia Cattouse first met Paul Robeson, actor and activist, in 1946.

CHAPTER THREE

HEALTH, WELFARE
AND SCIENCE

The National Health Service has been one of the largest employers of Black people in the twentieth century, and as a consequence is a major repository of the history of Black Londoners. However, few are aware of the pivotal contributions in its earliest phases of evolution made by health workers and care-givers such as Dr George Rice, Dr Harold Moody and Colonel Christine Moody.

Dr Rice took the pioneering work of Joseph Lister, 'the father of antiseptic', out of the operating theatre and turned it into a matter of general public health, in hospitals and schools in South London and the surrounding districts.

During his lifetime, Dr Harold Moody did much to change the employment patterns of Black women within the National Health Service by challenging the 'colour bar' to their employment as nurses in British hospitals in the 1940s. Also, as a father he supported the education of his daughters in the fields of education and medicine, inspiring his daughter Christine to follow in his footsteps and beyond. Dr Harold Moody's experiences of hardship and racial discrimination within the medical profession and society at large led him to found the League of Coloured Peoples in 1931, a powerful national political pressure group, representing the interests of Black people. When asked what he died from, family friend Dr Alex Buxton-Thomas, who performed the autopsy, said 'overwork'.

Christine Moody went on to make history in her own right. As a trailblazer in the early days of the World Health Organization, she led many of the earliest development and health programmes in Africa, the West Indies, the Far East and South America. Not bad going for a Peckham GP!

Modern techniques in primary care and specialist treatments now make it possible for people to survive who would not have done so decades ago. These changes are not dependent upon a single invention or revelation, but on many techniques developed over time by healthcare workers, sharing knowledge and observations which then become common practice. Black Londoners have been ever-present where such advances have been made, and directly and indirectly may lay claim to many innovations in medicine, nursing and public health.

Dr George Rice, who extended antiseptic research to South London hospitals and schools.

Above: **Dr Rice** was born in 1848, the son of freed slaves. He settled in Plumstead, South London, after studying medicine under Dr Lister at Edinburgh Royal Infirmary; Lister was famous for his work in antiseptic treatment in surgery. Rice was appointed superintendent of Woolwich Union Infirmary in 1877, and in 1884 he was selected out of eighty-four candidates as resident medical officer of the Sutton District Schools. From 1886 to 1917 Rice did some trailblazing research into epilepsy at Belmont Workhouse. In the group photograph of Belmont staff, Dr Rice is seated second from the right, second row. He died in 1935.

Right: **Surgeon Major J.B. Africanus Horton MD** (Edinburgh), an eminent nineteenth-century Igbo (of Nigerian origin) physician, political scientist and banker in British Army Uniform.

Mary Seacole distinguished herself heroically treating soldiers on the battlefields during the Crimean War (1854–56), and for treating cholera epidemics in Jamaica and Panama.

Seacole, a doctoress and nurse, often administered to soldiers' wounds, 'where they fell'. She even carried many away for treatment on her back or shoulders. And in an era where there was no NHS and medical treatment had to be paid for, she treated the poor for free. To many soldiers, from 'the labouring classes', who would never attend a military hospial, Seacole's was often the only treatment available to them. A British patriot, Seacole did not discriminate and nursed wounded soldiers from both sides, while under fire. Despite not being formally trained in medicine, she received informal training from medical visitors to her mother's guest house. Seacole also derived experience from her mother's training as a doctoress and used her knowledge of African traditional medicine in her work.

Seacole's heroism was much celebrated in her lifetime, alongside that of Florence Nightingale. How they differed was that Seacole's name was spoken of with affection amongst the ordinary soldiers, whom she treated as well as officers and the military elite, whom she had also nursed and befriended. Seacole had saved the lives of some of the same British soldiers twice: in Jamaica from the cholera epidemic of 1850 and then from their war wounds in the Crimea. In the 1850 cholera epidemic 32,000 Jamaicans died, with another epidemic returning in 1853. Owner of her own military convalescence hotel, Blundell Hall, Seacole's services had been requested by the Jamaican medical authorities during both epidemics. She treated local victims and organised a nursing service for the hospital at Up-Park Camp, a British Army hospital just outside Kingston, Jamaica.

When Mary Seacole heard that some of her friends from the British regiments, formally garrisoned in Jamaica, were among those suffering in the Crimea due to lack of medical provision, her conscience drove her to immediately offer her assitance. Seacole had first asked the War Office to allow her to be sent as a volunteer to the Crimea via official channels, and had been turned down through a mixture of racism and sexism.

When nurses were eventually to be dispatched to the war under Florence Nightingale, Seacole was to be refused for a second time. Undeterred by what she percieved to be nonsense, after originally travelling from Panama to London she borrowed money to make the 4,000-mile (6,437km) journey to the Crimea by herself. She went to the Crimea as a Sutler, or civilian merchant who sold goods to army camps. She built a metallic and wooden building for £800, from which she sold food and medicine and everything from 'a needle to an anchor'. She optimistically called the small Crimean base in which she lived and worked 'Spring Hill', and set about her work selling provisions and take-away cooked foodstuffs and treating battlefield wounded, soldiers who had been previously dying of medical neglect and poor nutrition.

Affectionately known to the military as 'Ma Seacole', many letters from grateful mothers in England thanked Mrs Mary Seacole for being with their sons in their dying moments. Mothers stated that they were able to gain comfort from knowing that at least their young sons died, 'In the caring arms of a woman whom they looked upon as a mother'.

This daughter of a free Jamaican doctoress and hotelier and a Scottish military officer held a respected position within Jamaican and later British society. Born Mary Grant in 1805, in 1836 she had married Edwin Horatio Hamilton Seacole in Kingston, the godson (or some have suggested, illegitimate son, of Lord Nelson, 1st Viscount Nelson, and Emma, Lady Hamilton). However, with the passing of the generation who experienced the Crimean War, and her own death, Seacole's memory became hidden for almost a century, while Florence Nightingale's became enshrined as a national and international symbol of nursing compassion. Seacole's autobiography had been a bestseller in its day. *The Wonderful Adventures of Mrs. Seacole in Many Lands* (1857), was a vivid account of her experiences.

In addition to her roles of doctoress and nurse, scientist and pharmacist may be added to Seacole's achievements. Seacole had a demonstrable understanding of what we now know as the contagion theory, and was capable of conducting autopsies to increase her knowledge of death caused by cholera. Thus, Seacole may arguably be seen as a scientist in the nineteenth-century tradition. She had arrived at scientific conclusions to killer diseases through her own experimentation. Seacole's main advantage over her fellow nineteenth-century scientists was that she had been able to test her remedies and scientific theories en masse, quite literally in the field.

Seacole was known to make and dispense her own medicines, which were much sought after. These medicines have often been denegrated or underplayed, under the definition of 'remedies'. At a time when it was quite common and even expected for one to die from jaundice, diarrhoea, dysentery and inflamation of the chest, the evidence of patient testimonials showed that Seacole's medicines worked. Furthermore, those who had been former patients frequently asked for supplies of these medicines to be made up for them to take to their commissions in other theatres of war or imperial missions.

Seacole's efforts in the Crimea were to leave her bankrupt. However, it is the extrordinary story of her rescue from bankruptcy and return to financial solvency which testifies to the great esteem in which she was held by the British military. Efforts to help Mrs Secole, who had aided the soldiers, included the establishment of several relief funds and a 'Seacole Fund Grand Military Festival' in 1857 which was held at the Royal Surrey Gardens, and attracted an audience of 40,000 people. Over 1,000 artists performed at the festival, including eleven military bands and an orchestra.

Seacole was eventually able to return to Jamaica to re-establish her hotel, but later came back to England, possibly to offer her serices to yet another military campaign. Seacole became friends with members of the royal family, including Count Gleichen and Prince Victor Hohenlohe-Langenburg, both nephews of Queen Victoria. She also became masseuse to the Princess of Wales, who suffered with 'white leg' and rheumatism.

Seacole died in London in 1881, and was buried at St Mary's Roman Catholic Cemetary, Harrow Road, Kensal Green. In 1991 she was posthumously awarded the Jamaican Order of Merit. The British Commonwealth Nurses' War Memorial Fund and the Lignum Vitae Club have re-consecrated and restored her grave, and in 1981 the centenary of her death was celebrated with a memorial service. Additionally, 2005 saw the 200th anniversary of Seacole's birth and a year of community-based and NHS commemorative celebrations of her achievements.

Mary Seacole has featured on British stamps (2005), and part of the Home Office's new headquarters in Marsham Street is named in her honour; further, a Green Plaque and Blue Plaque have been erected on two of Seacole's London residences, 147 George Street in Westminster and 14 Soho Square.

Today, Mary Seacole appears in the National Curriculum and she has hospital wards and buildings in British and Jamaican universities, as well as research and training institutes named after her, these include the headquarters of the Jamaican General Trained Nurses' Association, the University of The West Indies, Mona, Jamaica, Leicester's De Montford University, Birminham City University, Thames Valley University, St George's, University of London, and the Mary Secole Research Centre and Specialist Library for Ethnicity and Health.

Dr Harold Moody, doctor, Congregationalist minister, community leader and civil rights activist. Born in 1882, the son of a druggist, Moody came to England in 1904 to study medicine at King's College, London. He qualified in 1910, having won several academic awards. Denied the post of medical officer to the Camberwell Board of Guardians because of open racism, he went on to run surgeries in South London at Queen's Road, Peckham, King's Grove, Pepys Hill and New Cross Gate. Moody's early experiences of hardship and racial discrimination led him to found, with Stella Thomas and others, the League of Coloured Peoples in 1931. Moody was responsible for enabling the first Black nurse to train in Britain and the first Black officer to join the British Army in the Second World War. He died in 1947.

Colonel Christine Moody, a pioneer in the early years of the United Nations World Health Organization (WHO). She was born in South London in 1914, the daughter of the Black community leader Harold Moody (see p.63). After qualifying as member of the Royal College of Surgeons in 1938 she joined her father's practices in South London.

Christine Moody became an officer in the Royal Army Medical Corps early in the Second World War, shortly after her brother Charles had become the first Black officer to sign up to the British Army in the Second World War (see p.53). In 1944 she was put in charge of the British Military Hospital in Ambala, Punjab, and after the war she spent ten years in Ghana as senior medical officer with the Ministry of Health, developing maternity, paediatric and public health projects throughout the country. She went on to act as consultant in development and primary care to the World Health Organisation and the World Bank, as health adviser to the Philippines and as Chief Medical Officer for Public Health in Jamaica. She was made Commander of the Order of Distinction, Jamaica, in 1988.

Mrs Kura Anne Mary King-Okokon, midwife and public health nurse, came to London in November 1958. 'I had already had a successful career in Barbados as a Staff Nurse and Night Sister, and was waiting to train as a Midwife. I came to England because I had achieved all that I could in Barbados. I came with the intention of furthering my nursing career.' Arriving at Paddington Station from the SS *Antilles* boat-train at Southampton, King-Okokon first lived in Stoke Newington, later completing her midwifery and public health qualifications at East Birmingham Hospital, Little Bromwich, and the Maternity Hospital, Loveday Street. It was in Birmingham that Kura King-Okokon subsequently met the late C.O.I. Okokon, a Nigerian doctor, whom she was later to marry, and who became a consultant at the West Middlesex Hospital. They raised three daughters – a scientist, a teacher and a social policy researcher.

The daughter of one of Barbados' early prominent Black merchants C.C. King and Iris Vestina King, herself a nurse and daughter of missionaries, Kura King-Okokon attended one of the leading girls' public schools in the Caribbean, Queen's College, Barbados. This school had for years been the exclusive preserve of White European upper- and middle-class expatriates, to the exclusion of the Black Barbadian majority. Queen's College school was established in the 1683 through the bequest of Colonel Henry Drax. 'mandat[ed]... to produce an education for girls similar to that in the top educational institutions in Great Britain'. Her successful school experience served to heighten Kura King-Okokon's sense of Black pride, and a belief that she could compete with anyone and upon any terms, internationally.

This attitude was to strengthen her character in the face of the ignorant racism which she was to later to encounter within the National Health Service and the wider British society of the 1950s. A bright woman, Kura King-Okokon had been encouraged to study medicine by her godfather, Sir Hugh Gordon Cummings, one of Barbados' most famous Black doctors. Gordon Cummings (later to become Barbados' Minister of Health), was astounded by Kura King-Okokon's exceptional powers of mental recall upon overseeing part of her training at the Barbados General Hospital (Queen Elisabeth Hospital), Bridgetown Barbados. In a Britain still in the grip of its negative assumptions of Black achievement, this over-confident nurse was to unsettle and disturb many a professional 'superior' on the road towards her nursing and health visitor qualifications in London and Birmingham.

In the late 1960s Kura King-Okokon emigrated to Nigeria. She was soon however to find herself caught up in the Nigeria-Biafra Civil War. This war, which was to last from 6 July 1967–13 January 1970 and arose from the attempted secession of Nigeria's south-eastern provinces to form the Republic of Biafra; the death toll was eventually to reach approximately 1,200,000. To many of her peers, Kura King-Okokon became a Barbadian legend in her heroic bid to escape from war-torn Nigeria with two babies and two young children, eventually returning to London as a refugee 'with the clothes on my back'. This traumatic experience was to transform her life, with her home becoming a refuge to many families fleeing domestic violence, abuse and personal crises over the years. As a nurse, Kura King-Okokon also had to contend with the challenges of raising a family of severe asthmatics and extreme eczema sufferers.

Although briefly coming back to his London home, Dr Okokon was to return to Nigeria to help in the reconstruction of medical services of his war-torn homeland, eventually building a hospital. Kura Okokon made ends meet in London by returning to private geriatric nursing through church welfare organizations, and working as a sales representative for products such a Tupperware, Pippa D, Holiday Magic, AMI, East Lane Fabrics and Avon.

Mrs King-Okokon continues to be an active member of community and voluntary sector organisations, and has worked as a Phlebotomist at Northwick Park Hospital (at that time, one of the leading research hospitals in London). She left Northwick Park and became co-founder and the first female coordinator of the W.I.S.E. (West Indian Self-Effort) Project. The Black community and voluntary sector organisation has done much to redefine statutory provision in education, health and senior citizens' care, often addressing unmet needs, and mediating between care agencies and the Black community. Without the Black community and voluntary sector, statutory health and welfare providers in Britain would be less effective and sensitive to the needs of our diverse communities.

An example is the WISE Project's Supplementary School which emerged in response to Black parents who demanded action when the education

system was failing their children. Before its Luncheon Club, there was little recognition of the dietary needs of African-Caribbean senior citizens in Brent, one of London's most diverse boroughs. Mrs King-Okokon has also served on the Education Committee Advisory Group to the Barbados High Commission, London, since 1996, establishing it in its formative years and acting as a key recruiter. This role has been keenly acknowledged by outgoing High Commissioner Herbert Yearwood and former Prime Minister Rt Hon. Tony Blair.

The vital role of female community networkers in supporting cohesive communities is one which needs greater social recognition. Kura King-Okokon has contributed to community cultural life, ensuring the successful attendance of thousands at African Caribbean fundraising events, dinner-dances, exhibitions, shows, concerts, memorial services and lectures, as a key contact point for the distribution of information and tickets. An Executive Committee and Choir Member of B.O.N.A. (Barbados Overseas Nurses Association) and the Choir of Virgo Fidelis Church, Upper Norwood, Kura King-Okokon continues to contribute to the community and to sing God's praises and is in the process of completing her autobiography. Mrs King-Okokon has served on the Education Committee Advisory Group to the Barbados High Commission, London, since 1996.

Adelaide Tambo was the London NHS nursing sister who became the recipient of the Nobel Foundation Life Award for initiating the anti-apartheid movement in Britain. It was Adelaide Tambo who led the anti-apartheid movement in London and was at the forefront of demonstrations calling for Nelson Mandela to be freed.

Born Matlala Adelaide Frances Tsukudu, 18 July 1929, 'Ma Tambo' was the wife of the late Oliver Tambo, president of the African National Congress in exile (they married in 1956). Adelaide Tambo is however seen as a hero of the liberation struggle against Apartheid in her own right. She joined the ANC Youth League as a courier at fifteen, and by the age of eighteen was its chairwoman. Adelaide was one of the 20,000 women who marched on Pretoria's Union Buildings in protest against the Pass Laws in 1956. Later, in 1994 Adelaide Tambo became one of the first democratically elected members of the South African parliament, serving as an MP from 1994–99.

It was at 51 Alexandra Park in Muswell Hill, North London that Adelaide Tambo spent most of her thirty years in exile from South Africa. London was to become her home and the base for a permanent ANC office. Following the Sharpville Massacres (1960), in which mostly children protesting against the Pass Laws were gunned down, the ANC became a banned organisation and the Tambos were ordered to leave South Africa by the ANC's leadership. Their mission – to establish what effectively became a South African Government in exile. While Adelaide Tambo established the ANC's London Office, Oliver Tambo travelled the world. Both Tambos sought to inform the world about what was happening to Black people in South Africa and to put pressure on the White South African Government for democratic reform. (See p.179)

Dr Elizabeth Okokon is a State Registered Principal Clinical Scientist, specialising in Paediatric and Metabolic Biochemistry at King's College Hospital, London. Dr Okokon has an honours degree in Biochemistry (with medical options), an MSc in Cancer Sciences (Oncology) from University College, London, and a PhD on the steroid metabolism, genetics and the metabolic syndrome in children ('The steroidal causes of premature adrenarche in girls' or the onset of early periods).

As Paediatric Liaison, Dr Elizabeth Okokon assists paediatric clinical specialists (hepatologists, neurologists, metabolic endocrinologists, neonatologists and cystic fibrosis specialists) in the diagnostic investigation and management of children with rare metabolic disorders, as part of a multi-disciplinary team. Her other responsibilities include the management of a sweat-testing service for the Regional Cystic Fibrosis Specialist Centre.

Born in Britain in 1964, to a Nigerian father and a Barbadian mother, Okokon feels that she can truly define herself as African-Caribbean. She has lived in London since the age of three, attending school in Harrow. The racism and sexism she experienced nearly prevented her from pursuing her chosen career; as a result she is a member of Southwark Council's Black Mentor Scheme, where Black professionals provide guidance to teenagers, encouraging them to fulfill their educational potential.

Dr Okokon's commitment to mentoring is evident from her professional responsibilities: 'Training is one of my key roles and one I feel passionately about, as we can not only help staff reach their full potential but also ensure maintenance and improvements of laboratory standards'. Dr Okokon also plays an active role in the training of laboratory staff towards NVQ, state registration and MSc, assisting in their case presentations and portfolio preparation and frequently giving seminars within her department and at paediatric meetings.

Dr Okokon is one of an army of key professionals responsible for developing the next generation of doctors. Three times a year she trains the new intake of junior medical doctors and specialist registrars in laboratory procedures, investigative work-ups and pre-analytical sample preparation – the essential tools required for good paediatric liaison.

Elizabeth Okokon sat her MSc Part 1 exam a week before giving birth to her son, Kwame, and had a daughter Ama, in time for her graduation ceremony, while managing a laboratory at the same time. From 1989 to 1995 Elizabeth Okokon ran the Diagnostic Research Unit in the Academic Department of Obstetrics and Gynaecology, King's College, where she published research on infertility, the menopause and hormone replacement therapy.

A practical woman, not complacent about existing systems, Dr Okokon has introduced and managed new specialist tests to improve the speed of patient management and has evaluated new procedural methods. She also prepares training and standard operating procedures, costings and submits interpretive comments.

Membership of professional organisations presents important opportunities to communicate with other lab-bound colleagues nationally and internationally, and enables the sharing of important pieces of the research jigsaw. To this end, Dr Okokon is a member of the Association of Clinical Biochemistry, which recently nominated her for the Siemens Award at the Focus Conference (2008). Dr Okokon is also a member of the Society for Endocrinology and the British Inherited Metabolic Disease Group, attending South East Metabolic Group (re: commissioning of metabolic services).

A 'perpetual student', for Dr Okokon the quest for knowledge is never-ending. This quest is always practical and is seen as a natural part of her life. She is currently studying towards her FRCPath (Fellowship of the Royal College of Pathologists). 'Following my PhD, I have two papers under submission and have initiated further research projects that could be MSc projects'.

This Principal Clinical Scientist is keen to infect young people with her quest for knowledge, as a school governor and with regular visits to schools in London to encourage healthy living and to promote the study of science. Following a recent school science fair Dr Okokon has became a health ambassador, currently helping to organise National Pathology Week.

A matriarch with a deep love of community, Dr Okokon has also been a life-long fan of the institution of Carnival, and the responsibilities which being part of an all-year-round mass band engenders in the young. She has served on the Committee of South Connection Carnival Group, and plays mass with her family as a costumed masquerader (See p.186, bottom right).

November 2006 saw the publication of a textbook of *Postpartum Haemorrhage*, edited by **Dr Christopher Balugun-Lynch**, who was also a major contributor. The book's foreword was by HRH Princess Anne, who also helped to launch the publication at the Royal Society of Medicine. This not-for-profit Sapien publication (and a pocket version, *Guide for Immediate Action*) was distributed free to obstetricians in the developing world and is the first stand-alone textbook which covers haemorrhage in childbirth and how to prevent it. It contains the contributions of over 106 international experts.

Dr B-Lynch's major achievement is the invention of a surgical procedure to prevent or cease haemorrhage in childbirth – one of the major causes of death in childbirth internationally. Originally published in the *British Medical Journal* in 1997, Dr B-Lynch's procedure has become the number one worldwide procedure to prevent post-partum haemorrhage. It is simple, effective and cheap, costing approximately £10, as opposed to previous methods which costed an average of £10,000. In 2006, Dr B-Lynch was a guest speaker at the World Congress Federation of International Obstetricians and Gynaecologists, attracting 4,000 delegates.

The son of a bishop and Oxford graduate, born in Sierra Leone in 1947 Dr B-Lynch came to the UK in 1964, studying Law, and then Medicine at Oxford University and St Bartholomew's Medical College. In 1972 he contested London University Student President election and served as Vice President. An academic high-flyer, that same year he was awarded the University Union of Colleges Gold Medal (Christopher Balugun-Lynch danced with the Queen Mother at the University Graduation Presentation Ball in 1974, see photograph opposite). Graduating in Medicine in 1974, Dr B-Lynch was to become the youngest consultant of his generation, aged thirty-six (1983).

Clinical Director, Obstetrics and Gynaecology, Milton Keynes General Hospital NHS Trust (2000–04), and Lead Colposcopist (2004–present), Dr B-Lynch has also been a pioneer in the study of modern medicine, training doctors in the latest medical procedures. For example, as one of the earliest exponents of keyhole surgery, B-Lynch proceeded to train others in the technique. He was nominated for National Trainer of the Year in 2000 and 2001, receiving an Honorary Doctorate from the Open University (1997). Dr B-Lynch is a founder of the Myrtle Peach Trust, originally formed for the prevention of genealogical cancers, and currently a charity fundraising for pioneering medical equipment, keyhole surgery, education and research and women's health campaigns (1985 – to the present).

The name Balugun originates from the Oguns, the original sixteenth-century warlords of West Africa, famous for their bronze weaponry and artefacts. Balugun translates as 'Sons of Ogun Ancestry'. Dr B-Lynch's mother originates from the Falasha, one of the twelve tribes of the Jewish Kingdom, not acknowledged until 1967.

Dr B-Lynch maintains sentimental attachments to East London, which boasts several hospitals that he has been associated with over the years, including St Bartholomew's, Homerton, Hackney and the London Hospital, Whitechapel. He has also maintained a practice in Harley Street for over twenty years.

A consultant obstetrician and gynaecological surgeon, with special interests in complicated surgical procedures, Dr B-Lynch is a pioneer of minimal access surgery, and has provided 'Expert Witness' opinion within all his fields of expertise for the Law Courts of England and Wales.

Professor B-Lynch's awards over time are too numerous to include in their entirety. The following two of particular significance should, however, be given a mention. B-Lynch was winner of the Serono Award for Assisted Conception – this trophy is proudly mounted in Ward 8 at Milton Keynes Hospital (1987). In 2000 he was granted recognition for his surgical achievements in the Silver Scalpel Award (Smith & Nephew Foundation). He was also granted 'Freedom of the City of London' from Sir Edward Tackwell, Sheriff of the City of London (pictured opposite). Finally, in the foreword to his book, a textbook of *Postpartum Haemorrhage*, the Queen's daughter, HRH Princess Anne sums up the significance of Dr B-Lynch's work:

> One of the tragedies of modern life is that 90% of maternal deaths are due to delays in decision-making, transfer and treatment of critically ill patients who have bled after child birth.

She concludes by hoping that healthcare communities worldwide will use the material in the book to save lives. They have and they do!

Dr Mabel Alli is the Coordinator of the North West London Haemoglobinopathy Managed Clinical Network. The network manages the treatment of sickle cell and thalassaemia in nine Primary Care Trusts (formally Heath Authorities) in North-West London. These include: Brent, Ealing, Hillingdon, Hammersmith & Fulham, Harrow, Westminster, Kensington & Chelsea, and Hounslow Primary Care Trust. Dr Mabel Alli is also a Specialist Registrar in Public Heath Medicine for Brent and Harrow Heath Authority.

Born in Lagos in 1950, to a family originating from Ijebu, south west Nigeria, Dr Alli's father was an accountant and her mother a nurse. Dr Alli was raised with a strong sense of history and found her maternal grandmother to be her greatest influence, describing her as a progressive Christian who was at the centre of her community's cultural life, formally and commercially as a ceremonial advisor and events organiser. Dr Alli's grandmother was responsible for the hire of traditional costume and equipment for special events for example the Idana or Brass ornamental bowls, platters and goblets for marriage and engagement ceremonies.

Her grandmother was proud to discover that her granddaughter was entering medicine, but advised her, 'The Lord hates a proud heart'. She taught her that becoming a doctor was a privileged position, but she reminded her to be humble and recognise her limitations. 'Remember you don't know everything!' Dr Alli's maternal grandfather was an esteemed 'London-Trained-Taylor', who, after running a stylish business in Lagos, later inherited the kingship of his village, becoming enstooled as: Mogun Seja of Mobalufon.

Dr Alli states that in addition to her three sons, her greatest achievement was in serving the World Health Organization as a Medical Officer, among the Rwandese refugee camps of north west Tanzania (1994–96). During this time she was able to control outbreaks of malaria, cholera and shigella dysentery.

Her most prominent work in the UK has been for the North West London Haemoglobinopathy Managed Clinical Network. Through the pressure of clinical and campaigning groups such as the network, the NHS has implemented the Sickle Cell and Thalassaemia Screening Programme, for all pregnant women in areas of high prevalence in the UK (all major cities). Evidence has shown that the earlier a diagnosis can be made, and treatment begins, the higher the chances of an individual living to a normal life span, with both diseases.

Sickle cell is a condition which largely but not exclusively affects the African and Caribbean communities, in which the normally circular blood cells are sickle shaped and consequently have problems flowing through the blood system. Sickled cells can also come together to block the supply of blood to vital organs. This can lead to necrosis or the death of cells in areas such as the eye, and 'crises' or episodes of severe pain.

Before the existence of the network, care for sufferers was uneven. Today, all nine hospitals share identical protocols in their Accident & Emergency departments, with a dedicated named specialist, and a named specialist nurse. That these measures are in place is a result of years of campaigning by patients, their families, health professionals and campaign groups.

The network also supports the everyday care of sufferers, and coordinates, trains and supports experts, patients, and clinical practitioners' groups. As a consequence of the network, sickle cell care is as close to home as possible, ensuring that sufferers in North West London do not have to travel long distances to receive specialist care.

Dr Mabel Alli hopes that sickle cell and thalassaemia will occupy an equal place alongside all other long-term genetic conditions in the UK within Primary Care Trusts. She states, 'This is a question of human rights…The UK can afford to lead by example'.

Charles Ifejika invented a device for cleaning contact lenses, for which he received the Lee Valley Business Innovation Award (1996) and scientific endorsement. He has gone on to establish a business with an annual turnover of over £1 million.

Born in Nigeria in 1957, Ifejika came to London at the age of three and trained as an engineer. After receiving hospital treatment in 1986 for an eye infection caused by the build up of harmful chemicals behind his contact lenses, he embarked upon his own research into more effective methods of eliminating bacteria from contact lenses, inventing a means of using electrical charges to do so. So far, one of the greatest challenges has been the costly registration of a patent for the device, which he now holds for approximately the next twenty years.

The Ifejika contact lens cleaning device has attracted the support of many academic, medical and research bodies, including an endorsement from one of Britain's leading eye hospitals, Moorefield's, and critical acclaim from the *British Journal of Ophthalmology* (B.J.O.) in 2000. The B.J.O. published evidence on the 'Efficacy of a contact lens cleaning device and its enhancement of the performance of contact lens care products', by the Centre for Applied Microbiology and Research, Porton Down, Salisbury.

The commercial turnaround came for Ifejika with his appearance in 2002 on the BBC programme *Tomorrow's World*. The contact lens cleaner won the programme's Best Inventions Award, with an introduction to Boots, which recommended the product to all contact lens manufacturers. The *Tomorrow's World* award led to thousands of enquiries about Ifejika's product, and in particular the interest of commercial companies such as AMO, an international eye-care company, which is now handling the product's distribution. Ifejika's company Lenscare now has an annual turnover of over £1m.

The daughter of Eudora (née Henry) from Tobago and James Campbell from Trinidad, **Noreen Goss** (née Campbell) came to London from Trinidad in 1967 to study photography and to become a Fleet Street journalist. Enrolling at Brunel University, Uxbridge in 1968, her first hurdle was purchasing photographic equipment, with a camera costing nearly a year's wage.

Goss started nursing as a means of subsidising her photography course. Eventually leaving Brunel to continue to train as a nurse at Herefield, Mount Vernon Hospital (1967–70), Noreen Goss was to maintain a parallel career as a freelance photographer, receiving commissions from family, friends and members of the community, to photograph weddings, funerals, christenings, family gatherings, carnival, and national and community events.

Inspired by the writings of Malcolm X, Noreen Goss became a Black Power activist, and a regular 'soap-box' speaker at Speakers' Corner, Hyde Park, every Sunday during the period 1967 to 1969. Goss had the distinction of being one of the only Black women on the scene, dominated by eminent fellow speakers such as Roy Sawh. Her speeches attracted crowds of people, including some skinheads, by whom she was once chased. Her subjects included: 'The Afro', 'Black is Beautiful', 'Black and Proud: Saying it Loud', 'Injustices Suffered by the West Indian People in Britain', and 'Being Called 'Coloured' in South Africa'. Goss became an activist for Anti-Apartheid (1968) and Amnesty International (1968), as well as a member of the Zanu Party (1969/70), in solidarity for an independent Zimbabwe.

Noreen Goss met her future husband (pictured above right), on the set of *Top of the Pops*, where they were both audience members; they married in 1972. Both shared a radical political outlook and hippy lifestyle, housing and providing a practical support network, as well as fundraising for South African and Zimbabwean asylum seekers.

In 1983 Goss and her husband went to live in an independent Zimbabwe, invited by friends whom they had supported during 'the struggle'. She was later to fall out of political favour with Robert Mugabe when she began to criticise the regime and Zimbabwe's tribalism. 'For all we fought for and for all those that died, let us unite as one nation', she once told Mugabe at a friend's party. Prevented from leaving Zimbabwe for two years, Goss eventually escaped the country in 1988 'Many friends have "disappeared" ... 'I am even asked today, at social events, "When was the last time you saw my brother or other family member?" by British-Zimbabweans.'

Noreen Goss has been an S.R.N. for thirty-nine years, working in the London borough of Brent for thirty-four years, managing the 'twilight' or Out-of-Hours Nursing Care Service (1988–2004). Proud to be called 'an encourager', Goss has fought hard for training and access routes to employment for Black men and women in Brent. Her expertise has also been sought by Thames Valley University for the development of Nurse Training Modules. During her career Goss has also worked as a Theatre Nurse for Sir Magdi Yacoub, the leading specialist in heart and lung transplantation.

Combining her activism with her clinical experience, Noreen Goss has diplomas in District Nursing (1985), Management Studies (1991), Social Work (1994), Community Practice Teaching (1999) and Nurse Prescribing (2001). In 1997 Goss became an early recipient of the new BA in Nurse Practitioning at the Royal College of Nursing. Recent years have involved Goss championing HIV support through charities and as London President of the British Soroptomists Society (2007–08) (she also serves as their official photographer), and at the helm of her own Health & Social Care Agency, THELMA.

It should come as no surprise to anyone who knows him, that geneticist **Dr James Adjaye**'s greatest achievements are his children and the inheritors of his own genetic legacy.

As Principal Investigator at the Department of Molecular Biology, Institute of Child Health, University College London, Dr James Adjaye's ambition was to study a single embryo and to analyse one gene. This ambition has been fulfilled, expanding to the study of over 200 genes. Dr Adjaye's count now stands at the study of over 20,000 genes. Today, because of the work of Dr James Adjaye, we have a greater knowledge of human genes and their function. This research and the discoveries it has initiated have significant consequences for both the understanding and curing of disease in modern medicine.

Today, Dr Adjaye is Group Leader of the Molecular Embryology and Aging group, Max-Planck Institute for Molecular Genetics, Berlin, Germany. The Max-Planck Institute is Germany's foremost scientific institute, and one of the world's leading scientific institutions. It has hosted a generation of Nobel Prize winners including Albert Einstein himself.

Dr Adjaye was invited to join the Max-Planck Institute by Professor Hans Lehrach, known as the 'Godfather of human Genomics', since he instigated the sequencing of the human genome. The year 2006 saw the publication of *Embryology*, the continuation of Dr Adjaye's own pioneering work in embryology (the study of the beginning of human life), which began with his scientific 'breakthroughs' of 1997 and 1999.

The son of an accountant at the Ghanaian Embassy, Dr James Adjaye, was born in Oda, East Port, Ghana in 1964. His was to be an unsettled but interesting childhood, as his father travelled across Africa on diplomatic missions. Home eventually became the London suburb of Neasden, at the age of thirteen, when his father retired to the UK.

James became a disciple of inspirational biology teacher, Brian Nobel, at John Kelly Boys High School, Neasden. As an inner-city school with many social challenges, James was one of only three boys (one African and two Asian) taking A Level biology and chemistry. These were the only three pupils to make it to university that year from John Kelly.

Mr Noble's regime of 'Guinness and sandwiches, and emphasis on practical experiment after experiment', fascinated James and propelled him to study a first degree at the University of Cardiff, and eventually a PhD at King's College, inspired by Professor Peter Eagle and Professor Klaus Weber, biochemist and one the world's leading evolutionary biologists.

Student life in Cardiff proved to be exciting and James was a popular student, a 'jazz dancer', sharing his 'London moves' with fellow students. He joined the Jazz Funk Society and the Rock Society, and later shared a chaotic student house with four housemates.

James relished trips back to his London stomping grounds, as a jazz dancing man-about-town. He fondly recalls his favourite London landmarks because of their happy association with the dance venues of his youth: The Metro Ballroom and Electric Ballroom, Camden Town, and the Lyceum on the Strand, every August Bank Holiday. Other sentimental London landmarks include Kingsbury Library, where he '…went to study and to meet the girls' from his sister-school John Kelly Girls' High School. Other favourite landmarks include Camden market for shopping, Brockley and Greenwich, where he lived for a time, and King's College, Bloomsbury, where he began his illustrious career. Dr Adjaye has remained an active and loyal member of King's College Alumni Society, participating in reunions and assisting with recruitment fairs on their behalf. Recent years have also included student recruitment for the university with the British Embassy in Germany, where he currently resides.

Originally encouraged by his parents to study Pharmacology, Dr James Adjaye couldn't get over the wonder of biochemistry and couldn't get its experiments out of his head. 'I became hooked on experiments, and I am to this day, engaged in ongoing experimentation, through the continued influence of my old teacher Mr Noble (I still try to keep in touch with him!).'

Dr Adjaye became interested in family history almost by osmosis. He was fortunate enough to have met Mr Sam, the gentleman cocoa trader, his mother's father, before he passed away in 1978. Mr Sam was well known and well respected, collecting cocoa in trucks from all the villages in his region, in Ghana and eventually trading it.

Dr Adjaye's guiding philosophy has been, 'Have respect for your parents, but still believe in yourself, and know what your limit is. Try and go higher, don't underestimate yourself. Have faith that everything is possible. Belief in God and hope. Nothing is impossible, if you work for it, despite prejudices caused by your colour.'

CHAPTER FOUR

TRADE, INDUSTRY AND ENTERPRISE

WHO PUT THE OIL IN THE LAMP?

That London emerged as a premier port is substantially due to the economic contributions of Africans and West Indians. Trade in West African commodities and the advent of the slave trade facilitated vast accumulations of wealth and propelled the growth of the British Empire and the Industrial Revolution. So substantial was the wealth generated and accumulated that the City of London, as a global financial centre, still trades on its residue.

Between them, Africa and the Caribbean put the wax in the candle, the oil in the lamp, the sugar in the tea, the copper in the kettles, the rum on the table, the fruit in the basket, the cotton on the back, the diamond on the finger, the gold in the pocket and, quite literally kept the wheels of the Industrial Revolution turning through industrial lubricants.

The men and women of sugar and banking funded an empire to whose greater glory such London landmarks as the British Museum and the Victoria & Albert Museum were created, showing off the spoils of imperial conquest. The core of The National Gallery's collection was based on pictures acquired by John Julius Angerstein, the famous Lloyd's underwriter who was associated with the slave trade. So entrenched with sugar and slavery in the Caribbean were London's banking interests that the Bank of England was referred to as 'The Bank of the West Indies'.

ENTERPRISE AS SELF-EMPOWERMENT AND EMANCIPATION

British history is not the comfort zone which some might hope to retreat into. London's economic structures have also benefited from the waves of Black immigration over centuries, in addition to the wealth of labour and resources extracted through a global empire. The relationship between enterprise and slavery has always been a complex one. Enterprise can make a freeman out of a slave or a slave out of the free. Economic emancipation often preceded freedom under slavery: among the enslaved, some men and women were able to buy their freedom, while at the same time the profitability of the slave economy led to its continuance over centuries. Sadly, generations of Black Londoners have learned that personal freedom does not always guarantee economic freedom. Without the means or opportunity to pursue a trade or access employment, they were well represented among the beggars and the poor of London.

However, some were fortunate and many Black Londoners were to become well-known local traders: Ignatius Sancho and his wife Anne ran a grocer's store in Charles Street, Westminster; Robert Wedderburn and William Cuffay were tailors; other trades in which Black Londoners took an active role were as publicans, publishers, cookshop owners, entertainers, carpenters and blacksmiths.

TRADING KINGS AND QUEENS

The trading power of Africa itself was often diminished by imperial propaganda, which sought to remove the perception of Africans as capable of successful economic activity. Despite the imperialist quest to wrest control of Africa's economic destiny, Europe continued to depend upon the co-operation of West Africa's powerful trading dynasties, without whom access to certain commodities would have been impossible.

Madam Ewa Henshaw, for example, from the royal trading house of Henshaw Town, Old Calabar, Nigeria, was linked to Britain in this way through the export of palm oil. Palm oil was a raw material in the production of soap, margarine, cosmetics, machine grease and candles. Pears' soap is a British brand name established worldwide through this vital ingredient.

Here are just some of the descendents of the Black traders, entrepreneurs and industrialists of early twentieth-century London.

Above: **A Black tailor, Whitechapel Mission**, 1900. Little is known of the Black tailor in this photograph, but Whitechapel in East London is an area long associated with tailoring. The trade attracted many refugees from persecution, especially Russian and Polish Jews.

Right: **Madam Ewa Henshaw** was from a trading family of Henshaw Town, Old Calabar, Nigeria, which was linked to London through the export of palm oil to Britain. Madam Henshaw was related to King Eyamba V and Archibong I. Her husband, Dr L.E.R. Henshaw OBE, Deputy Director of Medical Services in eastern Nigeria, was descended from an Efik royal house where names were often anglicized to facilitate trade communications.

Sir Edward Asafu Adjaye, the Ghanaian High Commissioner, inspecting logs from the Gliksten concessions in Ghana, with E. Terance Scott, managing director, and R.E. Groves, director, of J. Gliksten & Son, at Stratford Lumber Yard, 1961.

George Dryden, businessman and community activist, was the Director of Dyke & Dryden Ltd, a leading distributor of Black hair and beauty products in Europe. Born in 1926, George Dryden founded the Dyke & Dryden with Len Dyke (see below). He was also an active community organizer as vice-chairman of the Association of Jamaicans from 1965 to 1975, a member of the West Indian Standing Conference from 1970 to 1980, and as Chair of Hackney Commission for Racial Equality from 1978 to 1981. His 'Services to the Community' were recognized by the award of an MBE in 1985.

Dudley Dryden died in 2002 and along with his business partner 'Len' or Lincoln Dyke, will go down in history as owning one of Britain's first Black multi-million-pound businesses. It was Dudley Dryden who had sufficient vision, courage and faith in Len Dyke's original business idea in the mid-1960s, to invest in his business. Overnight, Dryden the investor and 'sleeping partner' was to become Dryden the full joint partner.

Although initially selling Jamaican imported records, Dyke and Dryden began to address the need for Black cosmetics and hair care products. It was Dudley Dryden who sold cosmetics from a stall in Ridley Road Market, Dalston, East London, with brands such as La India, Island Beauty, Kuss-Kuss perfume, and American Tan tights, which before 'barely Black', was the closest to skin colour for Black women. His business partner, Len Dyke ran the office in West Green Road, Tottenham, which acted as a one-stop-shop for the Black community, selling records, cosmetics, flights to the West Indies, and later offering legal and immigration advice.

Among the first Black British million-pound companies, Dyke & Dryden have inspired a generation, including the Black hairdressers, cosmetics and hair product distributors, and nail shops, which now throng the high streets of Britain's cities. Major beauty product manufacturers now include Black ranges, and Black 'style' dominates high street to high fashion.

The Dyke & Dryden empire eventually rose to include six shops and warehouses. Beyond distribution, Dyke & Dryden became one of the first companies to manufacture Black hair care products in Europe. They beat off competition from America to eventually dominate the British market, and fought for markets in Africa and the Caribbean. By 1986 Dyke & Dryden had achieved a sales turnover of £5m.

Len Dyke, businessman and community activist, was the co-founder of Dyke & Dryden Ltd, leading distributor of Black hair and beauty products in Europe.

Len Dyke was born in Clarendon, Jamaica in 1926, the last of eleven children. His father was a headteacher who set high standards for his children. A qualified electrician, Dyke began his own contracting business in Jamaica. Dyke arrived in England in 1955, with his first wife Evelyn, settling in Middle Lane, Crouch End, North London. Len Dyke worked as an electrician for British Rail, but was often excluded from contracting work as an electrician in Britain, due to racist protectionist practices within the trade.

An ordained minister, who had been used to evangelising while travelling for his contracting business, Dyke's conscience and compassion led to his community activism, co-founding the West Indian Standing Conference following the attacks on the Black community reaching their peak with the death of Kelso Cochrane in the 1950s. The Black community, depite shocking discrimination, had few forms of redress. The West Indian Standing Conference gave support and advice and campaigned for social justice.

Dyke also helped to found the Association of Jamaicans and the UK Caribbean Chamber of Commerce, among other organisations. Dyke benefited from the emergent Black economic markets, but ploughed much of his profit and energies back into the community, supporting projects and causes such as Ferme Park International Fellowship and the Ferme Park Housing Association. As a lifelong community activist, Len Dyke was the person to call when racial tension arose, with the police seeking his services as an independent observer in the 1980s.

In response to exclusion from access to banking facilities, Dyke helped to establish Britain's first Credit Union in Hornsey, North London. The Hornsey Credit Union, a savings and loan club, provided a vital financial resource to many. It was Dyke's community activism which drove him to start Dyke & Dryden Ltd. He believed that Black people should not leave their future precariously in the fickle hands of a racist society, but sieze control of their destinies and begin their own businesses to guarantee their employment, to cater for the community and the next generation.

In the 1970s, '80s and '90s Dyke & Dryden posters and advertising helped to 'glamorise' many a drab or overcrowded bedroom in the Black community, launch a worthy bulletin or pamphlet and keep community newspapers, journals and magazines afloat.

Dyke & Dryden was sold to an American competitor in the 1990s, as the partnership began to struggle to maintain market share in a multi-billion pound market, with many Asian and White businesses now awake to its potential.

Len Dyke died in 2006, but for the many who witnessed or even heard about the legendary Afro Hair & Beauty Shows, (a company subsidiary of Dyke & Dryden – the first show took place in 1982) Len Dyke and Dudley Dryden will forever be associated with Black beauty, elegance, cutting-edge fashion and hope for a glossy and well-groomed future in which we all have a place.

Dounne Alexander is founder and Chief Executive of Gramma's Ltd, a leading supplier of herbal pepper sauces and teas in the UK. Born in 1949, Alexander came to Britain in 1962 to join her parents and sisters in Essex. In 1971 she moved to Forest Gate, East London, but it was from her flat in East Ham that she began Gramma's Ltd in 1987. By 1991 the firm had won national recognition for introducing Black herbal foods to seven top supermarkets including Safeway, Tesco and Waitrose, a success that forced a redefinition of British food culture.

In 1991 Gramma's Ltd was forced to liquidate due to its rapid growth rate and the withdrawal of banking support. It was re-launched later that same year however, with new financial backers and a restructuring with an emphasis on the luxury food market and mail order sales.

Gramma's products now include herbal seasonings and a selection of herbal teas and drinks. Of her herbal tea, Alexander states, 'Zara's Herbal Tea contains the whole 'tree-of-life' (i.e. roots, barks, stems, flowers and leaves) plus the first commercial product to contain the rare herb African Bush Willow (containing Combretastatin), recognized by British and American scientists as the most powerful anti-cancer herb.' In 2003 Alexander launched her health awareness campaign – 'Joining Hands in Health'. The year 2008 saw Alexander's health products on sale in Harrods, Fortnum & Mason and Harvey Nichols.

Dounne Alexander became Vice-President of London Youth Clubs in 1991 and won a European Women of Achievement Award in 1992. Elected Woman of the Year four times (1991, 1992, 2006 and 2007), Dounne Alexander was made MBE in 2006 'for services to the food industry'.

Joy Nichols founded the Nichols Employment Agency with her brother and co-director Lennox Campbell in 1984. This multi-million-pound recruitment business has grown from being a small agency on Harrow Road, North West London, to expand into the public, private and voluntary sectors, with offices in Lewisham and Peckham in South East London and Shepherds Bush in West London.

Nichols Employment and Recruitment Agency currently provides temporary and full-time work to over 250 people a year in the fields of social welfare, secretarial work, administration and nursing. Joy Nichols originally trained as a secretary; her agency's big break came with the abolition of the Greater London Council by Prime Minister Margaret Thatcher in the 1980s. Her existing contacts in local government were able to rely upon Nichols to fill vacancies with quality personnel. NEA's investment in IT and a well-trained workforce enabled the agency to respond to increased demand, which to the unprepared could have proved overwhelming.

A highly respected businesswoman and mentor, Nichols has served on the Business School Advisory Team of Middlesex University and as Chair of the African Caribbean Business Network (2000–02), established by former London Mayor, Ken Livingstone, to facilitate Black businesses' access to finance and information. In 2005 Nichols received the Queen's Award for Enterprise – Lifetime Achievement in Enterprise Promotion.

In 2008 the Nichols Employment Agency ventured into South Africa's employment and training markets, following the successful first all-Black trade mission to South Africa in collaboration with UK Trade & Investment. A similar trade mission is currently being considered in respect of the Caribbean – the staging of international events in the Caribbean, such as the Cricket World Cup is believed to offer enormous business potential.

It is difficult to imagine what modern Britain in film, television, cinema, theatre or music would be like, without the transformative energies of **Pearl Connor-Mogotsi**. Pearl Connor-Mogotsi nurtured the talent of Black British actors, dancers, musicians and performers, and set about creating a market for these talents to be employed and enjoyed. Because of her, modern British cinema, television and theatre, and the music industry, were forced to come to terms with the diversity of modern Britain, and to reflect this in their content and representations.

Pearl Connor – the 'Impresario'. As an Impresario Pearl Connor promoted, managed and directed public entertainment. However, as a Black impresario in Britain from the 1950s to the 1990s Pearl Connor did much more. She recognised that in order to perform the role of impresario, British arts and the entertainment industry needed to change. They needed to be lobbied, campaigned against, harangued, charmed and gently persuaded to accept Black British talent. This was Pearl Connor – the 'Activist's'- role.

Indeed, her impact was so great that we now take it for granted. Every time we see a Black face on a British soap opera, film or television advertisement, our thoughts should go to Pearl Connor, who challenged television producers and advertisers about casting roles which Black actors could apply for and for enabling Black writers to have the opportunity to reflect their cultural viewpoints.

Born Pearl Nunez in Diego Martin, Trinidad, Pearl Connor was the ninth of twelve children. Her father Albert Nunez was a strict headmaster of Portuguese and African origin, who took pride in his ancestry of freed slaves. Pearl Connor came to England originally to study law in 1948; she later became an actress and impresario. Even at eighty, Pearl continued to work as an arts consultant, and ran a literary agency and Black music publishing company until her death in 2005.

In 1956 Pearl Connor established, with her husband Edric, the Edric Connor Agency, later renamed the Afro-Asian Agency in the 1970s, following Edric's early death. Edric Connor (1915–68) had become a well-respected Black actor on British television; his television contacts, combined with Pearl's networking abilities and persuasive charm, made for a powerful machine. Their agency was located at the heart of London's television and theatre district in the West End's Shaftesbury Avenue.

Recognition must be granted to Pearl Connor from Britain's arts community for encouraging it to make a bold transition into modernity. Britain began to look more modern, more 'funky' on screen. The reputation of 'Swinging London', was not only due to the post-war impact of immigration on music, but was also matched by film and the arts. Far from casting Black people only, the Edric Connor Agency/Afro-Asian Agency had a virtual monopoly on all ethnic groups, representing Caribbean, Malaysian, Japanese, Indian and African actors, writers and filmmakers in Britain.

Diverse ethnic groups joined crowd scenes, became neighbours, villains, and sometimes heroic leading men and women. Some classic British films were cast by the Edric Connor Agency/Afro-Asian Agency: *Susie Wong*, *Alfie*, the *Carry On* films, the *James Bond* films, and West End shows such as *Hair*, *Jesus Christ Superstar* and numerous TV drama productions.

Pearl Connor was a Pan-Africanist with a keen political interest and awareness, regularly holding salons of artists and intellectuals at her home. She was supportive of Colonial independence, and the self-assertion, confidence and freedom of expression which Black political empowerment brought to the arts. An activist and strategist, Pearl was aware that this post-colonial new Black British 'cultural revolution' needed to grow and nurture writers, technicians and performers.

In 1963 Pearl Connor was instrumental in establishing the Negro Theatre Workshop, one of the first Black theatre workshops in Britain. *A Wreath for Udomo* was one of their earliest plays, adapted from the novel by Peter Abrahams and featuring Earl Cameron, Edric Connor, Lloyd Reckord and Joan Hooley. These workshops were held at London's Lyric Theatre. Later came *The Dark Disciples*, an enactment of the Easter story by a company of twenty-five Black actors. *The Dark Disciples* is an example of Connor's two-pronged approach of preparation and nurturing of excellence, while pitching her product/client/concept to producers. *The Dark Disciples* was later produced for television by the BBC in 1966.

In 1971 Pearl Connor married Joseph Mogotsi, leader of The Manhattan Brothers, the famous South African singing group. They formed another winning team, with Pearl acting as agent/manager/business partner and beloved wife. They continued to live and work together until the end of her life.

In a post-war, post-colonial Britain, it would have been tempting for the arts to retreat in into the glories of the past, but Pearl Connor demonstrated the excitement of a diverse future. Pearl Connor-Mogotsi – the 'Cultural Pioneer'.

Isobel Husbands (née Grant) was born in 1917 and settled in West London in 1955. She bought a succession of houses in London from the 1950s to the 1980s, demonstrating economic independence and shrewd financial management at a time when there was great discrimination in the housing market for Black men, let alone Black women. While working as a cook in a succession of West End restaurants, she developed an interest in dress design, collecting and mixing fabrics. William Husbands, who was born in 1913, worked at Selfridges in the West End from 1955 to 1980, beginning as a porter and retiring as a supervisor. He believes that he was the first Black man to work at Selfridges and into the 1950s when labour was in short supply he acted as a recruiter for the company within the Black community.

Christopher Adeshinaro Oluwatoyin Shokoya-Eleshin arriving at Heathrow Airport from Nigeria in 1965 with his parents (*above*). Christopher Shokoya-Eleshin settled in Plaistow, East London, at the age of four; the photograph (*below*) shows him outside his first London home. He became owner of one of the most successful Black building contractors in the UK.

After attending Upton Cross School and Clarkes School, **Chris Shokoya-Eleshin** went to Forest Public School, where he survived six racially motivated fights in his first week. Despite this hostile beginning, he excelled academically, socially and on the playing field to become a popular Head of School House. The photograph above shows him at the Old Boys' dinner in 1981.

A schoolboy county cricketer for Essex, Shokoya-Eleshin went on to join the MCC as a full playing member; in 1991 he assisted in organising the first MCC tour of West Africa for twenty years. He taught mathematics at secondary school level before founding the Shokoya-Eleshin Construction Company in 1992, which became one of Britain's largest Black-owned construction companies with branches in London, Liverpool, Freetown, Lagos and Shagamu. In 1996, the company's £2.3 million housing development in Musgrove Street, Liverpool, was identified by the UK Council to the United Nations as 'a model of good practice', and as a result Shokoya-Eleshin Construction Ltd was invited as part of the UK Council's delegation to the Habitat II Conference on Regeneration in June the same year. Christopher Shokoya-Eleshin is seen (right) with Jack Straw, then Shadow Home Secretary, and Eric Armitage, Chief Executive of Northern Housing Association, at the launch of a £1.5 million housing scheme in Blackburn.

In 2001 Shokoya-Eleshin Construction Ltd was nominated for The Inner City 100, an initiative to identify 100 of the most successful businesses located in fifteen of the UK's inner cities. Devised by the New Economics Foundation and supported by the Royal Bank of Scotland and NatWest, it was launched by the then Chancellor of the Exchequer, now Prime Minister Gordon Brown.

Whilst Liverpool celebrated its nomination as European City of Culture 2008, the Shokoya-Eleshin School of Small Business and Construction Training, with the assistance of European Union Objective 1 Funding, established a scheme to encourage more women and Black and minority ethnic communities into the construction industry through training.

The emblem of **Shokoya-Eleshin Construction Ltd** is a coat-of-arms representing Shokoya-Eleshin's ancestral descent from several royal houses in Nigeria. This photograph shows one of Shokoya-Eleshin's ancestors, the Alake of Abeokuta, taken by a royal court photographer in 1947.

Margaret Busby became the UK's youngest and first female Black book publisher when she co-founded Allison & Busby in the 1960s. Her impact upon the world of international publishing has been enormous, as a publisher, writer, critic, literary awards judge, mentor and cultural activist.

Apart from the award of an important place within British literary history, Margaret Busby's other awards include in 1999 being made a Ghanaian chief, also known as an 'enstoolment' (almost unprecedented recognition for the publishing achievements of a Black British woman of Ghanaian origin). Busby was enstooled in Cape Coast (Oguaa traditional area) in Ghana's Central Region, as Nana Akua Ackon I of Asafo Company No.1. The Open University awarded Busby an Honorary Doctorate, which she received at Ely Cathedral in 2004. In 2006 Margaret Busby received an OBE in the Queen's New Year's honours list, 'For Services to Literature and to Publishing'.

Other historical honours received by Margaret Busby include a Society of Young Publishers Award (1970), the 1993 Pandora Award (from Women in Publishing) and in 1997 an Excellence Lifetime Achievement Award (from The Write Thing). In 1998, in Chicago, Illinois, she was made an Honorary Member of AKA (Alpha Kappa Alpha, the oldest Black sorority in the USA).

As editorial director for Allison & Busby, Margaret Busby's visionary leadership was to break down literary barriers for a whole new generation of writers of all backgrounds and nationalities, many of whom have now become household names. Her numbers of titles run into the hundreds, including an international list of fiction, non-fiction, poetry and children's books. Without the foresight of Busby's twenty-year tenure at Allison & Busby, the following literary voices may have never been heard: C.L.R. James (for whom she is executor), Buchi Emecheta, Sam Greenlee, Chester Himes, George Lamming, Roy Heath, Ishmael Reed, John Edgar Wideman, Nuruddin Farah, Rosa Guy, Michael Moorcock, Val Wilmer, Hunter S. Thompson, Anthony Burgess, Colin MacInnes, B. Traven, H. Rap Brown, Clive Sinclair, J.B. Priestley, James Ellroy, Agnes Heller, Geoffrey Grigson, Julius Lester, Alexandra Kollontai, Ivy Compton-Burnett, J.G. Ballard, Mervyn Peake, Brian Aldiss, Budd Schulberg, Miyamoto Musashi, Christine Qunta, Lautréamont, Giles Gordon, Carlos Moore, Adrian Mitchell, Michael Horowitz, Jill Murphy, Anthony Barnett, Boris Pasternak, Claire Rayner, Tom Lowenstein, Michele Roberts, Molefe Pheto, Arthur Maimane, Maurice Nyagumbo, Hilary Wainwright, Tom Pickard, James Reeves, Libby Houston, etc.

As a cultural activist, Busby's determination for all human voices to be heard led to her foundation of GAP (Greater Access to Publishing) in the 1980s, a group campaigning for diversity in the UK publishing workforce, a precursor of the Arts Council's publishing training bursaries for Black candidates, for which she was also a mentor. Busby also served on the steering committee of the Arts Council's Diversity in Publishing programme.

Busby's commitment to breaking down barriers in literature has seen her appointment to the council of a breathtaking variety of organisations, spanning the breadth of the literary and cultural world, including the Africa Centre, Royal Literary Fund, Arts Council of England, International Book Fair of Radical Black and Third World Books, English PEN, Africa 95, Panafest (Ghana), Zabalaza ANC South African Festival, International Centre for African Music & Dance (Ghana), Yari Yari (USA), Minority Arts Advisory Service and the Black Theatre Co-operative.

Margaret Busby is currently on the boards of the African & Caribbean Music Circuit, *Wasafiri* magazine, Africa Remembrance Day, the Organization of Women Writers of Africa (USA), Hackney Empire and the Huntley Archives, and is patron of Independent Black Publishers (IBP). In 2004 she gave the keynote address at the Bath Literature Festival, and she has chaired and spoken at many conferences and seminars in the UK and abroad.

A measure of the great esteem to which Margaret Busby is held is reflected in her invitation to act as judge to a whole host of literary awards such as the Orange Award for New Writers, the Caine Prize for African Writing, Decibel/Penguin Prize, Guardian/Heinemann African Short Story Competition, the Commonwealth Broadcasting Association's Writing Contest, the Saga Prize, and the Arts Council/Independent Foreign Fiction Prize.

Appointed editorial director of Earthscan (a post which she held until 1990), with a commitment to post-colonial writers, Margaret Busby later began the epic project *Daughters of Africa: An International Anthology of Words and Writing by Women of African Descent from the Ancient Egyptian to the Present* (1992). Busby continues her role as highly respected, glamorous elder stateswoman of 'Letters' for British television, radio and newspapers.

A structural visionary whose glass and chrome buildings are at the forefront of architectural innovation, **Albert O. Williamson-Taylor** has built cafés in the shape of sea waves and bendy office blocks which appear to defy gravity. Albert O. Williamson-Taylor is creating architecture and civil engineering with a distinctive 'wow factor'. Today, Williamson-Taylor is doing for the rest of the world what he has done in London.

In 1995, Williamson-Taylor, one of Britain's most senior Black civil engineers, became a founding partner in the practice of Adams Kara Taylor, a multicultural firm of consulting civil and structural engineers. In December 2006 AKT took over and merged with the firm White, Young & Green, adding significantly to its scale of operations and creating a staff of 198.

Albert O. Williamson-Taylor believes that AKT, through its African, Asian and Jewish partnership, founded upon friendship and excellence, reflects the best that a diverse London of the twenty-first century has to offer. AKT's commission portfolio includes: East Corydon Station, The Sackler Galleries, Piccadilly, The Royal Academy of Arts and 'The Floating Bridge', West India Quay, Docklands, as well as the celebrated Peckham Library (see p.9).

Recent years have seen AKT amass a range of prestigious projects, and awards for creative virtuosity in architectural structure, design, innovation and sustainability. 'Firsts' have included the UK Centre for

Carnival Arts – the world's first purpose-built Carnival Arts Centre. However, it is upon London herself that AKT has made its greatest impact, establishing a new London Hilton Hotel at historic Tower Bridge, fashioning a high-tech urban landscape linking commuters to transport, and orchestrating power, energy and light in the King's Cross Development (pictured right), London's most important transport hub. And it is AKT which will surround the Olympic torch with light, through its Olympic Energy Centre, one of a total of four Olympic projects won by the firm.

Born in Bethnal Green, East London in 1959, Albert O. Williamson-Taylor grew up in Lagos and Freetown. Like many British-born children of African parents, Williamson-Taylor was to return to the UK for his higher education, first attending college, then studying for a Higher Diploma in Building Construction at Brunel University, and later studying for a degree at Bristol University (1976–78).

Williamson-Taylor was to spend a further four years studying for a Batchelor of Engineering at Bradford University (1978–82), followed by a masters degree in the same subject (1982–84). After

working for a small engineering firm in Bedford, Gregory and Associates, Williamson-Taylor finally returned to London to work with Pryce & Myers (1986–88).

Mr Williamson-Taylor Senior had studied architecture in London in the 1950s but did not practice. Britain of the 1950s was apparently not yet ready to embrace Black architects, with architecture falling outside the tightly prescribed categories of jobs for which 'immigrants' were to be 'accepted'. Williamson-Taylor Senior, however, was to eventually achieve his life's ambition, and become a City Council Surveyor, in Freetown Sierra Leone.

The Williamson-Taylor's 'London connection' is consolidated by Mrs Williamson-Taylor Senior's, nursing training at Kings College Hospital, London, finally ending her working life as Head of Paediatrics at the Military Hospital in Lagos.

To inspire him, at fourteen years of age, his father took Albert Williamson-Taylor to visit the chief engineer at an architectural and engineering consultancy in Lagos. The fourteen-year-old Albert was extremely impressed by the 'Victorian' layout of the firm, with the chief engineer sitting at a 'Double-elephant' (large-size) drawing board on a raised platform, surveying the whole practice from on high.

Williamson-Taylor determinedly studied science, mathematics and art. Both father and son shared a common artistic talent. The young Albert enjoyed sketching his comic-book heroes for pleasure, while studying drawing and painting.

Returning to England for college in Bristol at the age of sixteen, Albert Williamson-Taylor witnessed a 'great divide', between West Indian students who were encouraged to become technicians, and African students who were encouraged to undertake higher education, since it was assumed that they would be returning 'home'.

When he went on to Bradford for university, to Williamson-Taylor, the city, like the rest of the UK of the 1970s and '80s, 'felt like a psychological war-zone' for him as a young Black man: 'There seemed to be a fine balance being trodden between integration, and segregation'.

To Williamson-Taylor the actual university appeared to have created its own quota system, allowing one Black man a year. 'In an entire Engineering intake of seventy-five, there were three Black students. Unsurprisingly, one was later to leave due to the "pressure".'

Coming to his assistance, was International House. Williamson-Taylor believes that as the youngest student living in International House, the residence for 'foreign students', this provided him with vital emotional support, and an alternative model for living. Surrounded by students from China, Eastern Europe, Africa, Belize and Guyana, one African senior student advised, 'No matter what's coming at you – keep your sights on the end goal'.

By 1986, Williamson-Taylor had returned to London, establishing London Regional Taekwondo Martial Arts Clubs, (see p.47) and joining the prestigious engineering consultancy of Pryce & Myers. For two and a half years, Williamson-Taylor ran one of London's largest development projects at the time: the Lotts Road Development, Chelsea. Eventually leaving because he felt that his opportunities were being restricted, Williamson-Taylor then joined Anthony Hunt Associates. This proved to be a more encouraging experience, with major commissions. Williamson-Taylor left Anthony Hunt in 1995 to start a new engineering practice at a time when most individuals, let alone businesses, were coming to terms with economic recession.

The new company, Adams Kara Taylor, sought clients from emerging markets. The fledgling company was bolstered by the support of old clients who were attracted to them because they were known to deliver. This track record was to stand AKT in good stead as a practice determined to take on the most complicated engineering challenges and find solutions. 'We wanted to cover the front end of Engineering and the back end of Engineering.'

Asked when they felt they had arrived? Williamson-Taylor responded, 'It felt that we had arrived after six–seven years. People began to recognise us in Millennium year. We won the Stirling Prize, five years into our Practice'. When asked the secret of the success of such a relatively young practice, Williamson-Taylor, smiles and speaks modestly from the heart 'My two colleagues are the most talented people I know of in this business. I trust them implicitly'.

Williamson-Taylor's one regret is the lack of Black engineers across the industry: 'You can count us on one hand'. This fact makes Williamson-Taylor all the more remarkable.

December 2006 saw AKT merge with White, Young & Green. In the past, the industry was more about business than the individual, with growth at an unsustainable rate. Opportunities were often missed. Today Williamson-Taylor is poised to access international markets, spreading his values on a global scale.

Adams Kara Taylor have won 101 awards since their inception, which include: RIBA Stirling Prize (2000), RIBA design Award (2000) and Civic Trust Award, special Award for Social Contribution (2001) for Peckham; The Art Commission Trust – Building of the Year (2000) and RIBA Design Award (2000) for Southwark Station; Building of the Year (2002), BDA Award, and Supreme Winner of best Public Housing and an Environment Award (2002–04); FX Best Medium-Sized Office (2005), British Council Office Innovation Award (2005), Civic Trust Award for Sustainability (2007) for Heelis National Trust HQ; Civic Trust Award (2006), RIBA Award (2006), Structural Steel Design – Shortlist (2005 & 2006) for QMWC School of Medicine & Dentistry.

Known by some jealous rivals as the 'Starchitect'[1] or 'Prince Charming'[2] **David Adjaye**, is associated internationally with the creative use of industrial building materials[3]. He also happens to have taken the world of architecture by storm. An architect who loves to be seen as an artist, Adjaye has attracted famous enthusiasts from the celebrity world, such as Ewan McGregor, Jake Chapman, Alexander McQueen, Chris Ofili (with whom he has also collaborated, see p.20) and Juergen Teller.

However, putting the glamour aside, Adjaye should be seen as a driven architect of substance. Adjaye studied for his first degree at South Bank University and completed an MA at the prestigious Royal College of Art (1991–93). After qualifying as an architect in 1995 he started his own practice Adjaye Architects. Despite many commissions of gravitas, Adjaye describes his nomination for the Stirling Prize (2006), one of architecture's most coveted awards, as his proudest achievement. The award of an OBE in the Queen's Birthday Honours for service to architecture (2007) was to follow. The Whitechapel Idea Store (pictured above and on p.96), a large community library in East London, distinctive for its striking elongated windows of green and blue coloured glasss, echoes the stripes and colours of the stall awnings of the famous Whitechapel Market nearby.

With a father in the Ghanaian Diplomatic Service, Adjaye was born in Dar-Es-Salaam, Tanzania in 1966, the family finally settling in the UK in 1979. At one time Adjaye found himself floundering and confused over his choice of architecture as a profession, due to its lack of role models. For him, being unable to actually see oneself and one's role within the profession was, 'very traumatic'. Adjaye was not alone in struggling to find positive Black male role models, as the late 1970s were a turbulent time for many youths as the second generation of African and Caribbean immigrants from the 1950s and '60s were coming of age within a hostile social environment.

Although he had pursued a very different professional path, Adjaye's father had always been 'incredibly supportive' of his son. Ultimately, Mr Adjaye senior is credited with giving his son the 'backbone' to pursue architecture. This has led David Adjaye to conclude that, 'A father's blessing of a son or daughter, can do much, in the absence of any other references. It became a mode of potential power which said it was OK'.

Adjaye's mother was also very sympathetic. She came from the same area as his father, Asafu Village, Akins region in Ghana and she provided a strong spiritual base for David and his two siblings. Adjaye attributes his architectural successes to his parents' cultural and philosophical grounding. In his upbringing the philosophical belief engendered was that 'nothing is impossible'. David Adjaye is steely in this belief. A self-belief that is sometimes baffling to other colleagues: 'Mine is a blind belief which has enabled me to jump through fires, guided by my intuition. I am not a follower but intuitively driven, underpinned by intellect.' 'Through my belief system, I have been able to make things happen.' This has enabled Adjaye to enter new arenas and to compete at the highest international level within the field of architecture. Adjaye asserts that 90 per cent of his clients are looking to enter new arenas or to utilize his innovative ways of thinking about buildings.

He attributes recently winning the commission to create Oslo's Nobel Peace Centre, to the recognition by the Commissioners that he was a kindred spirit who understood their vision. Other recent commissions have included Boston's performing arts centre, New York's Museum of Contemporary Art and the new Museum of Contemporary Art in Denver.

David Adjaye always talks with great passion about London. Neasden, in North West London where he grew up and North London, where he has lived in more recent times, are seen as a 'Microcosm of a diasporic London universe'. Having lived among local Black, Irish, Asian and White English communities, Adjaye proudly announces, 'London is home!'

Adjaye is enthused about his future and the potential of East London, his current work base. 'East London is like an airport. You check in and go to other places. It keeps changing.' Stimulated by and interested in East End energy, David Adjaye loves to see individuals and communities negotiate difference, negotiate the built environment and what he refers to as 'cultural scripts'. For instance he loves the process of seeing Ethiopian boys becoming London boys, finding this inspirational; he believes that this tells us something about the human spirit.

For him, origin is never an issue, with both parents coming from Ghana, and having an early nomadic lifestyle as the child of a diplomat. Perhaps this confidence in a dynamic changing environment arises from Adjaye's strong sense of personal historical roots. Emerging from a very oral history, Adjaye was made aware of where his grandparents came from, and even paternal great-grandparents. He always had a sense of never needing to question who he was or where he was from, 'I always knew where I came from'. 'There is a whole generation of African kids, displaced because their parents haven't told them where they come from.' For Adjaye this is not an inevitable phenomenon, since he opines that, for most, immigration has been relatively recent, spanning only two generations: 'There is always a link, always a root source, and always one person in the family who will know... This is a powerful grounding tool.'

Adjaye has recently collaborated on the launch of BBC 3 and BBC 1 with Charlie Luxton and Justine Frischmann, former lead singer with Elastica, presenting *Dreamspaces* – Wallpaper* magazine TV, set to drum 'n' bass and club graphics.

Notes:

1. 'Don't Call David Adjaye a Starchitect', *New York Magazine* (2007)
2. *The Guardian*, Tom Dyckoff (Saturday, 8 February 2003)
3. 'David Adjaye's MCA/Denver Opens', *Architectural Record*, David Hill (26 October 2007)

David Thompson has, to date, built six international sports stadia. This international architect was presented to Her Majesty the Queen (1997) at his Indoor Sports Complex, the International Olympic Sports Stadium, Kuala Lumpur. Thompson describes himself as 'A Black maverick who tried to set an example, irrespective of the institutionalized racism entrenched in this country'.

His father, George Ayensu Thompson, who served as a tank driver during the Second World War in North Africa, also studied Structural Engineering at Willesden Polytechnic (1949), later lecturing in Structures & Mathematics at East Ham Polytechnic (1960s). His mother Georgina Quartey was a seamstress who worked at Lyons Teashop, and later as a technician at Elliot Automation, Watchmakers, London. They married and settled in London, until summoned by Kwame Nkrumah to help with post-independence reconstruction.

David Thompson went to the St Peter's Kindergarten and Essendine Primary School, Maida Vale, where he was the only Black child in the class. 'They always made me sit in the front row, so that I wouldn't be distracted by the others' taunts'.

Inspired to follow in his father's footsteps, after a visit to Chicago and seeing the Lake Point Tower, by Meis van der Rhoe, Thompson began the first Black British architectural practice, David Thompson Associates in 1982, after winning a competition to build an international Black arts centre in association with one of Britain's most famous architects, Lord Richard Rogers.

Trevor Robinson runs Quiet Storm Advertising Agency, and is the Chairman of Diversity at the IPA (Institute of Practitioners in Advertising – Britain's leading trade and professional body for advertising, media and marketing communications). Robinson had originally established the advertising practice DNE, with his former partner Alan Young. A dynamic partnership, which was to net highly sought-after contracts within the industry, creating some of the most memorable television adverts of their time.

DNE became one of the leading creative teams in the UK. Famous campaigns in the 1990s included multi-award winning ads for Pot Noodle, Martini, Tango and Golden Wonder Pots. By far, his most controversial and successful advert was the famous Tango advertisement with the catch phrase: 'You know when you've been Tangoed'. This ad was eventually modified, its mischievous nature provoking extreme pranks among excitable British youths, and the campaign receiving intense press attention (not necessarily a bad outcome in the world of advertising). Robinson's recent successes have continued with equally renowned campaigns for Ford Motor Company, Kerry Foods and *Heat* magazine in the 2000s.

Trevor Robinson was born in London in 1964, to Jamaican parents, hailing from Kingston and Port Antonio. His father was a skilled builder and electrician, and his mother a cook. Robinson was encouraged to pursue his own very different path from that of his parents, when it became clear that he was quite literally 'drawn towards art', as he drew friends and family, and designed and built go-carts.

Art, fashion and graphic design beckoned, with Robinson eventually completing study at Hounslow Borough College and Chelsea College of Art in the 1980s. Robinson claims to have been influenced by his father's, 'Go for it attitude', and being reminded that West Indians of the 1950s and '60s, who had come to Britain, were in a very real sense 'a frontiers people'.

His mother was also keen to encourage Robinson's artistic ambitions, as it kept him out of trouble and out of harm's way. After studying graphic design at art college, Trevor Robinson drifted into the world of advertising almost by accident. In order to pay off his college debts, Robinson took a job with the Richmond-based advertising agency Connel and Price, and 'Got bitten by the advertising bug'.

Trevor Robinson was to discover that he had a real aptitude for advertising, and recognized that he had found his true vocation. Robinson has always maintained a strong sense of the past. He learned to appreciate his family history through his mother. Also, his grandfather was able to pass on a great deal of knowledge of his family's origin, living to be 100. Ten years ago, Robinson began a direct dialogue with Africa, visiting Kenya. An encounter at Kenya airport left him seeing a mirror image of himself and his family among a group of travellers. This led Robinson to contemplate the possibility of a family heritage in East Africa.

Robinson also has a keen awareness of his historical journey within an industry not known for its Black professional input. Awards represent a stamp of recognition. He explains also that, 'Winning awards within the advertising industry means that a firm can command higher rates, and becomes sought-after, with team members being "head-hunted"'. Apart from industry accolades, one of Robinson's greatest achievements was falling asleep on the tube and waking up to hear one of his advertisements being talked about. Robinson also gets a kick out of watching people laughing at his adverts at the cinema.

The year 2007 saw the commemoration of the end of the British slave trade 200 years ago and the involvement of Quiet Storm in a campaign in association with the Anti-Slavery Society. The salient point being made was that a form of modern slavery continues, with the international trafficking of women for the sex trade.

Robinson's community commitment has led to his involvement in the 'Create not Hate' advertising campaign (2009). This ad campaign, created in association with the Lambeth Academy, Robinson's old school, is an attempt to stem gun and knife crime.

Trevor Robinson as CEO of Quiet Storm advertising agency, and Chairman of Diversity at the IPA, aims to educate diverse young people, schools and parents into believing that advertising can be a career for a diverse modern Britain.

Terry Jervis is Executive Producer and CEO of one of Britain's most successful Black-owned media enterprises, Jervis Entertainment Media Ltd. The centre of a 'bidding war' between the BBC and the new Channel 4 at the age of nineteen (1981), Jervis became the youngest BBC Head of Department by the age of twenty-eight (1988), covering music and special projects (including documentaries, live events and festivals). His special projects have spanned international popular culture, including documentaries such as *From Bat Man to Star Trek*.

Born in 1962 to a Guyanese mother who was a nurse, and a father who was a Jamaican electrical engineer, Jervis was raised with his two brothers and two sisters in North London and later on the Kingsmead Estate, Hackney, East London. He recently returned to the Kingsmead Estate to launch the All Mead Garden.

Jervis' mother had arrived in Britain in 1957 and his father in 1958. His father was eventually to achieve his ambition of running his own independent company, G.E. Electrics. 'My father was a big Pan-Africanist, and was highly political.' 'My mother wanted me to be a teacher or a social worker.' However, it was his mother's love of the music of Sam Cook that provided the subject of Terry Jervis' first documentary film about Sam Cook's life, featuring contemporary luminaries such as Sydney Poitier, Cy Grant (the voice of Lieutenant Green in children's sci-fi series, *Captain Scarlet and the Mysterons*, pictured opposite), and Harry Bellefonte. Cook had written the songs 'Cupid', 'Twisting the Night Away' and the moving civil right's era anthem, 'Change is Going to Come'. Mining the rich historical seam of Black popular culture, was to form a theme throughout Jervis' career.

As a young boy Jervis had an aptitude for drawing cartoons, which his entrepreneurial spirit transformed into making his own cartoon books and selling them to other students. The money saved from this enterprise was re-invested into cheap flights to the USA, where he bought American classic records to sell in the UK. Jervis' American adventure became groundbreaking in other ways, affording him the opportunity of meeting his music industry heroes, such as Alan Kline, former manager of Sam Cook and the Rolling Stones, as well as Jackie Wilson, who had popularised the song 'Reet Petite'.

These experiences were to result in the film, *From Gospel to Soul*, the UK premier of which was to be held at a hired cinema in Hackney. It was this film that attracted the attentions of a BBC talent 'scout', and later, the interst of BBC's Sue Woodward and Jeremy Isaacs (the producer responsible for the acclaimed series *The World at War*).

Ironically, the BBC first made Jervis aware of the imminent launch of Channel 4 and it was with Channel 4 that Jervis was to receive his first formal film school training. Until then he had been self-taught on Super 8 film (1981–82).

The BBC came calling in 1982, offering to send Jervis to train at the Polytechnic of Central London (now called the University of Westminster), for a degree in journalism and law. Upon completion of his degree, Jervis undertook training at Elstree Film School, Borehamwood in news and current affairs, events and music.

Jervis' 'trans-Atlantic' years began in 1992, when word of his talent had spread and he was invited to work in L.A., New York and Washington, eventually working for the Motown record label. These new opportunities enabled Jervis to work as a Freelance Executive Producer for the BBC, and to travel between the UK and the USA (1992–2000).

Terry Jervis has produced and directed well over forty documentaries, entertainment series and television programmes since 1988. Jervis was Producer/Director of *Soul of Soul* (1988), featuring Quincy Jones, Eddy Grant and Paul Young; Producer of the *Behind the Beat* series; *Stevie Wonder's Birthday Celebration*; and *The Making of Moonwalker* (1988); Director of the pioneering comedy *Real McCoy* (1992–93), and of Jeremy Clarkson's earliest offerings on TV – *Clarkson's Star Cars* (1993), for the BBC. Jervis produced *Baadasss TV* (1994), *Rapido TV* for Channel 4, presented by Ice-T and Andi Oliver – telling the story of their rise to world dominance; produced and directed the documentary *Raising Tennis Aces: The Williams Story* (2001), featuring Venus and Serena Williams, and he was producer of the Multicultural Achievement Awards, hosted by June Sarpong (2002) for Carlton Television.

Today, Jervis Entertainment Media Ltd is one of the few live global producers in the world. For the first time in history it used global satellite to relay the Millennium New Year's Eve celebrations worldwide, broadcast through UK operated satellites. Pioneers of satellite technology have thanked Terry Jervis, and Jervis Entertainment Media, for its services to British satellite operating systems. By using satellite, Jervis has raised awareness of its global potential.

Jervis Entertainment Media has recently signed a major contract with the Ministry of Defence, aimed at the promotion of the Royal Air Force, and raising awareness about its links with technological innovation in the twenty-first century.

Jervis' philosophy has been, 'You have to understand who you are. There are no boundaries for me. Even where we encounter cultural differences, we need to learn how to negotiate these.'

Noel Uche was one of the first wave of bright, young self-taught computer games creators, who understood the true potential of thetechnology for the mass market. 'At that time computer courses were too expensive, so I simply decided to teach myself the technology.' This resourceful attitude meant that within a year of this decision, Uche's skills and grasp of computer technology could not be denied, and he was offered a job in Milton Keynes for the company MINDSEYE. Following an interview, 'I got the job the same day'.

His first project was the *Thomas & Friends* computer game, based upon the popular children's character Thomas the Tank Engine. What this lacked in street credibility, it certainly made up for in sales (The game remains a 'bestseller' to the present day). In fact, the popularity of this game was to land Noel Uche his next job, and to begin his lifelong association with big name international branding companies.

Noel Uche was born in Dulwich, South London, and grew up in Brixton. His mother, a teacher, and his father, an architect, had known each other in Nigeria and were married at Our Lady of the Rosary, Knowle Close, Brixton. Noel's mother's career took an interesting turn when she re-trained as a computer programmer and went to work for the Inland Revenue. This undoubtedly fed Uche's awareness of the then 'new technology', and he learned at close hand the transformative nature of computer skills on the prospects of the individual.

Uche attended Stockwell Primary School and Tulse Hill Comprehensive. Both Uche and his parents became dissatisfied with the low expectations and the indiscipline within the British comprehensive school system, in particular in relation to young Black males in the 1980s, so they decided to send him to Nigeria to complete his education. This move in 1985 was to prove to be both a revelation and a turning point for the young Uche. Soon Uche was to discover that Nigerian schools were very competitive, strong on study and discipline. Far from being isolated, he found himself in the company of a wave of other British-Nigerians whose parents had acted upon similar concerns. A Nigerian university was to follow, with the same sort of camaraderie carried on into campus life that he found at boarding school. These were very happy times for Noel Uche and contacts fostered during these days have continued as strong business alliances to the present day, enabling him to trade confidently with western and southern Africa.

Returning to Britain, Uche applied to study architecture at Westminster University (1992). While economic recession had a negative impact upon the world of architecture, Uche's graphic design portfolio was to prove attractive to the advertising industry. In 1995 Uche made the move to a career in video games.

For many years Uche lived in Kensington, where he recalls enjoying its relaxed café society, which he shared with his wealthy neighbours. Having returned to the Brixton of his childhood, Uche has noticed the growth of affluence within some sectors of the Black community, and feels safe, comfortable and enjoys the familiarity in the old faces that he still sees around. 'When my mother comes to visit from her retirement in Nigeria, they all know her.'

One day Noel Uche met an elderly gentleman buying a *Thomas & Friends* computer game for his four-year-old grandson in a South Kensington branch of Dixon's. The man was flattered to meet one of the game's producers. This meeting made Uche realise his computer game mass-market breakthrough and its long-term potential, transcending age, income and culture.

Uche went on to form his own companies, MIDA and RV1 BDX. Later, travelling to Silicon Valley (USA), the home of the modern computer games industry.

Games subsequently produced by Uche have included *Micro Prose* for Atari, as well as the Formula I game for X-Box and PlayStation II. Projects have included computer animation and graphics for terrestrial, digital and cable television, as well as visualisations for architectural design models.

Today, Uche is chief executive of Africa United in Music Group (AUMG), which manages and promotes international artists to and from Africa. Artists have included Sean Paul, 50 Cent, the Nigerian super-groups P-Square and Style Plus, and South Africa's Lebo. AUMG has sponsored the Best African Music Category at the 2005 MOBO (Music of Black Origin) Awards. Uche's multimedia projects have included AUMG Live TV, Sky 148 and BEN TV. Today, sees Noel Uche's company backing new mobile phone advertising technology, involving digitised moving images.

The Royal Free Hospital, Hampstead was the birthplace of **'The Ringtone King', Alexander Amosu**, in 1975, who was born to Nigerian parents studying in England. Amosu's mother was a nurse originally from Ikorodu and his father, an accountant, was from Abeokuta. Amosu spent his formative years between the ages of three to twelve in Nigeria, after which he returned to England for his secondary education at Hampstead School. 'We lived in a small flat off Kilburn High Road at my grandmother's'.

From the age of sixteen Alexander Amosu's twin interests of business and technology were to be reconciled through a business studies course at North London Technical College, Seven Sisters Road; a BTEC and a degree in aeronautical engineering at St Alban's College, and at Queen Mary and South Bank Universities.

Alexander Amosu discovered the potential of the ringtone by accident. After buying a mobile phone in the 1990s, Amosu's natural curiosity got the better of him, when trying to programme an original ringtone for his own use. It was Amosu's brother who asked him to replicate the ring tone on his phone and took it to school. The phone went off in class, and the response by students was overwhelming, announcing the birth of a desirable commercial product. 'They came up to my brother and said, I want that ringtone. By that evening I had twenty-one people queuing outside of our house requesting ringtones. I said to myself, if all these people wanted ringtones, surely they would be prepared to pay for them?'

Amosu was to realise the power of word of mouth when people began asking each other, 'Where did you get this?' In his first year of trading Amosu received a telephone call from his accountant to ask him if he was aware that his business had made £1.6 million over the past year. He was only twenty-four years old and the *Independent* had already dubbed him 'The King of Ring Tones', Britain's premier provider of mobile ring tones and graphics. Amosu is credited with bringing urban music, such as Hip Hop and R&B to mobile ring tones and, arguably, in so doing, leading to its crossover mass-market appeal.

Amosu's greatest success with R&B ringtones came with the ringtone *Big Pimping* by Jay-Z. As was the case with all licensed music, Amosu's company was required to pay 10 per cent of its gross profits to M.C.P.S. (Musical, Mechanical and Performing Rights Society).

Business acumen was not new to the Amosu family. It was Amosu's great-grandfather who was the first person to begin a business making and selling singlet-vests or waistcoats in Nigeria. This business proved to be extremely successful. During the next generation Amosu's grandfather made money from building houses and buying land in Ikorundo.

Involvement in a broad range of ex-curricular interests, taught Amosu self-belief and resourcefulness; he joined the Air Cadet Force, based at Edgeware. Here, he became a Chipmunk and later a Glider, learning to fly a plane, registering plane hours towards his license. He also went camping and swam with the Air Cadets.

A budding entrepreneur since boyhood, Alexander Amosu found 'a gap in the market', at school in Hampstead when pupils were not allowed to buy chewing gum and prevented from leaving school grounds during break times. Using 'seed' money from his £10-a-week paper round, Amosu sold chewing gum to his fellow pupils. Between the ages of fourteen and fifteen other moneymaking ideas came in the form of organising five-a-side football tournaments – each team paid £25 to compete and food and refreshments were provided free of charge, with a trophy for the winner. One such tournament netted Amosu £1,200. Once he was made aware that people were prepared to pay to compete, Amosu was to go on to organise basketball and tennis competitions. During this time, Amosu was to emerge as 'Shadow King' or the college dance impresario. What to do with an under-used huge hall? He managed to persuade the college authorities that he had a plan, and would invest £100 of his own money and equipment (turntables, mixers and a DJ) in the venture. A one-off dance led to a seasonal fixture of college dances, covering Christmas, Easter and the end of term.

Amosu had always relied upon his own capital, and ploughed much of his money made from Saturday jobs back into projects. Between the ages of sixteen and eighteen, he worked for the high street electrical retailer Tandy's. One of Amosu's most successful business ventures as a teenager came at the age of eighteen, when he decided to establish a contract cleaning business. The idea came to Amosu by accident when his aunt asked him to clean her house. An obedient Amosu complied and she was so pleased with his efforts that she gave him a £20 thank you. It occurred to Amosu that his aunt was not the only over-worked professional looking for cleaning services and he asked himself what about businesses requiring cleaners? Within a short while Amosu had won twelve cleaning contracts and was forced to go to the Job Centre to recruit more staff!

As a young Black man in business Amosu has been met with both curiosity and suspicion in equal measure. He humorously relays the story of attempting to purchase his first Porsche. Knowing that this transaction could prove problematical, Amosu had contacted his bank manager in advance, to his puzzlement. Lo and behold, Amosu was all but ignored by the first person whom he encountered, a senior car salesman; following a pep talk from his formidable mother of the 'don't let them spoil it for you', variety, Amosu entered the dealership for a second time that day. It was a young trainee salesman who 'not knowing any better', came up to him and lavished attention upon the young entrepreneur and from whom he bought a £42,000 vehicle there and then. Amosu insisted to the dealership manager that this trainee, who had been at the job for less than a week, should receive the commission from his purchase and not the senior salesman (Amosu's bank manager, was called as expected, and was standing by to confirm that funds were available).

With a better track record than most, Amosu admits that not all of his projects as a youth were successful. However, he likens himself to an athlete: 'You've got to train, you've got to fail and at an early age make mistakes.' This philosophy has been more than vindicated by Amosu's achievements as an entrepreneur. In 2007 he launched a range of his luxury mobile phone products at Harrods. These luxury phones, aimed at celebrities and the super-rich, are made from gold, diamonds and precious gemstones, and range in price from £5,000 – £1 million. P. Diddy has bought a gem-encrusted Amosu Blackberry phone worth £45,000.

Today, Amosu is developing a brand of luxury products, making news in 2009 for designing a one-off creation – the world's most expensive suit. Selling for £70,000, it was made from the world's most luxurious fabrics, with gold and diamond buttons. Now regarded as a business guru, Alexander regularly appears as a judge on Nigeria's *Dragons Den*, and will be launching the AA Trust to support young entrepreneurs who have a business plan, between the ages of sixteen and twenty-seven.

Amosu has been keen to encourage creativity and innovation within multimedia, investing in the Screen Nation Awards, owning 25 per cent of its shares. Accolades for business have come in the form of African Business Organisation of the Year (2005) to Young Entrepreneur of the Year, The Institute of Directors (UK) (2005).

CHAPTER FIVE

CIVIC AND POLITICAL

AFRICANS WHO BROUGHT DEMOCRACY TO LONDON

Londoners of African and Caribbean origin have contributed to the civic and political life of the capital in many ways. Being among its most oppressed citizens, these Black Londoners have been at the forefront of the struggles of the poor and disenfranchised. The brutality of slavery lit flames of political zeal, which inspired some of the finest political orators of the nineteenth century who helped to transform the campaign for the abolition of slavery into one of Britain's first mass political campaigns.

Among the first campaigners for democratic government and the freedom of the press, as leaders of the Chartist movement, were Robert Wedderburn who had docked in London from a British warship from Jamaica at the age of seventeen, and William Cuffay, one of the three London delegates to the Chartists' national convention, who was born in Chatham to a Jamaican ship's cook. Both were eventually deported for their seditious activities. The Chartist movement was eventually to result in the extension of universal adult suffrage in Britain – the foundation of our modern democracy.

At the end of the Victorian age, another Black Londoner was to champion the poor and oppressed – John Archer. Although born in Liverpool to Barbadian and Irish parents, Archer settled in Battersea around 1890 and founded a photography studio in Battersea Park Road. John Archer is an example of a British-born Black man who held civic office in Britain as a councillor, alderman and mayor in the early twentieth century.

The ranks of often neglected women who have been political activists in London's history include Amy Ashwood Garvey. She co-founded the United Negro Improvement Association in collaboration with Marcus Aurelius Garvey (1914), which at its height in 1919 boasted a membership of 3 million people internationally. The Florence Mill Restaurant in London that she opened in 1929 with Sam Manning became a meeting place for Pan-Africanist intellectuals, writers, artists and visiting celebrities, and served as a centre of political discussion and organization for Black Londoners. Amy Ashwood Garvey later became an active campaigner against the fascist invasion of Ethiopia through the campaign group The International African Friends of Ethiopia.

POLITICAL ACTIVISM: THE BEST SOLUTION TO THE WORST INJUSTICE

What makes a man or woman enter political life? Undoubtedly, a certain amount of personal ambition. However, many are fired by the injustices that they have witnessed. To individuals such as Robert Wedderburn, who had witnessed his grandmother and his pregnant mother suffer under the slave-master's lash, the concept of freedom and justice was not an abstract ideal.

Privilege did not dampen John Archer's local commitment to the poor, the sick and the young in Battersea. Indeed, Archer believed that the greater one's economic capacity, the greater were his social and civic responsibilities.

Amy Ashwood Garvey's Pan-African ideals were fired not by the worst of human nature, but by witnessing its heights – the capacity of cultural survival. Through the role model of her grandmother, who retained memories of an Africa before her enslavement, Ashwood Garvey cultivated a cultural pride in her African heritage, which was rare for those who had undergone a British education. She was instrumental in the formation of political philosophies of Garveyism, Pan-Africanism and Black Power. In her striving to create support structures for the African Diaspora in London, Ashwood Garvey had an enormous impact on the political education of those were to lead the independent states of Africa and the Caribbean.

Lord John David Beckett Taylor of Warwick became a Life Peer in 1996, succeeding the late Lord Pitt of Hampstead as the only Black person sitting in the House of Lords. The House of Lords now includes twelve Black and Asian peers, since Lord Taylor's ennoblement.

A barrister since 1978, his involvement in community politics began as a Solihull borough councillor between 1986 and 1990. Lord Taylor participated in a Home Office/Department of Trade and Industry inner-city think-tank in 1988 which led to his appointment as a special adviser to the Home Secretary and introduced the Criminal Evidence (Amendment) Bill.

Taylor came to national attention when he stood as prospective parliamentary candidate for Cheltenham in 1992 for the Conservative Party; despite his candidature receiving the support of the party hierarchy, alleged racism within Cheltenham and among the local Conservatives manifested itself in a hostile campaign against Taylor's selection. Lord Taylor's legal expertise and high profile have led to his involvement in the media, as vice-chairman of the All Party Parliamentary Media Group and as presenter with ITV, Sky and the BBC (e.g. *Crime Stalker*, BBC1's *System on Trial with John Taylor*, and *The John Taylor Programme* on BBC Radio 2).

Lord Taylor of Warwick is a member of the NUJ, the Bar Council, and is also Vice-President of the British Board of Film Classification and is a member of the Association of Conservative Peers. Lord Taylor of Warwick is also a member of the Industry and Parliament Trust. He was also Chancellor of Bournemouth University (his term of office ending in 2006).

Olaudah Equiano was a major figure in the Abolitionist Movement. He was a popular and articulate headline speaker at anti-slavery gatherings in England and America. His speeches and later his autobiography revealed to the British public the evils of slavery, experienced from a former enslaved man's point of view. He also lifted the veil on the barbarity of the slave trade as it was practiced in America and the West Indies. Author of one of the earliest autobiographies of an African in the English language, one of the book's revelations was the muzzling of enslaved household servants on a permanent basis, to prevent them from speaking to each other. These metallic muzzles were often placed in the mouth and over the face even at night, preventing sleep. In 1783 it was Olaudah Equiano who alerted Granville Sharp and the Abolitionist Movement of the Zong massacre (1781) in which 133 slaves were thrown overboard in mid-ocean for the insurance money.

Olaudah Equiano was born in what we now know as Nigeria, near the River Niger, to Igbo-speaking parents. Today, his origin has been disputed by the alleged emergence of a record of his birth in America. Of this debate, all that may be said is that, at a time when international acceptance of the enslavement of Africans meant that even those who had bought their freedom, were forever in danger of return to the condition of slavery, we may never know if or why Olaudah Equiano may have chosen to give a false origin for a ship's record. Under these circumstances, he surely could be forgiven for doing so?

Equiano had been kidnapped and enslaved at the age of ten, with his younger sister, and taken to Barbados and then America. Testimomies written, in his autobiography, of the sexual abuse meted out to African women, who were enslaved, often found Equiano asking what had become of his own sister and how might she be similarly suffering? One of Equiano's enslavers, Pascal, was a naval captain who taught him seamanship. It was Pascal's sister who taught him to read and write. Another enslaver was a Quaker merchant by the name of King, for whom Equiano worked on his shipping routes and stores.

In 1765, King promised that Olaudah Equiano could buy his freedon for £40. Equiano was in his early twenties when he raised the money and bought his freedom, beginning a new life of adventure. Equiano became a seaman and visited the Americas, Turkey and the Mediterranean, and also participated in major naval battles during the Seven Years' War. Determined to make the most of his freedom, Equiano's wanderlust made him join the Phipps expedition of 1772–73, as an explorer in the search of the Northwest Passage to India. Returning to London following this, Equiano was aware of his uniquely privileged position, as first-hand witness to a slave trade, which he had survived, when so many others had been worked to death or murdered by sadistic enslavers, upon capture, transportation or within a couple of years of their kidnapping, on the plantation. Olaudah Equiano married Susannah Cullen, a local woman from Soham, Cambridgeshire (1792). The forces of destiny had conspired to create in Equiano an African who would be listened to: a baptised Christian, who was literate, articulate, well-groomed and conversant with European eighteenth-century social graces, in short – an African gentleman.

In 1788, as a leader of the Abolitionist Movement, along with Granville Sharp, Equiano submitted a petition to the British parliament to end the slave trade and petitioned England's Queen Charlotte, wife of King George III. Having addressed the Queen of England, Equiano was now ready to address the world, writing his autobiography in 1789, *The Interesting Narrative of the Life of Olaudah Equiano or Gustavus Vasa, the African, Written by Himself*. Equiano's book was not only an important work of propaganda in the campaign against slavery, but also a compelling read, which became a bestseller, and holds up today as a fascinating, stylish and acomplished work of literature, with an ironic and surprisingly modern authorial voice.

Equiano's appointment as head of the expedition to settle London's poor Black population in Sierra Leone either suggests that Equiano's leadership was highly valued by some members of the British establishment, or that they were trying to get rid of him! Either way, he did not live to complete this particular journey.

An abolitionist and a campaigner for parliamentary rights for working-class men, Equiano lived a life of enormous risk, constantly having to negotiate an increasingly hostile environmment caused by those fearful of seeing their slaving and hereditary interests undermined. A wave of anti-radical feeling was further aroused in England by the French and the American Revolutions. Equiano appears to have died in 'hiding', with even his enemies unaware of his death. He left a considerable estate of £950 (or approximately £100,000 in today's money) to his second and only surviving daughter, Joanna. Joanna and her husband, a vicar, are both buried at Abney Park Cemetary, Stoke Newington, London.

After such a traumatic early life, rather than choosing to enjoy the relative privilege of his freedom and education, Equiano could not ignore the plight of his fellow enslaved Africans. He risked the retribution of a society still run by slave traders to speak out about slavery's shameful and barbaric practices. Today, a Blue Plaque from English Heritage commemorates Equiano's last known London address. Formally a Congregationalist Chapel, it is now the American Church in Tottenham Court Road.

May the time come – at least the speculation to me is pleasing – when the sable people shall gratefully commemorate the auspicious era of extensive freedom.

(Olaudah Equiano, *The Interesting Narrative of the Life of Olaudah Equiano or Gustavus Vasa, the African, Written by Himself*, 1789)

Free Natives of the West Indies, engraving by Agostino Brunias, 1790. Courtesy of the Barbados Museum and Historical Society

Mary Prince was a major figure in the Abolitionist Movement. She became a spokeswoman for enslaved people, giving her first-hand eyewitness testimonies of the horrors of the slave trade to packed public meetings the length and breadth of Britain and America. In 1831 *The History of Mary Prince* was to become one of the first narratives of the life of a Black woman to be published in England. It documented Prince's journey from plantation enslavement to slavery in a 'sophisticated' metropolitan London of the 1820s and '30s: from Bermuda to Leigh Street, Bloomsbury, by way of the Turks and Caicos Islands, and Antigua. This book was an important abolitionist propaganda document, in the campaign against the slave trade. Prince's book reveals the build-up and motivation, which led to her eventual escape from captivity in London, after years of endurance, torture and sexual abuse under slavery.

The History of Mary Prince became a bestseller, with three editions being reprinted in the year in which it was first published. Also, by the publication year, 1831, the anti-slavery movement had had an enormous impact upon public opinion. No longer could British society plead ignorance of plantation cruelty, with the mounting evidence of slave and missionary testimonies detailing a catalogue of human degradation upon the plantation and within homes in Britain.

The timing of Mary Prince's testimony has great significance. In 1829, the year of her 'escape', Prince and her supporters in the Anti-Slavery Society presented a petition to parliament regarding her case. The publicity gathered from this parliamentary petition may be said to have spurred on the Anti-Slavery Society to sponsor the publication of Prince's book.

The year 1831, the date of Prince's publication, falls during the last decade of legal slavery upon British soil, and may be said to have been part of the final campaigning push towards complete abolition. By this time the slave trade, or the shipping of slaves for the purpose of sale, had been made illegal since 1807 and Black servant-slaves in London, like Prince herself, were deserting their captors in ever-increasing numbers. In 1833 the Slavery Abolition Act was passed. The abolition of slavery came into effect on 1 August 1834. In reality, however, slave children under the age of six were actually freed, and children over six and adults became 'apprentices', working for their 'former' enslavers. It was the enslavers who were financially compensated by parliament for the abolition of slavery, to the tune of £20 million, and not the formerly enslaved masses.

Prince's contribution to the Abolitionist Movement and support of her enslaved sisters cannot be underestimated. As a poor but 'respectable' Christian woman, to have spoken out about the brutality of slavery would have been sufficient. However, her courage is magnified by the fact that she risked social opprobrium by daring to speak of her own and other women's endemic and systematic sexual abuse under their enslavement. The impact of this was to undermine the moral basis of slavery and by implication all those who would defend it. It should be remembered that even at the time many in the Abolitionist Movement wanted to censor her history of sexual abuse by her enslavers since girlhood. Her former enslaver's response – to sue the publishers for defamation of character!

I am often much vexed, and I feel great sorrow when I hear some people in this country say, that the slaves do not want to be free... How can slaves be happy when they have the halter round their neck and the whip upon their back? And are disgraced and thought no more of than beasts? – are separated from their mothers and husbands, and children, and sisters, just as cattle are sold and separated? Is it happiness for a driver in the field to take down his wife or sister or child, and strip them, and whip them in such a disgraceful manner? – women that have their children [forced to give birth to their children] exposed in the open field to shame?

Since I have been here I have often wondered how English people can go out to the West Indies and act in such a beastly manner... they forget God and all feelings of shame.
All slaves want to be free – to be free is very sweet.

(Mary Prince, *The History of Mary Prince, A West Indian Slave*, 1831)

John Archer was a British-born Black man who held civic office in nineteenth-century London, as councillor, mayor and alderman. Archer was born in Liverpool in 1863 to a Barbadian father and an Irish mother. He settled in Battersea around 1890 with his Black Canadian wife, and opened a successful, award-winning photographic studio in Battersea Park Road. A highly respected member of London's Black and wider community, Archer was a friend of Samuel Coleridge-Taylor (see p.36) and a delegate at the 1st Pan-Africanist Conference, which was held at Westminster Town hall in 1900. One outcome of the conference was that he was elected to the Executive Committee of the Pan-African Association. Battersea was London's most progressive borough; when Archer was elected Mayor of Battersea in 1913, he declared, 'You have made history tonight... Battersea has done many things in its past, but the greatest it has done is to show that it has no racial prejudice, and that it recognizes a man for the work he has done.' He played an active part in the civic life of the borough, especially in tackling poverty and public health. Archer later became election agent for the Asian MP Shapurji Saklatvala, both as a Labour Party candidate and then as a Communist Party candidate. Archer died in 1932.

Mr. J. C. Archer, a photographer and a man of colour, who is the Progressive nominee for the Mayoralty of Battersea. A close fight is promised next Monday. "I am prepared," he has said, "to meet any man on a public platform on the question of colour prejudice." He has lived in Battersea twenty-three years.

Amy Ashwood Garvey, political activist, impresario and historian. Born Amy Ashwood in Port Antonio, Jamaica, in 1897, she inherited a highly developed political sensibility from her grandmother, the daughter of Paramount Ruler of Juben (Ghana), in the independent state of the Ashanti Confederacy, who was brought to Jamaica as a slave. In 1914 she was co-founder, along with Marcus Aurelius Garvey (later to become her first husband), of the United Negro Improvement Association, which boasted a membership of 3 million people at its height in 1919. When she came to London in 1922 she quickly became aligned to the Pan-African movement, eventually chairing the fourth Pan-African Congress in 1945. In collaboration with Sam Manning, however, she is also credited with promoting the all-Negro revues that toured in London and Europe in the 1920s, with such critically acclaimed shows as *Hey, Hey!* and *Brown Sugar*. In 1929 Amy Ashwood and Sam Manning opened the Florence Mill Restaurant in London, which became a meeting-place for Pan-Africanist intellectuals, writers, artists and visiting celebrities.

When fascist Italy invaded Abyssinia (Ethiopia) in 1935, Amy Ashwood Garvey became an active campaigner for the Abyssinians, founding the International African Friends of Abyssinia in 1936, and being part of the deputation that welcomed Haile Selassie when he arrived at Waterloo Station (see p. 163). During the Second World War, she negotiated with the Roosevelt government to offer wartime work to unemployed Jamaican women. This photograph depicts Amy Ashwood Garvey (right), wearing Ghana Kinte cloth robes, at 1 Basset Road, Ladbroke Grove, which she established as an African and Caribbean students' hostel and a women's resources centre in the 1950s. In later life she lived in Nigeria, Ghana and Liberia, studying the history and culture of these countries. She died in 1969.

Claudia Jones in the offices of the *West Indian Gazette*. Born in Trinidad in 1915, Jones emigrated to America when she was seven. In 1956, however, she was deported from America because of her communist links and she settled in London. She was a prominent Communist Party leader and trade unionist. On her arrival she formed a committee to support the victims of the McCarthyism that was sweeping America and driving so many left-wing activists and sympathizers to seek asylum in London. The following year, concerned that

the Kenyan revolutionary movement was receiving biased treatment in the press, she initiated a bulletin comprising press cuttings and original articles. In 1958, the year of the Notting Hill riots, Claudia Jones founded the *West Indian Gazette*, the first ever mass-circulation Black newspaper in Britain. She continued to campaign on behalf of Kenyan political prisoners, and the issue of African independence and racial violence in Britain. This also inspired her to form the African, Asian and Caribbean Organization. In 1958 Jones founded the Notting Hill Carnival to foster better relations between the Black and White community (see p. 186). She died in 1964.

Lord Pitt, with Lady Pitt, at his eightieth birthday celebrations, 1993. David Thomas Pitt was born in St David's, Grenada, in 1913. He came to Britain to study medicine in 1932 after winning one of the island's top scholarships, qualifying in 1938 and eventually setting up his own general practice in Gower Street, Central London. His political life in London began in 1947 when he was part of a Commonwealth delegation of the Federation of the West Indies. Pitt played a full part in the political mobilization of postwar immigrants to Britain, as chairman of the Campaign Against Racial Discrimination, and as chairman of the Community Relations Commission from 1966 to 1977. He represented Hackney as a member of the London County Council and the Greater London Council in the 1960s. Although he was an unsuccessful parliamentary candidate for the seats of Hampstead and Clapham, he forged a path for the Black MPs who followed.

In 1985 he was created **Baron Pitt of Hampstead**, and the following year he became the first Black president of the British Medical Association. He was patron of the Black Contractors Association until his death in 1994. This photograph shows him (right) at the inaugural gala dinner of the Parliamentary Black Caucus in 1987 (others shown are, from left to right, Keith Vaz, Bernie Grant, Ronald Delloms and Diane Abbott).

This picture depicts **Bernie Grant**, then Leader of Haringey Council, with Dolly Kiffin, head of the Broadwater Farm Youth Association, 1985.

Born in Guyana in 1944, Dr Grant came to Britain in 1963. After working as a railway clerk and telephonist he became a full-time union official in 1978. Bernie Grant was elected as Labour councillor for Haringey in the same year, becoming leader in 1985. Grant came to prominence in the British press when he defended the young people whose frustration at police harassment resulted in the Broadwater Farm riot, in which a police officer was killed. Bernie Grant went on to represent Tottenham as one of Britain's first Black MPs in 1987, until his death in the year 2000 at the age of fifty-six.

A firebrand activist Grant campaigned for reparations for the British enslavement of Africans, and the repatriation of African artefacts from British historical collections in museums and galleries. Bernie Grant caused equal delight and consternation by wearing African dashiki to parliament, particularly in 1996 at the state opening of parliament. These dashikis were to become something of a Grant signature.

In addition to the three sons who succeed him, Bernie Grant leaves the living monuments of the Bernie Grant Centre, Tottenham – a 300-seat theatre and education centre, which Grant fought to establish for the people of Tottenham before he died, designed by David Adjaye Architects (see p.95), and the Bernie Grant Archives at the University of Middlesex.

Former Prime Minister Tony Blair said of Bernie Grant:

> He was someone for whom I had immense respect and affection… He was a dedicated and diligent constituency MP who worked tirelessly for the less well-off, whose commitment to social justice was unwavering and who also made a powerful contribution to development issues… He advised me regularly on issues relating to development and on our relations with Caribbean countries.
>
> [Bernie Grant] was someone who always made efforts to understand and respect other people's point of view. Bernie was also an inspiration to Black people throughout the country. One day I hope it will be commonplace to have Black and Asian MPs at Westminster… When that happens, it will in no small measure be a tribute to Bernie Grant and the inspirational lead he gave. ('Labour MP Bernie Grant dies', BBC News, Saturday, 8 April 2000)

Gertrude Paul was appointed commissioner for the Commission for Racial Equality (CRE) in 1980, and reappointed in 1984. The London-based CRE was hugely instrumental in the fight for equality for all Black Britons. It had the power to investigate cases of discrimination, to examine documents and to redress discriminatory practices. A total of fifteen commissioners sat on the governing body; Mrs Paul was one of the earliest Black women to become a commissioner. The CRE has now been succeeded by the Human Rights Commission.

Born in London in 1950 and raised in Brixton, **Linda Bellos Adebowale** gained public recognition as part of the Greater London Council Women's Unit, and as vice-chair of her local Labour Party Black Section. She was elected leader of Lambeth Council in 1986. Bellos' political philosophy has centred around two key issues: the involvement of working-class people in decision-making and equal opportunities.

While leading Lambeth Council, Bellos undertook many initiatives, including a move to increase the representation of Black contractors from two to 100. In the 1990s Bellos forged a new career in broadcasting at Greater London Radio. She was also coordinator of the Global Trade Centre in London, which existed to increase the trade links between the Black community in the UK and the rest of the world. Until 2007 Bellos was Chair of the Southwark Lesbian, Gay Bisexual Trans Network, and in December 2005 Bellos, now a grandmother, and her partner, Caroline Jones, were among the first couples to sign a Civil Partnership Agreement, witnessed by family and friends.

She is currently chair of the Southwark Action for Voluntary Organisations (SALVO), and is treasurer of the African Reparation Movement (UK). Bellos works on mainstreaming equality and diversity within the the British Army, the Metropolitan Police, the Crown Prosecution Service and the Association of Chief Police Officers. Today she runs her own consultancy, Diversity Solutions Ltd.

In 2002 Linda Bellos received a Metropolitan Police Volunteer Award 'in recognition of outstanding contribution in supporting the local community'. In 2006, she was awarded an OBE in the Queen's New Year's Honours for services to diversity.

Merle Amory was the first Afro-Caribbean woman to lead a district council in Britain. Born in 1958 on the West Indian island of St Kitts, Amory came to Britain at the age of five, settling in London, and joined the Labour Party in 1974. She stood as Councillor for the Stonebridge ward at the age of twenty-three and later for Queen's Park. She became Leader of Brent Council in 1986, the first Black woman council leader in Brent and the youngest Labour council leader in London. As leader of the London Transport Board for the GLC in 1987–88 she was responsible for the regulation of all transport in London.

In 2005 **Gloria Mills** made history as the first Black woman president of the TUC (Trades Union Congress). This election took place on the last day of the 137th Congress in Brighton. Gloria was awarded an MBE in 1999 for her services to trade unions, and a CBE in 2005 for services to equal opportunities.

Whilst working in legal publishing, Mills joined the National Society of Operative Printers, Graphical and Media Personnel (NATSOPA) in 1978. This was to be her first involvement with the trade union movement.

Gloria Mills worked as regional and then national equal rights officer for the National Union of Public Employees (NUPE) before becoming the director for equal opportunities at UNISON, Britain's biggest trade union, in 1993. In the following year she became the first Black woman to be elected to the TUC's ruling body, the General Council. She also sat on the Department of Employment and Education's Race Relations and Employment Advisory Group and the TUC's Race Committee.

Through her campaigning Mills has fought for equal opportunities to be extended to women, Black people and lesbian and gay workers, and the young; she has also campaigned for the national minimum wage, as well as lobbying on migrant and human rights issues. Mills became a senior manager/senior trade union officer for UNISON with responsibility for strategic equality and employment policies. She has also served as CRE (Commission for Racial Equality) Commissioner representing the TUC, and was a member of the Labour Party National Policy Forum.

Mills was instrumental in lobbying for an amendment to the European Union's 1957 Amsterdam Treaty of Rome (1997). The revisions to the treaty ensured that there were legal provisions to protect people on the grounds of race, disability, sexual orientation, age and religion, 'to have legal redress if people are discriminated against in any EU country was very critical'.

In 2000 Gloria Mills was elected to the Executive Committee of the TUC as chair of its Race Committee and a member of the TUC Women's Committee, before becoming TUC President (2005). During her presidency Mills strove 'to make British workplaces, towns and cities more inclusive places to work and live'. In her thirty-year Trade Union career Mills has witnessed equal opportunity policies move from the margins to become 'mainstream' employment practice, enshrined in law.

This image depicts **Lord William (Bill) Manuel Morris**, when he was Deputy General Secretary of the Transport and General Workers Union (TGWU), with Ron Todd (General Secretary). Born in Jamaica in 1938, and educated at Mizpah School, Lord Morris came to England in 1954 to join his mother, later becoming qualified in mechanical engineering. After 'a baptism of fire' in union posts at Hardy Spicers engineering firm in Birmingham, he became full-time TGWU officer in 1973. His influence on national trade unionism emerged in 1979 when he was responsible for leading negotiations in the bus and coach industry as national Trade Group Secretary for Passenger Services. He was elected General Secretary of the TGWU in 1991. Morris has also served on a wide range of bodies including the European Community's Economic and Social Affairs Committee and the TUC's Race Relations Committee. He is currently a member of the Employment Appeal Tribunal, the England and Wales Cricket Board, and Chancellor to the Universities of Technology, Jamaica and Stafford, England.

Honoured with an Order of Jamaica (2002), and Commander of the Order of the British Empire or KBE (2003), Lord Morris was ennobled in 2006, as Baron Morris of Handsworth.

Diane Abbott MP, featured with the late Bernie Grant MP. Born in 1953, Abbott was educated at Cambridge University before working for the Home Office. A former member of Westminster City Council (1982–86), Abbott also worked for TV-AM. In 1987 she was elected Labour MP for Stoke Newington, making history as Britain's first Black female MP. Diane Abbott became a member of the Labour Party's National Executive in 1991.

In the 1980s and 1990s Diane Abbott was instrumental in campaigning for the pioneering and controversial Labour Party policy of women-only shortlists to encourage the election of women to parliament. However, despite the success of this policy in the 1997 election in yielding a greater number of female MPs in parliament, Abbott laments that this has not included a single Black woman. She has only been joined in parliament by one other Black female MP, Dawn Butler in 2005, who replaced Paul Boateng as MP for Brent South (following his appointment as British High Commissioner to South Africa – see p.137). The year 2005 also saw the previous Black female MP Oona King Loose her seat in Bethnal Green (King was a Labour Member of Parliament in the UK from 1997 to 2005).

Abbott has become known to millions of television viewers, as a political commentator on the popular and topical BBC TV current affairs and politics programme, *This Week*. This programme, hosted by Andrew Neil, in which Abbott, a Labour MP, gives commentary alongside former Conservative MP and Minister Michael Portillo, received an award in 2006 from the Hansard Society Award for 'Opening Up Politics', at the Channel 4 Political Awards Ceremony.

Above left: A tireless community and race relations campaigner, **Ambrosine Neil** came to Britain in 1962 to pursue a career in dress design. She was founder of the Parents Association Educational Advance in 1976, and was elected Labour Councillor for Brent in 1982, although she gained notoriety by 'crossing the floor' of the council chamber to join the Conservatives, thus turning Brent into a hung council after twelve years under Labour. Brent later passed into Conservative control, but Neil lost her seat in 1986 when she stood as Conservative Councillor for Manor Ward, Brent South.

Above right: **Rudolph Daley** trying out an exercise bike while opening Lambeth's fourth day centre for people with severe learning difficulties, late 1980s. Daley came to Britain in 1958 from Jamaica. After a career in administration he was elected to Lambeth Council in 1986, becoming Mayor of Lambeth in 1988.

Above: **Valda Louise James** as Mayor of Islington, 1988. Born in 1927, she came to Britain in 1961 and raised her six children alone, in conditions of some hardship while working in catering, dressmaking and eventually nursing. In 1986, she became the first Black women to be elected to Islington Council, where she applied her experience of raising a family in difficult circumstances to her work on the Social Services Committee, the Review Committee and eventually as chair of the Children and Family Committee. She has been vice-chair of the Pensioners Forum, council committee member, and serves as church warden and chair of the pastoral committee of her church.

Two years later, she transformed the face of Islington local government by becoming mayor, with her daughter as deputy mayor[1]. James had lost six children out of twelve she carried and because of her first-hand experiences of 'cot death', she chose Focus as her mayoral charity, raising over £60,000 for the baby unit at the Whittington Hospital. Some of her most memorable moments include officially welcoming the late Diana, Princess of Wales, during her time as mayor of the borough on four occasions. She remembers her youthful outlook and laughter on one occasion when she sat on their table at a Young Photographers Graduation Dinner, at Sadler's Wells.

1. Her daughter later studied at the London College of fashion, and is now a teacher and herself sits on several Council Committees.

Randolph Beresford with his wife, displaying his MBE outside the gates of Buckingham Palace, 1986.
Carpenter, former mayor of Hammersmith & Fulham, trade unionist (representing every category of
tradesman and technical employee), public servant and Chief Na Na Abenpong Nko Sohene Anwi (the
Development Officer), Randolph Beresford was also one of London's first post-war Black mayors (1975).

Randolph Beresford was born 20 March 1914 in New Amsterdam, Berbice, British Guyana. Randolph had
joined the family carpentry business at fifteen. The war years brought some prosperity to the Beresfords in
the form of carpentry contracts for the building of American air bases in Guyana. Randolph later joined the
army as a bandsman, playing the trumpet.

A wartime marriage to Clavilda came in 1944. A schools manager, Clavilda had previously worked for
the Jordanian Ambassador in Washington D.C. In his first mayoral address Randolph Beresford was to
acknowledge his wife's support in his professional and civic achievements.

Randolph Beresford arrived in Britain on 27 December 1953 with his carpentry tools. By New Year's Day
1954, he had registered as a carpenter. The 1950s saw Randolph Beresford's enthusiastic involvement in the
world of trade unionism: joining the Amalgamated Society of Woodworkers (A.S.W.) (1954), becoming an
active member; elected officer of his local branch of the A.S.W. (1955); Elected Delegate to Hammersmith
& Kensington Trade Council (1955–1967), representing all the trade unions in the region, where he served
for twelve years; Beresford also served as Convening Shop Steward to G.L.C. Housing Department, Western
District (1958) and was elected Federation Steward (1959–79).

The 1960s and '70s represented a turbulent period within British industrial relations, during which many
of the rights which contemporary workers enjoy today were fought for and eventually won. Where would
we be today without health and safety, anti-discrimination, equal pay, industrial injury legislation, welfare
and housing entitlements? These were some of the local battles which Randolph Beresford fought that were

to have national significance, when he was appointed to the London Federation of Trades Councils (1962); the Industrial Tribunal (1976) and the Confederation of British Industries (C.B.I.) (1978) – the organisation representing employers in manufacturing and nationalised industries.

A councillor for the White City Ward for eighteen years, Randolph Beresford was London's first post-war Black mayor. Even before becoming mayor of Hammersmith & Fulham (1975), he was to set new trends in Black political and community involvement, which have enriched the civic life of a diverse London:

> Your year in office has been an exceptionally happy one and this has spread through your great personality. We are indebted to you for all you have done during your term in office.

(Barrie Stead, Leader of the Council Hammersmith & Fulham, 1978)

This speech was delivered at Mayor Beresford's farewell grand civic reception, marking his departure from office, at which 600 invited guests were hosted, including twenty mayors from the Greater London area, Lord Pitt and Lady Pitt, and Lord and Lady Carter, from the Guyana High Commission.

During his Mayoral year in office, Randolph Beresford also received the Golden Keys to Georgetown, Capital of Guyana, and New Amsterdam, the town of his birth (1975), from the prime minister, Forbes Burnham.

A BEM (British Empire Medal) in 1979, in the Queen's Birthday Honours List was to follow, in recognition of his representation of every category of tradesman and technical employee, London-wide and nationally, during his trade union career. This award also recognised his public service, which culminated in his election to Mayor. His BEM citation read:

> Mr Randolph Beresford was a Convenor Steward since 1955, diligently carrying out his duties, and work as a Tradesman [Carpenter with the G.L.C.'s Housing Department]. He had a particular interest in the safety and welfare of his fellow workers, and was awarded a Certificate by the London Safety Group.
>
> He has maintained excellent trust between Management and Operatives...
>
> He was also responsible for maintaining good Race relations, in a district that has a mixed community.

(MBE Citation by Mr L. Bennett, Director of Housing, Greater London Council 1979)

Upon his retirement in 1979, Randolph Beresford decided to make a full-time commitment to public service. His organizational and negotiation skills were in great demand, and he co-founded, and served on the management committees of numerous voluntary sector organizations and charities. His achievements included organizing training for youth groups, fundraising for children and seniors' organizations, and creating new facilities for the community. In turn, the community has named two public buildings in his honour.

In 1987 Randolph Beresford was awarded the MBE (Member of the Order of British Empire), for his commitment to the voluntary sector. Randolph attended his second Royal Investiture, accompanied by his late wife Clavilda, and two of his daughters, Elaine and Giselle.

In 1994 Randolph Beresford ascended to the African Throne of Ashanti and was enthroned as a Tribal Chieftain. His new Chieftaincy name is Na Na Abenpong Nko Sohene Anwi (the Development Officer). In recognition of his work in Ghana with the MISSION DINE CLUB, and his lifelong contribution British society.In a reversal of the history of kidnapping and enslavement of Africans, the British-West Indian was kidnapped, dressed in ceremonial robes and enthroned on the royal seat, undergoing an ancient ceremony to become a Tribal Chief. This honour from Africa, his ancestral homeland, to a man born in British Guyana, brought Randolph Beresford full-circle.

Dr John Roberts QC (Queen's Counsel) has many firsts to his name, such as being the first person of African ancestry to become head of a legal chambers in England and Wales; appointment as Queen's Counsel; appointment as Recorder of the Crown Court; and appointment as Master of the Bench at Gray's Inn ('with Voice and Vote').

As Queen's Counsel Dr Roberts has been appointed to 'Her [or His] Majesty's Counsel learned in the law', a post granted to senior lawyers, often referred to as taking silk, after the special silk gowns worn by QCs and having the privilege of sitting within the Bar of the court.

Not interested in perpetuating the Bar as an exclusive old boy's club, Roberts was to break rank with the legal establishment and to create new opportunities for women at the Bar, accepting seven female Barristers into his Chambers between 1975 and 1976. These female appointments were extremely rare and constituted a highly significant strategy at that time. Today, these former Roberts appointees now constitute Britain's legal establishment.

Judge Roberts' reach was to extend to the British Dependent Territories when he became the first person of African ancestry to be appointed High Court Judge to the British Virgin Islands and Anguilla, British West Indies.

Born in Sierra Leone in May 1928, Judge John Roberts can trace his relationship to the UK to 1720 and his maternal Welsh great-grandfather. Roberts takes even greater pride in his paternal great-grandfather, Joseph Jenkins Roberts (pictured below right), who was the first President of Liberia; a state founded by formerly enslaved Africans. Roberts Airfield, named after him, was to become one of the most important strategic airbases for the British and Americans during the Second World War.

Of Judge Roberts' own parents, his father was a teacher and his mother was a successful tradeswoman in general merchandise. Tradeswomen in West Africa represented a highly respected and politically powerful matriarchy (they had the capacity to de-throne chiefs), and have traditionally controlled significant areas of commercial activity. Their exercise of economic autonomy was to baffle colonialists decades before the days of women's liberation in the West. Perhaps this was to impact upon Judge Roberts' own ideas about gender equality?

Originally drafted into the American Army during the Second World War, Roberts joined the Royal Air Force in 1952, serving in the Near East, the Far East and Australia. In 1962 Roberts qualified as an air traffic controller. (*Above*: Roberts inspects policemen at Hendon Police College).

In 1961 Judge Roberts was to meet his Jamaican future wife, formerly Eulette Clarke, at a dance competition in Walsall, the West Midlands. For this reason amongst others, Roberts proudly possesses a Jamaican passport. The Robertses have been married for nearly fifty years.

In 1988, Dr John Roberts became the first person of African ancestry to be appointed Queen's Council to the English Bar. In addition to the English Bar, John Roberts has set a record in being called to the Bar in nine other countries: Jamaica (1973), Sierra Leone (1975), Trinidad & Tobago (1978), Bahamas (1984), St Kitts & Nevis (1988), Antigua (2002), Barbados (2002), Bermuda (2003) and Anguilla (2006).

A Member of the Guild of Freemen of the City of London (1996/7), with an Honorary Doctorate of Civil Law, from City University London (1996) and an African Achievers' Award for outstanding contributions to Justice and Race Relations, Judge Roberts says, 'No matter how high you go in the world, never forget your roots'.

Baroness Amos has the distinction of being the first Black person appointed Leader of the House of Lords, and the first Black woman to be a member of the British Cabinet. Made a Life Peer in 1997, Baroness Amos was appointed a Government Whip in the House of Lords (1998); Parliamentary Under Secretary of State at the Foreign and Commonwealth Office (2001), later joining the Cabinet as International Development Secretary (2003). Of her achievements, Baroness Amos believes that it is very important for the Black community to be represented in serious positions of state, and that Black people are seen as part of the society in which we live and to be accepted as such. 'It is vital that our contributions to this society are recognised, and for us to possess strong role models.'

Changes brought about within her office since her appointment include the House of Lords now having an independent Speaker, who does not represent specific Party interests. This important change to the House of Lords was achieved by Baroness Amos being able to take people with her and employ her strategic skills, first honed in her former role as chief executive of the Equal Opportunities Commission. Amos' stewardship of the EOC was instrumental in the creation of rights which part-time workers enjoy today. This has had an important impact upon Britain's workforce, and working women in particular.

Baroness Amos has also made her presence felt in the international arena, as government minister for Africa. In this capacity, she has worked with colleagues in the G8. Baroness Amos has helped to develop the Africa Action Plan, which led to Britain setting up the African Commission, and eventually the Gleneagles Agreement at the G8 Summit. As host of the 2005 G8 Summit the British Government set its agenda to include economic development in Africa, and to write off Third World debt. One of the achievements of the 2005 G8 Summit was the agreement to write off $40 billion of debt from the poorest countries between the International Monetary Fund, the World Bank and the African Development Fund. Amos asserts that tackling poverty needs to be addressed by all in an integrated way. Issues which have featured prominently on Baroness Amos' agenda have been women's equity, race equality, and social justice.

With both parents who were teachers and a grandfather who was a headmaster, education and the value of education was a central theme in her family. Amos maintains that this educational focus has helped her in everything that she has achieved, beginning with her career in community education, research and local government. Her interest in knowledge and commitment to public service have guided Baroness Amos' aims to promote fairness, justice and equality.

Arriving in London in 1961, and settling on Richmond Avenue, Angel Islington, later moving to Stoke Newington, Baroness Amos' father began her families' long connections with North London. North London is also home to Amos' favourite football team, Tottenham Hotspur, which she has loyally supported since 1963. A Londoner for most of her life, Baroness Amos departed the capital for a short time for Kent, and to attend Warwick and Birmingham universities in the 1970s and '80s.

A Trustee of the National Portrait Gallery since 2003, Deputy Chair of the Runnymede Trust, and a Trustee of University College Hospitals, Amos made the decision to support the building of one of London's newest hospitals, UCL (University College London, on Euston Road). Other health-related commitments have included membership of the Board of The Kings Fund, the Royal College of Nurses and the AFIA Trust, which serves the health interests of Africans and Caribbeans in the UK.

Family history is important to the Amos family, who are currently consulting relatives in the Caribbean, USA and Canada in the compilation of a family tree. The family fulfilled a great ambition in 2006 when they were all able to make a pilgrimage to Ghana to explore their Gyanese-Ghana heritage. Baroness Amos recalls stories from her father of 'The old women who could talk about slavery times in Guyana'. The visit to Elmena Castle and Gore Island proved to be a moving confrontation with the past for the Amos family. Both of these landmarks continue to resonate with the historical atmosphere of their previous inhabitants, the kidnapped slaves imprisoned in dungeons, which would be their last experience of Africa, before 'the middle passage' and enslavement.

CHAPTER SIX

LONDON INTERNATIONAL

Nationality and our sense of place are often constrained by the notion of a world in which populations remain within a single geographical region, and the notion of one's national loyalty is fixed and simple. 'Black Londoners', we shall see, have been part of a shifting population in which movement has occurred to and from Africa and the West Indies, not just among individuals, but among different generations of the same family.

Throughout this book an attempt has been made to broaden the concept of what it is to be a 'Londoner' in order to include those who themselves may not immediately perceive themselves as such. It may be contended that instead of sticking rigidly to birth or length of residence, it may be more useful to assess Black Londoners' 'credentials', by more complex notions, such as contribution, sense of belonging, impact upon a wider community, and international consciousness.

One group which has often been forgotten in our focus on Africa's disempowerment at the turn of the century has been that of African kings and queens, and their emissaries. It is important, however, that the movement of African royal houses and diplomatic corps be acknowledged, since their activities became particularly intensive in the run up to the European 'scramble for Africa'. If we do not acknowledge them, we risk the confirming the stereotype of Africa as a helpless child. It must be remembered that before military annexation of African territory, many African leaders had instigated protracted diplomatic missions to London. They would arrive via Greenwich, and then make their way up the Thames to Westminster.

Such a journey was made by the Chief of Bamangwato of the British protectorate of Bechuanaland, now known as Botswana. Chief Khama led a deputation to London, which included Chief Sebele of the Bakwena and Chief Bathoen of the Bangwaketse to see Queen Victoria in 1895. Their diplomatic mission aimed to prevent their territory from being transferred to Cecil Rhodes' British company in South Africa. The deputation was a success, and Bechuanaland became a protectorate, against the encroachment of White settlers. This deputation was to leave an indelible mark on the memories of Londoners. These great African chiefs' dignified carriage, flamboyant dress and Christian piety, combined with the moral appeal of their cause, made them welcomed visitors. Several years later when the grandson of chief Khama entered London newspapers for quite different reasons, the memory of his forebears was invoked.

As in all walks of life, the diplomatic arena has seen significant changes in the role of women. Women's disposition for bonding and establishing trust in new environments and their conciliatory style have perhaps made them natural diplomats. The late twentieth century has seen this natural advantage put to international use, with increased representation among the senior members of an international diplomatic corps. Mrs Agnes Aggrey-Orleans came to London in the 1960s as education counsellor at the Ghanaian Embassy; today she is the high commissioner in Geneva, a highly influential posting.

Interestingly enough, the Aggrey-Orleans have another high commissioner among their ranks: Mrs Agnes Aggrey-Orleans' husband – who was appointed high commissioner to the Ghanaian Embassy in London in 1998. Thus, the Aggrey-Orleans, like many others, have had ongoing London connections, which are used by the embassies of Africa and the Caribbean to make their national voices heard effectively among their international peers.

When one's children have been raised and educated in London and one's everyday existence is living and working in the capital, who can say that one is not a Black Londoner at the end of the diplomatic mission when it is time to be called 'home'?

Dr Kwame Nkrumah photographed at the Commonwealth Conference of Prime Ministers, London. Dr Kwame Nkrumah was born in the Gold Coast (now Ghana) in 1909. Nkrumah became an active member of the Pan-African movement in London, which worked for political independence from imperial domination during the 1940s and 1950s. He was also editor of the *New African* from 1945–47. Dr Kwame Nkrumah went on to become the Prime Minister of Gold Coast in 1952, then Prime Minister of an independent Ghana in 1957 – the first independent African state of the British Empire. Although a product of Western education, Kwame Nkrumah made a point wearing robes of Kente cloth as a statement of national identity and pride.

Born in Nkroful, Nzima, Nkrumah belonged to his mother's Clan of Anonas. Nkrumah's heredity was determined by his matrilineal line, in contrast to Western principles of heredity, which flow from the father's or patrinilial line. It was his mother, who produced and sold vegetables and who, as a Catholic convert, demanded that her only son received the formal education which had been denied her. Nkrumah's father, who had several wives under the polygamy system, was a goldsmith in the region of Half Aassini. Nkrumah describes his childhood as happy and harmonious, and himself as a much adored slightly spoilt younger child of the compound.

Nkrumah graduated from Lincoln University, USA, in 1939 with a BA in Economics and Sociology. He was then invited to become an assistant lecturer in Philosophy and later admitted to Lincoln Theological Seminary, attaining a BA in Theology (1942), graduating head of the class. A Master of Science Degree in Education from the University of Pennsylvania (1942) was to follow, with a Master of Arts Degree in Philosophy from the University of Pennsylvania (1943) thereafter. A popular lecturer in Greek, Philosophy, Negro History and Social Philosophy, Nkrumah's classes were always full, with students being drawn to his oratorical skills. He was voted, 'The most outstanding Professor of the year', by the Lincolnian University journal in 1945.

It was, therefore, a natural progression in his academic career for Kwame Nkrumah to be drawn to the London School of Economics, since it was one of the most progressive and radical centres of social and economic theory, attracting statesmen and women and policy makers throughout the twentieth century, with eminent professors, such as Laski. Nkrumah had originally come to London to study for his doctorate in Philosophy at the London School of Economics and Law at Gray's Inn, when a fateful meeting with George Padmore, who was to become his lifelong friend and political mentor, resulted in Nkrumah helping to organize the 5th Pan African Congress in Manchester in 1945. This congress was co-chaired by Dr W.E.B Du Bois the Afro-American scholar and founder of the National Association for the Advancement of Coloured People, USA and Dr Peter Milliard a Black British doctor from British Guyana.

As founder of the West African National Secretariat, Nkrumah was responsible for defining its principal aim — the decolonization of Africa. The ethos of African unity was a golden thread running throughout Nkrumah's politics from his student days when he served as Vice-President of the West Africa Student's Union (WASU) in London, to his contribution to the founding of the Organisation of African Unity (OAU). The Pan-Africanist ideal of unity among African states was seen as key to sustainable independednce for all post-imperial nations.

It was Nkrumah's attempts to create economic self-sufficiency from the colonial powers which was eventually to lead to a coup with him being ousted from power and exiled to Conakry, Guinea. A harsh programme of industrialisation and curtailment of democratic rights, to this end, sowed the seeds of political unrest. Nkrumah's claims of CIA involvement in his coup have had some light shed on them in recently released CIA documents, detailing collaboration between the coup organisers and the then American Embassy through the 'overt diplomacy and covert actions', of President Lyndon B. Johnson's administration from 1964–68.

Nkrumah, literally and figuratively laid the first stones in the foundation of the Kwame Nkrumah Ideological Institute in 1961, a training institution for the Ghanaian civil service, also promoting Pan-Africanism. In addition to a political and idealogical influence on colonial independence struggles worldwide, Nkrumah's Akosombo Dam (pictured on p.127), although heavily criticised in its day for its expense, remains a lasting legacy to Nkrumah, the visionary, producing most of Ghana's hydroelectric power to the present day.

Although dying in Romania while receiving treatment for skin cancer in 1966, Nkrumah's international reputation during his lifetime is reflected in the range of countries which gave him horourary degrees: Lincoln University, USA; Moscow State University; Cairo University, Egypt; Jagiellonian University, Krakow, Poland; and Humboldt University, East Berlin; amongst others. Nkrumah was also the recipient of the Lenin Peace Prize by the Soviet Union. As recently as 1989 a Russian stamp was produced to commemorate the legacy of Kwame Nkrumah and in 1999 BBC listeners in Africa voted Kwame Nkrumah, the first head of an independent Ghana their 'Man of the Millennium'.

Above left: **Eleazar Chukwuemeka (Emeka) Anyaoku**. Born in 1933, Eleazar Anyaoku became Executive Assistant in the Commonwealth Development Corporation in London and Lagos in 1959, and a member of the Nigerian delegation to the United Nations in 1962. For three decades he acted as Commonwealth observer of elections, referenda and talks, one of the most senior positions in international diplomacy, and was based in London. Since 1990, Anyaoku has been Secretary-General to the Commonwealth, based at Marlborough House in London.

Above right: **Mabel Dove** at the counting of the votes for the seat of Ga in Ghana in the 1950s, as the first woman to become a member of the Legislative Assembly of Ghana. Before her political career, Mabel Dove was a prominent West African journalist in London.

Above: **Nnamdi Azikiwe**, journalist turned statesman. Born in 1904, he was editor-in-chief of the *African Morning Post*, Accra, from 1934 to 1937, and then of the *West African Pilot* until 1945. From 1945 Azikiwe was a representative of the National Council for Nigeria and the Cameroons, which began as a London student movement. He questioned Britain's continued domination of her subject nations and took the British Government to task on democracy and human rights. In 1963 he became the first President of Nigeria, having been governor-general and commander-in-chief from 1960. He was joint president of the Anti-Slavery Society, based in London, in 1970, and wrote extensively on economics, politics, history and poetry. Azikiwe died in 1995.

Left: **Mrs Azikiwe**, born Flora Ogbenyeanu Ogoegbunamn, awarding a plaque to A.E. Hoffman, chairman of the Palm Shipping Co., 1961.

Sir Asafu Adjaye, the first high commissioner to London, from Ghana (1958). Having graduated in Philosophy and Law at University College London in 1925, he won the Profumo Prize in law in 1927 and went on to enjoy a distinguished legal and political career, playing an active part in Ghana's transition to independence. He was the kind of intellectual heavyweight needed to grapple with the new trade contracts with Britain that were forged after independence was granted in 1957.

Sir Edward Asafu Adjaye signing the UK–Ghana Air Services Agreement in 1958. He was knighted in 1960 and made a fellow of University College London the following year.

H.V.H. Sekyi, High Commissioner to Ghana, en route to present his Letters of commission to the Queen, 1970s.

Sir Seretse Khama arriving for talks at the Commonwealth Relations Office, Whitehall, 1950. Born in 1925, Khama was the son of an African chief of the Bamangwato, a British protectorate of Bechuanaland. He came to London to study law, but was exiled by the British state when he married a White woman, Ruth Williams, a *cause célèbre* that enlivened dreary postwar London. Because of this he was only allowed to return to Britain in 1956 on renouncing his chieftainship, and it is now clear that Britain succumbed to pressure from the South African Government, then pursuing a policy of racial segregation, to deny Khama his rights. South Africa held the key to Britain's status as a world power because of her uranium reserves, which were vital for Britain's nuclear programme. In 1966 Khama became the first Prime Minister of an independent Botswana, and was knighted.

The dictator **Dr Hastings Banda** on a state visit to London in the 1960s. Hastings Banda was a GP in London from 1945 to 1953 and represented Nyasaland at the Pan-African Congress of 1945. He was President of Malawi from 1966 to 1994. Below, Mrs Banda and the Duke of Edinburgh.

Haile Selassie on a state visit to London, October 1954. When Abyssinia was invaded by Italy in 1935 the violent and duplicitous nature of imperialism was exposed anew. Black Londoners, through such organizations as the International African Friends of Abyssinia, united with mass movements in Africa and the West Indies to formulate a new ideology of colonial liberation.

Send-off party given by **Mrs Kwesie Armah** for the outgoing wives of councillors at the Ghana High Commission, 1965. Women at the High Commission often acted as administrators and were responsible for establishing and maintaining links between Ghana and London's Black and indigenous communities, as well as between national and international embassies.

George and Dorothy Owanabae with their son, Anthony, 1964. Originally from Owarri, Nigeria, Mr and Mrs Owanabae lived in Wales for three years, where Mr Owanabae was a student, before settling in Kilburn, North West London, in 1964. In the same year, Mr Owanabae qualified as an accountant. Mrs Owanabae later became a fashion and beauty consultant and fashion designer, starting her own company. The Owanabaes returned to Nigeria in the early 1980s.

Mrs Asafu Adjaye welcoming M. de Guiringaud to the Ghana High Commission in France. Formerly Martha Violet Randolph, Mrs Asafu Adjaye was one of the many 'first ladies' of the independent African High Commissions to help to build trust and good relations within the world of international diplomacy in the post-colonial era. In addition to being Ghana's first high commissioner to the UK (see p.130), Sir Edward Asafu Adjaye was Ghana's first Ambassador to France (1957–61).

John (twelve) and William (eleven), the sons of the president of Liberia, discovering how a TV set works, at the Radio Show, Earls Court, 1957. They are accompanied by their tutor, Mr P. Fry.

Paul Boateng in front of the Palace of Westminster. Born in Hackney in 1952 of Ghanaian-English origin, Boateng took an active interest in politics from an early age, joining the Labour Party at the age of fifteen. His skills in political rhetoric were honed by his training as a solicitor in the 1970s and later as a barrister. Boateng represented Walthamstow on the Greater London Council before becoming MP for Brent South in 1987. An active member of the opposition for a decade, he became the most senior-ranking Black politician in the House of Commons, with a ministerial appointment as Under-Secretary of State for Health in the Labour government of 1997. Boateng is also a Methodist Lay Preacher and former Vice-Moderator of the World Council of Churches programme to combat racism. In 1988 he won the prestigious Martin Luther King Memorial Prize for social and racial justice.

Paul Boateng became closely associated with the New Labour project, characterised by a more centrist Labour political agenda, a distancing from the union origins of the party and financial conservatism. In 1998 Boateng became Under Secretary of State for the Home Office and then Minister of State for Home Affairs. The year 2001 saw Boateng ascend to his appointment as Financial Secretary to the Treasury, followed by a Cabinet post as Chief Secretary to the Treasury. It is interesting that Boateng did not rise to Home Secretary in 2002. Instead, Charles Clarke, who had been his junior, replaced David Blunkett upon his resignation the same year.

It was during this period that Boateng announced his decision not to stand for re-election as MP in 2005. He was appointed British High Commissioner to South Africa after the election of a new Labour government in 2005 and was replaced as MP for Brent South by Dawn Butler MP (the third Black woman to be appointed to the British parliament).

Adelaide Tambo was the London NHS Nursing Sister who became the recipient of the Nobel Foundation Life Award for initiating the anti-apartheid movement in Britain. It was Adelaide Tambo who led the anti-apartheid movement in London and was at the forefront of demonstrations calling for Nelson Mandela to be freed.

Born Matlala Adelaide Frances Tsukudu, 18 July 1929, 'Ma Tambo' was the wife of the late Oliver Tambo, President of the African National Congress in exile (married in 1956). Adelaide Tambo is however seen as a hero of the liberation struggle against apartheid in her own right. She joined the ANC Youth League as a courier at fifteen and by the age of eighteen was its chairwoman. Adelaide was one of the 20,000 women who marched on Pretoria's Union Buildings in protest against the pass laws in 1956. In 1994 Adelaide Tambo became one of the first democratically elected members of the South African parliament, serving as an MP from 1994–99.

It was at 51 Alexandra Park, in Muswell Hill, North London that Adelaide Tambo spent most of her thirty years in exile from South Africa. It was her home and a permanent ANC office. Following the Sharpville Massacres (1960), in which mostly children, protesting against the Pass Laws, were gunned down, the ANC became a banned organisation, and the Tambos were ordered to leave South Africa by the ANC's leadership. Their mission – to establish what effectively became a government in exile. While Adelaide Tambo established the ANC's London office, Oliver Tambo travelled the world. Both Tambos sought to inform the world about what was happening to Black people in South Africa and to put pressure on the White South African Government for democratic reforms.

Number 51 Alexandra Park became a focal point for the large South African exiled community in Britain, providing practical and financial support to families in Britain and South Africa. In additional to political and welfare roles, as a nurse and mother 'Ma Tambo' provided emotional support to exiled South African students, such as former South African President Premier Mbeki, as a young man a long way from home.

A founder member of the Afro-Asian Solidarity Movement and the Pan-African Women's Organisation (PAWO), Adelaide also worked with the International Defence and Aid Fund (IDAF), to identify and financially assist some of the families whose main breadwinners or children left South Africa after 1976.

Adelaide Tambo had trained as a nurse in South Africa. Even as a student nurse at Pretoria General Hospital, she started a branch of the ANC Youth League. Her profession enabled her to support her London family, often doing twenty-hour shifts in NHS hospitals to enable her to send her three children Dali, Thembi and Tselane, to public school in England. This was for their future and their safety. She was often forced to work night shifts, and her house was under constant surveillance by the South African secret service and had on occasion been broken into.

It is therefore neither accident nor nepotism which made Adelaide Tambo the first recipient of the Oliver Tambo/Johnny Makatini Freedom Award in February 1995. This award recognises 'The faith, courage and sacrifice of an individual during the freedom struggle'. Adelaide Tambo's late husband Oliver Reginald Tambo died in April 1993 (see p.179). Adelaide Tambo also received the Order of the Boab in Gold, one of the highest honours bestowed by the post-1994 South African Government.

As a campaigner for human rights, disability and senior citizens' rights, Adelaide Tambo was also awarded the Order of Simon of Cyrene, in July 1997, for her, 'Active and outstanding and untiring commitment to the Anglican Church and disadvantaged communities'. The order is the highest honour that can be bestowed upon a layperson by the Church of the Province of Southern Africa.

A history-maker and historian, with an eye towards the future, Adelaide Tambo had collected all of her late husband Oliver's speeches, which she later published in 1991. Many monuments now stand to commemorate the life of Adelaide Tambo herself, who died in January 2007, these include the Adelaide Tambo School, Soweto (2005); a street named after her in Durban; The Adelaide Tambo Clinic, Gauteng; and the Adelaide Tambo Sub-Council 23, council building, in Delft (August 2008). Adelaide Tambo's greatest monument may however be said to be the new South Africa, which she helped to establish, and to which her children and grandchildren now contribute.

We've come back to a country where there's been no improvement in our people's lives. The future of the country is in our hands. Let's take up the challenge...

(Adelaide Tambo (1990), upon her return to South Africa from exile in London)

Winnie Mandela (centre) with members of the **Commonwealth Secretariat**, 1986. The Commonwealth Secretariat, based in Pall Mall, London, has been the administrative centre of the Commonwealth since 1965. The fifty-four independent nations and former British colonies that make up the Commonwealth have campaigned for human rights and humanitarian causes for over three decades, epitomized by the campaign against apartheid in South Africa. Under the Harare Declaration of 1991, the Commonwealth committed itself to the encouragement of democracy and good government, which has led to a reduction in the number of military and one-party states among its members, although the execution of the writer and environmental campaigner Ken Saro-Wiwa by the military government of Nigeria in 1995 led to the immediate suspension of that country's membership. The emphasis in the Commonwealth is now increasingly towards trade, investment and the global economy.

As Deputy High Commissioner, **Herbert Yearwood** (pictured on the left) is responsible for the representation of Barbadians and those of Barbadian origin in the UK. However his remit goes beyond passport and immigration matters, to stimulating trade between the UK and Barbados, the welfare of Barbadian community in the UK, to supporting the wider UK African and Caribbean community organisations and events.

Born in Barbados in 1936, Herbert Yearwood is one of seven children born to a well-known headmaster of St Luke's Boys School. Yearwood has enjoyed a long relationship with London since his arrival and long-term settlement in 1959–71. Joining the Royal Signals of the British Army (1959), Yearwood was later to join British European Airways, Communications and Telegraphic Section.

During his London residency, Yearwood raised a young family of two children and served as Vice-Chair of the Earls Court Labour Party, running for a council seat in the Earls Court Ward. He was also an active member of the Anti-Apartheid Movement since 1965.

Herbert Yearwood combined his civic commitment to the UK with his official role as representative of the Barbados Government, through his ongoing commitment to four key local committees. As deputy high commissioner, Yearwood saw his role as larger than the glamour of the ambassadorial reception, reaching out to the UK-Barbadian community founding local committees to utilise UK-Barbadian expertise within the community and to improve local conditions in education, justice, health and trade. This has been seen as an innovation and evolution in the modern role of a high commission. Yearwood is particularly proud of the achievements of the education committee, in its establishment of the C.V.R.P. educational initiative. This has become a London-wide scheme introducing Caribbean elder-support to schools, through a network of trained volunteers. This initiative, run by co-founders Mrs Esther Holmes and Mr Winston Best has been mentioned in the House of Lords and has received education award nominations.

Herbert Yearwood's legacy has also been to support UK–Barbados trade and cultural linkages, as lead organizer of the Barbados Expo UK (1997–99 and 2006) and the Caribbean Expo (2001). In 2004, Yearwood received a certificate of excellence from the National Council of Barbadian Associations in the UK for his tireless efforts on their behalf.

With a civic commitment that was to continue upon his return to Barbados from London in 1971, Yearwood was appointed a Senator by the Barbados Labour Party, under Prime Minister Tom Adam's leadership. Yearwood received a Silver Cross of Merit for his services to the Senate (1985). Herbert Yearwood has served as the Barbados Labour Party's National Election Coordinator since 1995. So indispensable was Yearwood to the party's electoral success that every five years he would be immediately relieved from duty as deputy high commissioner and summoned 'home' to Barbados, at the announcement of a national election.

Herbert Yearwood is the founder of the British branch of the Barbados Labour Party, being recognised in 2005 for this contribution to the BLP UK. The Grantley Adams Award for BLP in Barbados, 2006, saw Herbert Yearwood receive his most illustrious award to date – the Prime Minister's Award for Exceptional Service.

In addition to civic and state duties, Yearwood has internationally recognised expertise in large-scale event planning and organization, and before returning to the UK in 1995, he was responsible for running Barbados' major National Trade Exhibition, the BMX, and was rewarded for this in 1989, by the Barbados Manufacturers Association for his 'Outstanding Contribution'.

Recognised as one of the key individuals behind the creation of the Oystins Fish Festival Barbados, which has become a major national spectacle and tourist attraction, Herbert Yearwood received a medal for twenty-five years of service to the festival in 2002.

Thanks to the contribution of individuals such as Herbert Yearwood, Barbados is today regarded as a world 'model for sustainable development'. In 1994, this role was recognised by a commendation 'in appreciation for sustainable development, by the UN Global Conference on Sustainable Development on Small Island Developing States, and by the Barbados Agricultural Society Organising Committee of Eco-Forum'. Although not formally possessing 'dual citizenship' of Britain and Barbados, there can be few human beings who have served two nations more loyally.

CHAPTER SEVEN

CHURCH LEADERS

As early as 1765, Africans and West Indians came to London to be ordained as priests in the Church of England. As their numbers and seniority increased, they came to be consecrated as bishops (see p. 146). Examples are the Rt Revd J.T. Holly, who was consecrated Bishop of Haiti in 1874; the Rt Revd Samuel D. Ferguson, Bishop of Cape Palmas (now Liberia) in 1885; and the Rt Revd Isaac Oluwole, Bishop of Lagos in 1893. The pilgrimage of Black bishops from all over the globe to Westminster Abbey and St Paul's Cathedral may challenge some of our preconceptions of the involvement of Black people in the Anglican Church.

One particularly influential minister who forces us to reassess the involvement of Black Londoners in organized religion is Dr Harold Moody, Congregationalist minister and one-time head of the London Missionary Society. Such figures as Moody and the Trinidadian temperance lecturer Henry Sylvester Williams demand that we reappraise the concept of the missionary as being both White and Africa-bound. These ministers had a considerable presence in London and an enormous popular following among all ethnic groups.

THE MODERN BISHOPS OF THE INNER CITY

The Rt Revd Wilfred Wood, Bishop of Croydon, represents the experiences of postwar mass immigration. Originally from Barbados, his settlement in London forced Bishop Wood to be aware of the harshness of life for new immigrants, and the problems of the inner city. As a strong advocate of a relevant church, he became one of the founder members of Paddington Churches Housing Association, thus encouraging the dramatic growth of housing associations in general and, in particular, Black housing associations.

Despite the long association of London's African-Caribbean communities with the Anglican Church, they have only recently had the opportunity to make their presence felt in the decision-making body of the church – the General Synod. Between 1990 and 1996, for example, the Rt Revd Dr John Sentamu served on the General Synod, while maintaining his early links with the prison service as a committee member of the National Council for the Care and Resettlement of Offenders, the Family Welfare Association and the Health Advisory Committee of Her Majesty's Prisons. When he was the Bishop of Stepney, he defined his mission as 'To seek God's rule of justice, righteousness, peace and love; to be part of God's movement of change, to reach out with God's love to human need, and to be a vision-bearer for the area.' Today Sentamu serves as Archbishop of York.

Isaac P. Dickerson (standing centre), evangelical minister and temperance lecturer. Dickerson was born a slave in Virginia in 1852. When he was emancipated he became a teacher at a missionary school in Chattanooga and travelled to Britain with the Jubilee Singers, a choir that toured America and Europe to raise funds for Fisk University for Negro education. Dickerson remained in Britain when the choir returned to the USA in 1872 and studied to become a minister at Edinburgh University. He toured as an evangelist throughout Europe and Palestine, and when he began a small mission of his own in Plumstead, he supported himself by lecturing on these regions throughout Britain. Dickerson was a cheerful and well-liked figure in his local community.

Samuel Adjai Crowther
Bishop, Niger Territory
Oct 19 1888

The **Revd Samuel Ajayi Crowther** was the one of the first Black men to be consecrated as an Anglican bishop, to the See of the Niger in 1864. His consecration at Canterbury Cathedral was of national interest and was conducted before a packed congregation, which included Admiral Luke of the *Myrmidon*, the anti-slavery ship that had freed him, who became a life-long friend. The sermon at Bishop Crowther's consecration was preached by the Revd H. Longueville Mansel, Professor of Philosophy from Oxford.

Crowther was to become a pioneer of the London-based Christian Missionary Society; challenging many of our assumptions about missionary work in Africa in the nineteenth century. Although the monks of St Augustine and the Portuguese Capuchchin monks had brought Christianity to Nigeria in the fifteenth century, Crowther was seen as the best chance of establishing a Christian congregation amongst the followers of the myriad of African religious traditions in West Africa.

Crowther was elected Bishop for many reasons, most importantly due to his qualities of leadership and Christian scholarship, skill as a linguist and knowledge of a breadth of cultural traditions. Also, in the mid-nineteenth century, prior to European domination of West Africa, White missionaries had been defeated by the deadly malaria, and were treated with hostility or indifference by African Chiefs and the international traders, with whom they were often at odds.

Thus, the decision to put an African at the helm of missionary activity was seen as a sensible means of addressing a hard-to-reach constituency. This move was not without controversy and even met resistance from Crowther's own White missionary colleagues, who believed that a Black man should always occupy a subordinate position to the White man, and that his appointment would send the wrong message to the 'natives'. However, despite Crowther's humility and his own reluctance, the C.M.S. and Anglican leadership maintained that his symbolic appointment would signal the development of the African Church as a self-supporting, self-propagating institution.

Samuel Crowther was born around 1810 in Osogun, Yorubaland, three years after the abolition of the slave trade by Britain. A trade which had taken centuries to become established, was hardly likely to be transformed by act of parliament alone, in three years. Samuel Ajayi's early life was therefore tragically and repeatedly affected by the capture and enslavement of his entire family to feed the slave trade.

Ajayi himself recounted being exchanged six times before his slave ship was intercepted by the Royal Navy and he was set free. Once liberated he was sent to live in Sierra Leone, and was taught to read and write at a Church Missionary Society (CMS) school. He learnt English within six months, later becoming a pupil-teacher at a local school earning seven and half pence a month.

Having converted to the Christian faith in December 1825, Samuel Ajayi was baptised and he named himself Crowther, after the inspirational Vicar of Christ's Church, Newgate, London. Arriving in London in 1826, part of his London stay was in the Parish School in Islington until 1827, while he trained for missionary work in Africa.

Crowther led missions to many parts of the West African interior, establishing Christian communities using education as a tool. His achievements did not go unnoticed. The University of Oxford was later to confer upon him an honorary doctorate, 'in appreciation of his invaluable contributions to the development of Christianity in West Africa'. Following further study, Crowther was ordained in England in 1842 with the Revd Henry Townsend. After their ordinations, both the Revd Henry Townsend and the Revd Samuel Ajayi Crowther returned to Abeokuta (now in present-day Nigeria).

Visiting Britain to protest about the 'evil' being perpetrated in West Africa by recent colonialists, Crowther was invited to meet Lord Palmerston, the British Prime Minister, and invited to Windsor Castle to meet Queen Victoria and Prince Albert. He was able to inform both politicians and royalty about West Africa. It has been documented that, at this time, Crowther spoke at meetings throughout Britain. His style of speech is described as 'grave, eloquent and well-informed'. In 1852 Crowther published and revised the seminal book, *Yoruba Grammar and Vocabulary*. He also achieved the translation of four books of the New Testament. Crowther and King also completed a translation of the Bible and the Book of Common Prayer in Yoruba, Igbo and Nupe languages, which are still upheld as scholarly classics. Crowther is further believed to have written the first book in Igbo.

Bishop James 'Holy' Johnson was born in Sierra Leone to Yoruba parents who had been kidnapped by slavers and released by a British anti-slavery patrol. One of his greatest achievements was to value and incorporate African cultural forms of worship into the Anglican Church.

Johnson also managed to maintain unity within the Anglican Church in West Africa, when the African political elite was beginning to organise against colonialism and reject the paternalism of White missions and Anglican Church institutions. Africans were beginning to form their own Christian breakaway sects. The Anglican response was to appoint Johnson as Assistant Bishop of West Equatorial Africa, Niger Mission. In 1900 James Johnson arrived in London as the second African to be consecrated Bishop at Lambeth Palace Chapel. Eventually becoming known as 'Holy' Johnson because of his piety, his religious beliefs only served to strengthen his own political commitment to African nationalism.

The contradictions which sat the heart of the Christian mission in Africa were impossible to avoid at a time of imperial control and eventual annexation of most of Africa. Where does universal 'brotherhood' fit in to a context of imperial racist practices, which excluded Africans from high administrative office? Johnson was a fervent critic of imperialism, and encouraged the education of Africans and their uptake of high office.

Johnson, a graduate of Forah Bay Institute, was ordained and became a pastor of the Church Missionary Society (CMS). He constantly challenged his White missionary colleagues. His Christianity emphasised the biblical message of Jesus as the Lord and Saviour of the entire world, and not just Europeans. That some European missionaries had brought Christianity to Africa was seen by Johnson as a technicality. It could have been brought by any other group, but this did not automatically entitle them to exert power over Africans.

In fact, in Johnson's view, one of the few advantages that European arrival had brought to Africa was Christianity. He saw Western control of Christianity as neither inevitable nor desirable. Johnson advocated that Africa should be evangelised by Africans. 'It is more helpful that a people should be called to take up their responsibilities… than be in the position of vessels taken in tow.'

Johnson's take on African religions was liberal and relatively progressive, maintaining that many cultural practices could be incorporated as part of an Africanisation of the Anglican Church. Many decades before the emergence of the 1960s and the philosophy of 'Black Power', Johnson incorporated Yoruba religious names into Christian baptismal rituals. A century before the ecumenical movement Johnson was in dialogue with traditional healers and diviners. Johnson's Anglican Church, he asserted, should be one that reflected and respected African philosophies, culture and sensibilities, within the context of Christian fundamental beliefs.

The need for autonomy from European control should, according to Johnson, not merely be limited to religion and culture, but also to economics. His attempts to raise a £10,000 fund, to endow the Niger Mission and end dependency on England, created alarm and consternation among his critics within the missionary fraternity, causing him at one stage to be physically ejected from his parish.

By joining the Legislative Council in Nigeria in 1886, Johnson was able to advocate his religious, moral and political message of African nationalism as spokesman for African interests. It has been argued that Johnson was instrumental in the appointment of Isaac Oluwole, as Assistant Bishop of Western Equatorial Africa in 1893, following his criticism of the lack of African control of the Church Missionary Society.

Isaac Oluwole became Assistant Bishop of Western Equitorial Africa, and was consecrated at St Paul's Cathedral, London on 29 June 1893. Made Doctor of Divinity by Durham University, Oluwale was of Sierra Leonean and Egba origin. From 1879 to 1893 he served as the Principal of the Church Missionary Society Grammar School, Lagos.

George Makippe, also known as Watto or Watteau. Makippe was born a slave in equatorial Africa and was converted to Christianity by David Livingstone. He came to Britain as a young man in the late nineteenth century, as one of the six boys who were bearers of Dr Livingstone's coffin. Makippe was appointed gardener to James E. Vanner, in Chislehurst, where he worked for thirty years, being remembered by his employer in his will. He then worked as a gardener for a Mr Williamson for another twenty years. He was a local celebrity both in Chislehurst and in London, and his picture was taken by many court photographers. Makippe was an active member of the Wesleyan Church and a celebrated organ-blower for many years[1]. He married an English woman, Martha, who bore him three sons and he died at a great age in 1931.

According to George Watto, having been sold to a Portuguese slaving expedition by his wicked uncle, he was then 'rescued' by British soldiers who were accompanying the British explorer Dr Livingstone. Having 'liberated' the kidnapped African men, women and children, the British sent the women home and 'kept' the men as interpreters, and Dr Livingtone kept a young Watto as his 'boy' or boy servant.

Written sources pose Livingstone as the rescuing hero. To Watto, as to any child, dependent upon a significant adult, Livingstone would have represented a form of security. However, our modern sensibilities would probably take a less forgiving view of such a scenario in which a child rescued from a kidnapper was not returned to his parents or region, but kept by the explorer because he, 'Took a fancy to the small "Arab" Makippe'[2], to be his 'boy' or boy-servant.

1. *The Flesherton Advance*, Ontario Canada, 7 May 1924. Page 3.

2. Taken from *A Guided visit to Chislehurst Methodist Church*. This guide is adapted from a hand-written, hand-drawn original prepared for the Chislehurst Circuit Centenary in June 1992.

Rt Revd Wilfred Wood
became the Church of England's
first Black bishop in England,
when he was appointed as the
area bishop to the Suffragan
See of Croydon in the Diocese
of Southwark from 1985 to
2003. Historically, prior to his
appointment Black bishops,
although consecrated at
Lambeth Palace, Canterbury
Cathedral or Westminster, had
served overseas territories, such
as Equatorial West Africa since
the nineteenth century.

Born in Barbados in 1936, Wood came to London in 1962 and served as curate, then honorary curate,
of St Thomas with St Stephen, Shepherd's Bush, until 1974. Being struck by the harsh conditions that Black
immigrants had to endure and by the problems of the inner city, Wood maintained an active involvement
in race relations and social justice in London and the UK. He was a founder member of the Paddington
Churches Housing Association, as well as of Berbice Housing Co-operative, Notting Hill Community
Association and the Carib Housing Association for Black Elders. He was appointed bishop and London's
Race Relations Officer in 1966.

When a Community Relations Commission was proposed to replace the National Committee for
Commonwealth Immigrants, Wood and fellow campaigners submitted a set of conditions for the
establishment of this new commission, which became known as the 'Wood Proposals'. These proposals
demanded that members of this committee be directly elected by minority ethnic associations, to ensure
community representation and accountability. Wood subsequently became Chairman of the Institute of Race
Relations in 1971.

Bishop Wood maintained that the Church of England had a moral duty to respond to Institutional Racism
both within the church, and within the wider society and internationally. He was instrumental in the
development of the Committee for Minority Ethnic Anglican Concerns (CMEAC), the former Committee
on Black Anglican Concerns (CBAC). In 1998 Bishop Wood, became a signatory to the open 'Letter: Iraq:
Time to Think' by Rowan Williams, the then bishop of Monmouth, and former archbishop of Canterbury,
along with nineteen other British bishops calling for the British and American governments to think long and
hard before they decided to take military action in Iraq:

> We hope to see some sharper definition of what precisely the allied powers mean to achieve for Iraq and the
> region before our government embarks on a course that will undoubtedly involve more civilian casualties and
> more erosion of the bases of civil society in Iraq.
>
> In the name of all our brothers and sisters in the region – Christians, Muslims and others – we wish to add our
> own voices to this demand, before there is further terror and bloodshed...

Rt Revd Wilfred Wood has been honoured for his work in race relations in the UK and was awarded the
Knight of St Andrew (Order of Barbados) in 2000. In 2003, when Wood retired to live in Barbados, he was
succeeded by the Ven. Nicholas (Nick) Baines: 'Following Bishop Wilfred Wood is a considerable challenge
but, I shall do my best to serve the people there as faithfully and generously as he did for so many years.'

Paul Keynes Douglas, Jamaican orator, reciting a reading from 'Pa Pa God' on Caribbean Sunday at a London church.

Garth Moody (crouching, right) with his family, on holiday in Jamaica, 1940s. Born in London in 1925, the youngest child of Dr Harold Moody (see p.65), Garth Moody trained as a pilot in 1944, although the war finished before his training was completed. He then spent ten years in the Civil Service in London before emigrating to New Zealand in 1958, where he ran a hostel for Maori teenagers. Returning to London, he followed in his father's footsteps by becoming a Congregationalist minister in Wimbledon in 1971, combining Christian ministry with a strong social commitment. In 1985 he continued his ministry in Nottinghamshire.

John Tucker Mugabi Sentamu was born into Uganda's Buffalo Clan on 10 June 1949. The Most Revd and Right Hon. the Lord Archbishop of York was elected to Britain's and the Anglican Church's second most powerful ecclesiastical post on 21 July 2005, confirmed as ninety-seventh Archbishop of York on 5 October 2005 at St Mary-le-Bow, London, and inaugurated on 30 November 2005 at York Minster. This role is not only ecclesiastical but also parliamentary – the archbishops of Canterbury and York, with twenty-four other bishops constitute the Lords Spiritual in parliament. Hence, the additional title Rt Hon. Dr Sentamu, who is also primate of England and Metropolitan, a member of the House of Lords and a Privy Councillor: 'The Archbishop of Canterbury ranks next in precedence to the Royal Family, and above the Lord Chancellor. The Archbishop of York ranks next to the Lord Chancellor, and above dukes' (*Titles and Forms of Address*, 2007, A & C Black Publishers Ltd).

Archbishop Sentamu has served London Diocese for much of his career as: assistant curate, Ham St Andrew, diocese of Southwark, 1979–82; assistant curate, Herne Hill St Paul, diocese of Southwark, 1982–83; priest-in-charge, Tulse Hill Holy Trinity, diocese of Southwark, 1983–84; vicar, Upper Tulse Hill St Matthias, diocese of Southwark, 1983–84; vicar, Tulse Hill Holy Trinity and St Matthias, diocese of Southwark, 1985–96; priest-in-charge, Brixton Hill St Saviour, diocese of Southwark, 1987–89; honorary canon, Southwark Cathedral, 1993–96.

The first picture shows Rt Revd Dr John Sentamu outside the church that he helped to restore in Tulse Hill, 1988. Sentamu was born in Uganda, where, encouraged by English missionaries and teachers he studied law and enjoyed an illustrious career as chief magistrate and judge of the high court before he was forced to leave the country in the 1970s because of his criticism of Idi Amin's violations of human rights.

After studying theology at Cambridge University (Selwyn College, Cambridge, BA 1976; MA 1979; PhD 1984, Ridley Hall, Cambridge), Dr Sentamu became a minister in the Church of England, holding positions in Cambridge and London before serving as Vicar of Tulse Hill from 1983 to 1990. He was a member of the General Synod of the Church of England until 1996, when he was appointed bishop of Stepney (1996–2002). Much of Dr Sentamu's work has been concerned with the welfare of prisoners and the ethnic minorities. Between 2002 and 2004 he was Chairman of the EC1 New Deal. He became President of Youth for Christ in 2004 and President of the YMCA in April 2005.

Archbishop Sentamu has been at the forefront of several historically significant campaigns, which began in London, and grew to national importance. For example from 1997 to 1999, Dr Sentamu was adviser to the Stephen Lawrence Judicial Inquiry and he chaired the Damilola Taylor Murder Review in 2002. He has been the chairman of the NHS Haemoglobinopathy Screening Programme since 2001. (see p.74)

Before his appointment as Archbishop of York, Dr Sentamu had been appointed bishop for Birmingham in 2002. His commitment to Birmingham saw Dr Sentamu campaigning against drugs, knife and gun crime and youth violence, being instrumental in bringing the killers of Charlene Ellis and Letisha Shakespeare to justice. Dr Sentamu also 'stood shoulder to shoulder', with the workers of Rover car plant, supporting and advising those affected by plant closure.

Dr Sentamu is a fellow of the Royal Society of Arts. His interests include music, cooking, reading, athletics, rugby and football. He is married to Margaret and they have two grown-up children, Grace and Geoffrey.

CHAPTER EIGHT

TRANSPORT

From the turn of the century employment within the British Merchant Navy brought many Black Londoners to the capital – men such as Joseph Adolphus Bruce (see p.50) at the turn of the century, and Orlando Martins and Earl Cameron during the First and Second World Wars. Black Londoners have maintained strong links with London's transport industries throughout the twentieth century. In the 1940s there was an influx of Black British war-workers from the West Indies, charged with the responsibilities of keeping road and rail transport moving as part of the war effort. Many Black Londoners benefited from the strong connections of the military with the transport industries, through companies such as Alliance Haulage, Lambeth. It was a regimental link that gave Hector Watson his first job after the war – he went on to establish one of the first Black-owned haulage transport companies in Britain.

Many West Indians were recruited to work in London through the Barbados Migrants Liaison Service (BMLS) (1948–56), a body created by the Government of Barbados and encouraged by the British Government to tackle unemployment in both countries and labour shortages, originally for London Transport. It organized recruitment campaigns, medicals, training programmes for applicants, examinations, transportation and settlement loans. The BMLS proved such an efficient model that it was adopted by the British Government to encourage and settle new immigrants to Britain, not simply for London Transport but for the National Health Service, British Rail and the hotel and catering industries. In 1956 the organization was renamed the Migrants Liaison Service and extended to cover other West Indian islands.

Although originally proportionately small in numbers, Black transport workers in London were highly visible in their employment, and became an integral feature of the life of the capital. Their ubiquity has made London into one of the most cosmopolitan cities in the world.

For many workers, difficult conditions were made worse by the prejudiced attitudes of co-workers and superiors alike. 'Blacks were never given senior positions, regardless of clear ability or years of service. You could be a foreman but never a station master', according to Mr Ben Davis who has worked for London Transport for forty-seven years. 'Things have only recently changed.' While some had to fight their battles alone, others benefited from the increasing political assertion of a Black community growing in size and confidence. One important example of this was the West Indian Standing Conference's 1967 campaign against the *de facto* 'colour bar' against Black inspectors.

Joe Clough was one of London's first Black bus drivers. In 1908 he was the driver of the no. 11 on the route from Liverpool Street to Wormwood Scrubs. He worked for the London General Bus Company which later became known as London Transport. Mr Clough originally came to London from Jamaica in 1906. He married the daughter of a city publican. Mr Clough went on to deploy the driving skills he had honed on the streets of London working as a ambulance driver in France during the First World War. After 1918, Mr Clough left the city and settled in Bedford, working for a local bus company and then went on to run his own taxi firm.

Opposite above: **B. Johnston and J. Joff** at their tea break, 1942. This photograph of two Black workers, one from Jamaica and the other from the Gambia, reminds us of the wartime service provided to London Transport by Black people. Many Black people served as drivers, agricultural workers, engineers, coal miners and munitions workers as well as in the armed forces. Mr Johnston had already served in the navy before 1942, having had a lucky escape when his ship was torpedoed; before that he was reputedly a chauffeur for Mae West.

Opposite below: **Ben Davis** (*back row, left*) with the Emergency Breakdown crew, Neasden, 1959. In 1997 Ben Davis, the closest thing to a hero, celebrated forty-seven years of service for London Transport. Like Davis himself, celebrations were understated.

Emergency Breakdown are the first service called when there is a train accident or disaster. Frequently they work at the scene with a 'hot line' to the Minister of Transport. The team's skills range from highly skilled technical genius; accompanying surgeons to rescue passengers from mangled wreckage to the most grisly and demanding job of dealing with the aftermath of devastating accidents.

Born in 1932, he began work as an engineer at Ealing Common in 1951, joining the Breakdown Emergency Service in 1959. Despite much initial opposition to the presence of a Black engineer in this all-White service, Davis persevered, becoming a highly respected senior engineer, and was one of the crew that drove a lorry to the Moorgate Disaster in 1982 to aid the survivors of that train disaster, and sadly many more since.

Cynthia Palmer (left) clearing snow from Leytonstone Underground station in the harsh winter of 1963. Cynthia Palmer has now retired, but still conducts customer surveys for London Transport.

Ken Harper, bus driver, with his children, 1960s. Although London Transport helped to sustain many Black families in post-war Britain, there was little equality of employment. Despite the mass recruitment of Black workers in the 1960s, not a single Black bus inspector had been appointed by 1967, the year of *The Unsquare Deal: London's Black Colour Bar*, an influential report by the West Indian Standing Conference. This report revealed the restrictive employment practices and the racism of most White garage managers and made several recommendations to remedy the situation. These recommendations are now an accepted feature of employment practice.

Mrs A. Hart, bus conductor at Stockwell Garage, 1962, a classic image currently on show at the London Transport Museum. What this image does not show are the hardships, indignities and heroism of these women who managed to survive in jobs which were still male dominated and involved having to endure the hostile elements of the London streets. Black female bus conductors triumphed over these adversities, winning the respect of their peers and providing models of employment for a new generation of Black British women.

Joyce Jackman Edwards (née Jackman) was a railwaywoman on the London Underground for thirty-three years. Joyce Jackman came to Britain from Barbados in 1958 to study nursing at Leavesden Hospital, Watford. In 1960, however, she changed career, becoming a London Transport railwaywoman. After eight years as a ticket collector at Marble Arch and four as a Relief Ticket Collector, she moved to Wembley Park station and spent twenty years there – 'The most rewarding of my career', she says. In 1993 she received a Special Certificate.of Service, marking her thirty-three years' work for London Underground. This photograph features Joyce Edwards and her husband in the 1960s.

Many women were employed by **London Transport** in catering on an industrial scale, as large-scale demand took home-grown catering skills well beyond the domestic sphere. Black women met the challenge of creative menus within prescribed budgets. Mrs Norma Medford of Stockwell Garage, won the Hotel Olympia International Hotel and Catering Exhibition challenge cup and gold medal for the industrial catering section in 1966. The silver medallist, Miss Anita Smith of Acton Works, was also Black. Marva Braham, another award-winner, had one of her recipes immortalized in the London Transport Museum as 'Mrs B's Recipe for Caribbean Fish'. Such women introduced diversity to their menus and a richness to traditional English fare that reflected their cultural origins. (*Right*) Miss Lafinmakin serving tea in a London Transport canteen, 1965.

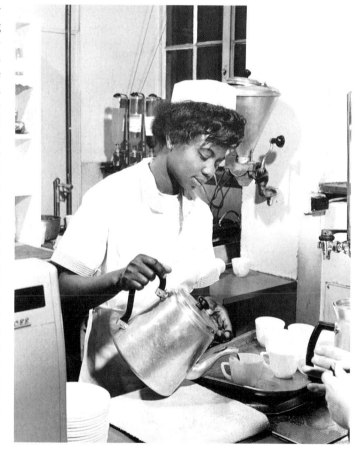

Centralized canteens were a necessity in an industry characterized by shift work and unsocial hours. British employers such as London Transport often recruited Black women directly from the West Indies to fill both traditional and non-traditional job vacancies, giving them extensive training. This photograph shows **Mrs Merna Miller** being crowned London Transport Catering Queen for 1971. This competition was designed to add glamour and excitement to a job which was as much physically demanding and a test of endurance as it was skilled.

A **Black woman bus inspector** in the 1970s. The first line of promotion for the ordinary busman and bus woman was inspector – from acting inspector to silver badge inspector and then gold badge inspector. Inspectors commanded a better salary and conditions of work, as well as higher status. It took many years, however, for the 'colour bar' to cease operating so that Black bus workers could become inspectors alongside their White colleagues.

The shared experiences of the **Underground** are part of what it is to be a 'Londoner'. There are unwritten codes of behaviour – silence, strict observation of personal space and avoidance of eye contact. Many recall when they first learnt 'the rules' of the London Underground, and compare these with some amusement to public behaviour in Africa and the West Indies.

CHAPTER NINE

EDUCATIONALISTS
AND WRITERS

Black Londoners have sought access to learning as a means of emancipation from the constraints of empire, class, race and geographical location. While some came to London on scholarships from Africa and the West Indies sponsored by Church missionary societies or wealthy parents, others came as travellers or workers. In their plans for the future, education and training featured significantly.

Students and educationalists of African, Caribbean and Asian origin were among the first to raise the clarion call against racial oppression within the British Empire. Individuals such as Trinidadian law student and temperance lecturer Henry Sylvester Williams had the opportunity to observe at first hand the conditions of life in the West Indies, and racism on the streets of London, and make the link between racial oppression and the political reality of empire. It was Williams who issued a call in 1898 for a world conference on Black people to take place in 1900. The Pan-Africanist Conference was held at Westminster Town Hall in 1900.

Before the mass recruitment in the transport industry and the health service, students were the most numerically significant group of the Black population, and were key allies of the resident Black population. Both groups relied upon each other for political organization and self-defence, in the broadest sense. The gathering of different national and ethnic groups, all of whom were under imperial control, resulted in better mutual understanding and provided a new perspective on the empire, a perspective that was at odds with imperial propaganda. Personal contact meant that different ethnic groups could reject the stereotypes inherited about each other, which made possible the political mobilization of the myriad independence movements of Africa and the West Indies. Thus to study in London became an education in Pan-Africanism.

Despite the influx of students from Africa and the West Indies to London, few were accepted in the professional life of London after graduation. While many had always intended to return to Africa and the West Indies, it also became clear that to remain in London to practise professionally was not always an option. Dr Harold Moody, for example, was refused employment at King's College Hospital despite being among the highest achievers in his year as a medical student in the same hospital (see p. 65). This stimulated his ambition to open his four London surgeries. Likewise, the father of the famous London composer, Samuel Coleridge-Taylor (see p. 36), had to return to Ghana in order to practise as a surgeon, where he was later to become surgeon-general.

Patterns of professional discrimination continued in the 1950s. Like many who came to London to study, Beryl Gilroy (see p. 165) was among the West Indies educational élite. Yet before being allowed to teach, she was forced to work as a washer-up at Joe Lyons' restaurant chain, in a factory and as a lady's maid. Her titanic battle for professional recognition led to her appointment as one of the first Black headmistresses within a mainstream London school.

A milestone in changing the educational climate occurred in 1966 when New Beacon Books was founded by John La Rose. He was been responsible for the publication and dissemination of books by Black writers such as Sam Sevlon, Derek Walcott and C.L.R. James. These publications have not only impacted upon the Black communities in the UK, but have altered the paradigms of the British educational establishment. Without such books, multiculturalist approaches to education would not have been possible.

Other individuals such as Gloria Lock have played a major part in introducing the books of African-Caribbean writers into mainstream education and the public at large. By offering teaching advice and support, and assistance to students working on class projects, Gloria Lock's remit as specialist Afro-Caribbean Librarian for some twelve libraries in Wandsworth included stock acquisition, display, training, publication, liaising with the public and educationalists, and organizing events. Wandsworth Library Services in the 1980s and '90s became a national resource for educational and library services, seeking to reflect greater diversity.

Opposite below: **Students in the 1940s.** Many people of Afro-Caribbean descent came to London as students. Some became permanent residents, others returned home, and a third group came and went, forming part of London's shifting population. Colonial secondary education was modelled closely on the English school system and largely administered by English men and women who set exams from the English examination boards. In theory a student could transfer from a classroom in Jamaica to a classroom in England without having to make any adjustment. Ironically, while British schools have moved away from more traditional teaching methods, some West Indian islands have retained them, with the result that Barbados, among other countries, has a higher literacy rate than England itself. Many Black teachers who were educated in Britain returned to Africa and the West Indies equipped to challenge the Europe-focused education systems of their countries. They include Dr Francis Akanu Ibiam, principal of the Hope Waddell Training Institute, in Calabar, Nigeria, who went on to become governor of the Eastern Region after independence.

Mary Lucinda Rice. Born in Plumstead in 1882, the daughter of Dr George Rice (see p.62), Mary Rice lived in the family home in Sutton from 1919. It was from this house, called Sagamore, that she ran the Sagamore Preparatory School from 1938. The family archive that she maintained on the Rice family was rescued from the local council rubbish dump by a Black council worker, Mr W. Ryder of Croydon. Her mother's family, the Cooks, owned Borstall Farm and were a wealthy family of contractors who played an active part in civic life.

Recruitment panel at **Nigeria House, London**, for the new University of Nigeria, at Nsukka, 1960 (Dr Nnamdi Azikiwe, chairman, is second left). From the 1950s, with the prospect of independence, came the need to reform the institutions of higher learning in Africa and the West Indies. Although ancient Africa boasted some of the earliest universities in the history of civilization, under colonialism the education of the élite was in the hands of their colonial masters; in Nigeria, for example, only 10 per cent of all civil service posts were held by Africans in 1945. New universities and colleges had to be built to educate Africans and West Indians so that they could take up key posts in their own countries, and Black graduates were recruited in abundance from London and elsewhere.

Gloria Lock served as specialist Afro-Caribbean librarian in Wandsworth, with responsibilities for twelve branch libraries and as African/Caribbean Community Librarian, Battersea (1985).

Gloria Lock (née Johnson) is depicted with her mother just before travelling to London from Sierra Leone in 1960. She studied at the University of London and Royal Holloway College, then taught English and Librarianship at Sierra Leonean, Nigerian and British Colleges and Universities.

In the 1980s and '90s Lock succeeded in making Wandsworth the model for the dissemination of information on Black people, both locally and internationally, through several landmark exhibitions, such as Focus on Africa (1987), 1492 and All That (1992) and the Caribbeans in Wandsworth (1992). Lock also produced a series of postcards on local Black historical figures, which challenge prevailing historical assumptions. Gloria Lock has served as Chair of the African Caribbean Library Association (ACLA), 1990; the African Caribbean Library Association, 1981–2002; and promoted Black writing in libraries across the country. In 1992 she won the Holt Jackson Library Association Award for Community Initiative and Good Practice.

Promoting child-centred approaches to teaching which are now commonplace, **Beryl Agatha Gilroy** (1924–2001), was one of the first Black head teachers of a British state school. An educational visionary and cultural pioneer, Gilroy was appointed deputy head, later attaining headship of Beckford Primary School, East London.

One of the key lessons which emerges from her story, are that unconventional-yet-challenging approaches to teaching can often yield greater successes than a formal system of education, which frequently failed Black and White working-class children.

Raised and home-taught by her maternal grandmother in Berbice, Guyana, Beryl Gilroy was not exposed to formal education until the age of twelve. This early formative experience of 'home-schooling', with the freedom of study and the liberty to read copious amounts of books, was to indeed give Gilroy an academic 'edge'. She was to graduate from Guyana's Teacher's College with first class honours (1945).

The insights gained from her grandmother's teaching philosophy and her own education were to be passed on to her children, who were 'home-schooled' in their early years. It can be no coincidence that her son, Professor Paul Gilroy, went on to become one of Britain's leading academics and original thinkers (see p.167).

Beryl Gilroy arrived in Britain in the early 1950s after being selected to study at the University of London. Gilroy graduated with a diploma in Child Development (1951–53). As was sadly the case with so many West Indians who had arrived in Britain, racism in employment meant that Beryl Gilroy was unable to take up a teaching post for many years after graduation.

How Gilroy struggled to overcome prejudices within teaching, and her successes in winning the respect and friendship of an initially hostile White working-class community, were later to be documented in her seminal book, *Black Teacher* (1979). Beckford was eventually to attract students representing over forty different nationalities. This book, which may be described as a grittier *To Sir, With Love*[1], managed to survive the best efforts of her publishers to tone down its portrayal of the stark reality of racism within British society.

Beryl Gilroy was to spend the second half of her career as a researcher at the University of London, Institute of Education, as well as nurturing a Psychotherapy practice primarily aimed at Black women and children. She was also a founder member of Camden Black Sisters, a successful women's campaigning and support group. She also served on the ILEA (Inner London Education Authority) Centre for Multicultural Education. This was very much a vanguard position in which her innovative research could find its way to the classroom, via teachers passing through these major teaching and developmental institutions.

Recognition was to follow in the form of an honorary doctorate from the University of London and an honorary fellowship from the Institute of Education (2000), alongside a PhD in Psychology (1982).

Racism and sexism conspired to delay Beryl Gilroy's writing career until later in life. We are all beneficiaries of a literary legacy, which despite its postponement, was well worth the wait. Her books include fiction and non-fiction, focusing on contemporary social issues: they encompass a rich tradition of Caribbean folk tales and historical novels addressing the subjective experiences of slavery: *Boy Sandwich* (1989), *Steadman and Joanna* (1991), *Sunlight on Sweet Water* (1993), *In Praise of Love and Children* (1996), *Inkle & Yarico* (1996) and *Green Grass Tango* (2001). In 1986, her novel, *Frangipani House*, won the GLC Literature Prize.

1. *To Sir, With Love*, written by E.R. Brathwaithe (1959), was an autobiographical novel about the struggles of a West Indian teacher in a London comprehensive school. It was later turned into a Hollywood film, starring Sydney Poitier.

Sources for this entry include: PeepaltreePress.com, website. Publisher's tribute to Beryl Gilroy, © PeepaltreePress 2001.

Beryl Gilroy, Monday, 28 May 2001, *The Independent* – 'Beryl Agatha Answick, teacher and writer'.

The Guardian obituary, 'Beryl Gilroy: An innovative Caribbean writer, novelist of the black diaspora and London's first black head teacher', Peter D. Fraser, Wednesday, 18 April 2001.

John La Rose, political and cultural activist, was born in 1927. La Rose came to London from Trinidad, where he had made a significant impact on political life as General Secretary of the West Indian Independence Party and in the trade union movement. From his North London base he co-founded the Caribbean Artists' Movement (1966), the Caribbean Education and Community Workers' Association (1969) and the Black Parents' Movement (1975).

La Rose was also one of Britain's leading Black publishing pioneers as publisher of New Beacon Books since 1966 and founder of the International Book Fair of Radical Black and Third World Books. The publication and dissemination of books by such Black writers as Sam Selvon, Derek Walcott and C.L.R. James has made the multicultural approach to education possible. La Rose was also a poet and essayist in his own right.

John La Rose died on 28 February 2006, leaving behind an important legacy and repository for the African diaspora in Britain and internationally: The George Padmore Institute and Archive is a library and educational research centre, housing materials relating to the Black community of Caribbean, African and Asian descent in Britain and continental Europe. Established in 1991, the institute carries on the name and historical memory of the Trinidadian Pan-Africanist George Padmore, who inspired the anti-imperialist independence movements in Africa and the West Indies. Padmore became a highly influential figure in the fifth Pan-Africanist Conference, Manchester 1945.

Andrew Salkey, writer, editor and teacher. Born in Panama in 1928 to Jamaican parents, Salkey travelled widely, coming to London in 1952 to study at London University. He spent the next twenty-four years in the capital as freelance broadcaster, book reviewer, teacher, narrator and writer, contributing to a host of political and literary journals and writing books across the fields of non-fiction, novels, poetry and children's stories. He has also written some fifty plays and other features, mostly for radio. His work deals with the themes of boundaries between people and national territories and the impact when these boundaries are crossed. These themes are as present in the folk tales of the Caribbean that he has retold, especially about the Anancy character (or mischievous spider), as they are in political studies of race and colonialism. Salkey was professor of writing at Hampshire College, Massachusetts from 1976 until his death in 1995.

Professor Paul Gilroy is one of Britain's leading academics, and social thinkers. His groundbreaking work on racism, nationalism and ethnicity and the history of the African Diaspora has done much to influence the way contemporary multicultural Britain views itself, and how others view it from abroad. With seminal books which have influenced a generation of students and others, such as *There Ain't No Black in the Union Jack* (1987, reprinted by Routledge, 2002), *The Black Atlantic* (1994) and *Between Camps: Nations, Cultures and the Allure of Race* (2000), Gilroy has demonstrated a multi-disciplinary intellectual background, which encompasses literature, art, music, cultural history and social science. His latest book is *After Empire: Melancholia or Convivial Culture* (Routledge, 2004).

Gilroy has lectured at some of the world's leading universities, and is currently the first holder of the Anthony Giddens Professorship in Social Theory at the London School of Economics (LSE), University of London. That post follows his Charlotte Marian Saden Professorship of Sociology and African American studies at Yale University (USA), where he also chaired of the African American Studies Department.

Gilroy received his PhD from the Centre for Contemporary Studies, Birmingham University, achieving a professorship in Sociology and Cultural Studies at Goldsmiths College, University of London in 1991.

Born in Bethnal Green, East London, in 1956, Paul Gilroy jokes that he comes under the technical definition of a Cockney. He was raised by an English father and a Guyanese mother from Berbice, in rural Guyana, who arrived in England in 1951. He has one sister.

Although born in East London, it is North London with which Gilroy has the great emotional connection, he went to University College School, Hampstead, on an 'assisted place', after winning an 11+ scholarship. 'About my school it may be said, they taught me how to educate myself... I remember with particular affection my very right-wing history teacher.' Gilroy was the first of three Black boys to enter the school during the 1960s. He rose to be head boy. Going to school in Hampstead, Gilroy became very familiar with Hampstead Heath 'I have loved Hampstead Heath, from the time I discovered it as a child. I love its old oak trees and its wildlife, especially the kestrels. I am also found of the Azaleas at Kenwood House. I love the book-lined room in which England's chief justice, Lord Mansfield is said to have written his famous judgement in the case of the slave James Somerset. It's a room in which I have had many a heated argument with the guides from English Heritage.' North London is also the location of the Whittington Hospital in which Gilroy's son was born and his father died.

Gilroy's eccentric historical map of London also charts Fulham Palace Road, site of the Greyhound pub which was another place where he had a life-changing experience. It was there that he met the late, great Bob Marley. 'I rushed down the stairs to meet him when he stopped for a breather after an amazing concert in 1973.'

Gilroy grew up in an untidy house full of books, which included the works of DuBois, Raymond Williams, C.L.R. James and many others 'But Marley's poetic, moral take on our history was to alter my life'. Gilroy's life was transformed by the *Catch a Fire* album. Marley's rebel, Garveyite perspective would redefine history and create a new cohesion, which was to impact upon Gilroy's own work. Marley brought the language of rights into the equation.

However, it was his mother, Beryl Gilroy, the educational pioneer and writer, who may be regarded as the greatest influence in Gilroy's choice of career. Beryl Gilroy not only encouraged her son's own education but from an early age, her anthropological and cultural interests demonstrated to him 'how culture works, and how it evolves'.

Gilroy's Guyanese heritage embraces a grandfather who was the son of an enslaved African-Dutch speaker from Surinam, English-German ancestry and a grandmother Sally James, who was of Portuguese origin. The Gilroys are also cousins of the journalist and musician Rudolph Dunbar, whose book, the first-ever *Treatise on the Clarinet*, remains a treasured possession of Gilroy's. 'Those who claim that British multiculturalism has failed can't have it both ways. You can't make that claim and yet celebrate the diversity of this modern city.' Gilroy maintains that the popular message that multiculturalism failed only serves to fuel the arguments of racism.

Of his greatest achievements, Gilroy lists being a good father to his son and daughter. He is also proud of having his writing translated into French, Italian, Portuguese, Danish, Swedish, Japanese, Arabic, Spanish and German. Gilroy believes that it has been his greatest mission to 'Assist in the fight against ignorance in a world where racism engenders suffering, to contribute to the fight against political and educational illiteracy, and for the relevance of political involvement.'

In keeping with these sentiments, one of Gilroy's favourite London landmarks is the statue of the nurse Edith Cavell, St Martins Place, London WC2. Edith Cavell was executed by firing squad for rescuing hundreds of British soldiers from German-occupied Belgium during the First World War. Gilroy is moved by the statue's inscription quoted by her on the eve of her death in which she states, 'Patriotism is not enough. I must have no hatred or bitterness for anyone.' This humanitarian sentiment profoundly speaks to Gilroy. 'Patriotism is not enough. People in this country need to re-negotiate our relationship with the rest of the world.'

Jessica and Eric Huntley, co-founders of Bogle L'Ouverture Publications in 1969 were among the earliest Black independent publishers in Britain. The Huntleys are also founders and co-directors of the International Book Fair of Radical Black and Third World Books. Jessica Huntley has also played a leading role as an educator, not only in the Supplementary School movement, responding to the crisis of the educational system surrounding Black children, but also by providing an Educational and Equal Opportunities Consultancy.

Challenging publications such as Walter Rodney's seminal book *How Europe Underdeveloped Africa*, as well as many of Andrew Salkey's explorations of the Caribbean folklore character *Anancy the Spider*, were championed by Bogle L'Ouverture, which in collaboration with *Race Today* also published *Voices of the Living and the Dead* (1974) and *Dread Beat and Blood* (1975), Linton Kwesi Johnson's first and second books of poetry, mixed reggae and Caribbean patios in commentary about the injustices experienced by second generation of Black people in contemporary Britain.

> To publish is to be radical, to write is a subversive act... to be a Black writer is by definition to be radical and revolutionary. (Eric Huntley)

In 2005, the London Metropolitan Archive announced a major accession of the archives of Jessica and Eric Huntley, 'Prominent members of the community and tireless campaigners for the rights and issues of Black and Caribbean people in London'. Important historical documents charting the Black presence in the late twentieth century are now available to the public. Documents include material on publishing and campaigning; papers and correspondence, including records relating to Kent County Council's Youth Service, the Black and Caribbean community, the Ealing Windrush Consortium; Bogle-L'Ouverture publications and the Friends of Bogle papers including correspondence, publicity and financial records and publications 1964–2004; and Common Lore Storytelling Company Ltd: minutes, correspondence, memorandum and articles of association, resource pack and publicity material 1986–2000.

Ben Okri is a writer and journalist. Okri was born in Nigeria in 1959 and came to London at the age of four. His writing career began even before he had finished studying comparative literature at the University of Essex, with the publication of *Flowers and Shadows* in 1980. This was followed by *The Landscape Within* (1982). In 1987 he was shortlisted for the Commonwealth Prize and the following year for the Guardian Fiction Prize, for *Incidents at the Shrine* and *Stars of the Curfew*.

Okri has become a literary luminary with an international reputation, not restricted to English language works. This fact is apparent from the nature of his international accolades. For *The Famished Road* Okri won the Booker Prize (1991), the Chianti Ruffino-Antico Fattore International Literary Prize (1993) and the Primio Grinzane Cavour (Italy, 1994). International recognition has been followed by The Crystal Award, given by the World Economic Forum (1995) and the Premio Palmi (Italy) for *Dangerous Love* (2000). In 2001 Ben Okri received an OBE from the Queen.

Okri has contributed to several leading newspapers and journals, including the *Guardian*, the *Observer* and the *New Statesman*, and holds honorary doctorates from the University of Westminster (1997), and his alma mater the University of Essex (2002). In addition, Okri is vice-president of the English Centre for the International PEN and a Member of the Royal National Theatre.

In recent years Okri has tended to explore more poetry and his work has shifted towards greater 'magic realism', and imaginative experimentation, keeping his readers on heir toes. *Starbook* (2007) was Okri's eleventh book, published after a five-year gap.

Kwame Kwei Armah lists his proudest achievements as having two plays at the National Theatre and having overnight significantly increased the National's Black patronage as a consequence, upwards of 60 per cent. These two plays were *Elmina's Kitchen* (2003) and *Fix-Up* (2005). *Statement of Regret* (2007), based upon former Prime Minister Tony Blair's 'statement of regret' about Britain's role in the slave trade, was his third National Theatre play. The year 2008 saw the launch of *Let There be Love*, opening at London's Tricycle Theatre, starring Joseph Marcell (formerly Geofrey from 'The Fresh Prince of Bel Air').

Kwame Kwei Armah first came to public attention as an actor and one of the most popular stars of *Casualty*, playing the paramedic Finlay Newton (1999–2004), and starring in *Holby City* (2001). His popularity and image as an all-round British entertainer peaked when he sang as a contestant in the BBC's *Comic Relief Does Fame Academy* (2003), consequently releasing an album and winning the Screen Nation Award for favourite TV actor (2003).

It was however the revelation of his talent as a playwright, which has met with the greatest acclaim for Kwame Kwei Armah. This critical success began with an Evening Standard Award for the Most Promising New Playright (2003) and a shortlisting in the Best New Play category at the 2004 Laurence Olivier Awards, following Armah's writing of *Elmina's Kitchen* (2003). The year 2003 also saw Kwei Armah's directorial debut in America at Baltimore's Centerstage, directing the award-winning Naomi Wallace play *Things of Dry Hours*. Following an *Elmina's Kitchen* adaptation for television, Kwame was to receive the film and entertainment's most prestigious BAFTA TV Award nomination for Best New Writer for *Elmina's Kitchen* (2005). Kwei Armah's success followed a writer's residency at the Bristol Old Vic (1999–2001), during which his drama *A Bitter Herb* was produced as well as two productions of his musical *Blues Brother Soul Sister*.

Kwame Kwei Armah was born Ian Roberts, in Hillingdon, 1967 to Grenadan parents, as one of seven children. Coming to England in 1962/1963 Kwame's father, a factory worker for Quaker Oats, and mother, a nurse, were to have high aspirations for their children. It was however Kwei Armah's mother who was to have the greatest influence over her son's future career, by insisting that he attend the fee-paying Barbara Speakes Stage School in Acton, working two jobs to afford this. Kwei Armah truly came to understand how, to his mother, education was central to everything, by her insistence upon finding time to return to college to complete her own O-levels in her forties, having left school at fourteen.

Kwame grew up in Southall, but feels a general connection to London as a whole, having lived at some time, north, west and east of the capital. 'Wherever my mother, and children are, that is home'.

Now an associate at Britain's National Theatre, and America's Baltimore's Centerstage Theater, Kwei Armah freely admits to having a second home in the rehearsal room of the National Theatre Studio. 'When I pass the rehearsal room, the hairs stand up at the back of my head. I love to find the life in a play. This is where I have found the most peace that I have found anywhere in life outside of church.' 'Coming from a working-class background, driven by a strong work ethic, you tend to think that unless there is noise and unless, you're doing things, its not working. When I first went into the National Theatre Studio, I was given a place to be, to just think, an intellectual rather than spiritual home.'

Genealogical research undertaken by Kwei Armah, revealed the family origin of his great-great-grandfather among the Cromante in Ghana. Having 'found his tribe', Ian Roberts, re-claimed a tribal name Kwame from the Ga, of significance. Kwame, means, 'To find a way'.

A prolific writer, 2006 saw Kwei Armah writing two feature films. The first film features one of Jamaica's greatest slave revolts, the Tackins Rebellion, 1769. The second film is the story of a Black mathematician and his burden of responsibility. Kwei Armah has also completed a music project for the Marley family, set among the child soldiers of the Congo. 'For years there was only one kind of Black story one was able to write. Now there are several of them.' On the discipline of writing, Kwame states, 'I am paid to sit at home and look at the news, read newspapers, books, and to write about what is happening, in the culture. When one considers the luxury of this position, concentration is the least of my challenges'.

Beginning the writing process, Kwei Armah is motivated to write when he has a feeling in his stomach that he has the physical energy to write. This sets up a system in which he can say; 'Now I'm ready to do battle with myself'. For Kwame the battle is not always what he puts down on the page, but what he has not.

As a writer Kwei Armah believes that empathy is a prerequisite, 'To enable me to look at humanity through the prism of love, whether it is looking at what we like or don't like'.

Kwame Kwei Armah was in 2008 appointed writer-in-residence for BBC Radio Drama, a role in which he developed his own original material, in addition to training and mentoring new writers.

'One of my proudest achievements is that I am the first Black female to write and star in my own show in the UK, *Little Miss Jocelyn*'. The only other female comedian to achieve this distinction has been Britain's leading comedian, Victoria Wood.

Jocelyn Jee Esien studied drama, at the prestigious Guild Hall (1994–97), counting among her contemporaries Brit-pack Hollywood exports such as Orlando Bloom.

Coming from Nigeria in the 1960s, Jocelyn's father, a qualified lawyer and mathematics teacher, was not entirely convinced about acting as a career choice, until he saw his daughter struggling to carry huge books on the works of Shakespeare. Then, convinced of the academic nature of her course, he mellowed. Jocelyn's mother, a chef, had by contrast always been quite encouraging and supportive of her career choice. Partly, because she saw in her daughter a kind of kindred spirit; Jocelyn Jee Esien's mother chose to train as a chef quite late in life.

Jocelyn Jee Esien has an historical connection with London's East End, having been born at the London Hospital, Bethnal Green. Esien has lived in Hackney for many years, and continues to support the Hackney Empire, performing her major charity events there. In fact, Hackney and Dalston could be said to have provided inspiration for many of her more 'off beat' characters in *Little Miss Jocelyn*.

A keen follower of family history for many years, Esien has watched her father preparing his 'Memoirs'. He has been forced to admit that Jocelyn is not alone in joining the entertainment industry, since his own grandmother was something of a local impresario, staging and performing plays, and touring shows from village to village. Storytelling and singing are mainstays of African culture.

Jocelyn Jee Esien had gathered previous experience for *Little Miss Jocelyn*, from collaborative writing on some of the material for the successful comedy show *The Three Non Blondes*. This series was itself an innovation, since never before had three Black British women been the instigators behind a 'hidden camera', comedy show. 'We had tried different things, a sitcom, a sketch show, then the idea for a hidden camera show came from performances at our live comedy shows.' The BBC funded a pilot show and the rest is history. *The Three Non Blondes* picked up a Screen Nation: Best Comedy Award (2003), at the time it also received the highest ratings for a programme on BBC 3, and was then destined to achieve success on BBC 1 & 2, respectively.

The year 2003 saw *The Three Non-Blondes* cast being invited to give an award to Ms Dynamite at the MOBO (Music of Black Origin) Awards ceremony. A nomination was also received from the British Comedy Award for Best Comedy Newcomer (2003). Jocelyn Esien found time to make an appearance on the *Lenny Henry Show* (2004). Other awards have included The Black Entertainment: Comedy Award (2004); Esien was to further receive a nomination by the Royal Television Society, Television Award Best Comedy Performance (2004).

The Three Non-Blondes received an Afro-Hollywood Award (2006). This American award reflects the fact that *The Three Non-Blondes* has been part of the regular programming of the BBC America Channel for the past three years, with all cast members building up a loyal American fan-base.

Jocelyn Jee achieved a nomination by Channel 5 Women in Film Awards for Best Newcomer (2006) and was nominated for a BAFTA Award for Best Comedy Programme (2007).

Jocelyn Jee Esien has also featured in the popular BBC comedy *After You've Gone* (2007) and *The Sarah Jane Adventures* (2008), the science fiction spin-off series from *Doctor Who*.

CHAPTER TEN

NEWS AND NEWSMAKERS

The individuals, events and institutions which have had an impact upon the cultural and political life of Black London are too numerous to mention. However, this chapter attempts to record a brief selection of significant historical events, institutions and individuals.

Black Londoners of African, Caribbean and Asian origin were among the first to raise the clarion call against racial oppression at the First Pan-African Conference on 23–25 July 1900 at Westminster Town Hall. This conference attempted to take steps to influence public opinion on existing proceedings and conditions affecting the 'Natives' in the various parts of the Empire, in particular, South Africa, West Africa and the British West Indies. It was at this conference that Dr W.E.B. DuBois, the Black American scholar and leader, declared that 'the problem of the twentieth century is the problem of the colour line'.

Significantly, John Archer, the first Black mayor of a London borough, Samuel Coleridge-Taylor, London-born musician and composer of Ghanaian origin, and Trinidadian law student and temperance lecturer Henry Sylvester Williams helped to organize the conference. One of its sponsors included the Asian ex-MP Dadabhai Naoroji. Here we have an early example of African-Caribbean and Asian Londoners' political solidarity. (John Archer later became election agent for his political mentor Saklavatla, one of the first Asian MPs.)

The organized political responses of the Black community have often come from events which have been far from organized but rather random and symptomatic of deeper social issues – the killing of a Black woman during an illegal police raid, the unexplained death in police custody of a young man, and so on. Such were the shooting of Cherry Groce, the killing of Cynthia Jarrett and the death of Colin Roach – events which affected Black Londoners but which attracted the protest of Londoners of all races, events which brought home to the Black community the fact that change could be brought about by both organized and disorganized mass protest and by mobilization through the political processes. Either way, apathy was simply not an option.

The cultural impact of Black Londoners on London life has been significant, from youth sub-culture and music, to fashion, food and literature. The Africa Centre and the Notting Hill Carnival are symbols of the contribution that Black Londoners have made to one of the most cosmopolitan cities in the world.

As a Pan-Africanist politician, lawyer and journalist, **J.E. Casely Hayford** successfully campaigned for African conservation and human rights, and against the British imperial government's attempts to take over African land in the Gold Coast (now Ghana). As a consequence of his campaigns, the Land Bill of 1897 and the Forest Bill of 1911 failed.

In 1919 J.E. Casely Hayford served on the Gold Coast's Legislative Council, and the same year went on to establish West Africa's first nationalist movement, the National Congress of British West Africa. He received an MBE from the British Government in 1919. In 1925 he was to represent the Congress at the League of Nations.

J.E. Casely Hayford had originally studied law at Cambridge University (1893). A member of the Inner Temple, Inns of Court, London he was called to the British Bar on 17 November 1896. Although Casely Hayford had studied to become a barrister, he found his calling as a respected journalist, campaigning for a Pan-Africanist and anti-imperialist agenda.

Casely Hayford contributed to and edited a slew of influential West African newspapers from 1885–1930. These newspapers included the *Western Echo*, *Gold Coast Echo*, *Gold Coast Chronicle*, the *Gold Coast Methodist Times*, *Gold Coast Aborigines* and the *Gold Coast*. He wrote several influential academic books on the Gold Coast, and the famous Pan-Africanist novel *Ethiopia Unbound*. Through the self-belief and passionate leadership of men and women like J.E. Casely Hayford, Ghana became the first African state to wrest its independence from British control in 1957.

Alex Pascall (*left*) interviewing for the radio programme *Black Londoners*. Pascall came to London from Grenada in 1959 where he had founded the island's most popular folk group and he soon built up a reputation as an experienced compere at some of the capital's leading nightclubs. In 1969 he formed the Alex Pascall Singers, which drew upon both African and Caribbean traditions of performance. In 1974 he was invited to host *Black Londoners* on Radio London, which he did for fourteen years. One of the longest running radio programmes hosted by a Black presenter, it was unique in its mix of music and community news and interviews. Pascall was an early champion of Soca Calypso and African/World music, and a pioneer in the development of African Caribbean teaching resources for schools, in Britain. Pascall has been an Educational Adviser for several television companies, and wrote and recorded stories and music for radio and television.

One of the co-founders of the Notting Hill Carnival, Europe's largest street festival, Pascall has been invited to serve on the Carnival Arts Committee of the Arts Council of Great Britain over many years. Pascall was among the earliest campaigners to fight for the recognition of carnival arts (the whole range of art forms which support carnival practice), helping to establish the Foundation for European Carnival Cities in 1985. Pascall with fellow carnivalists became exponents of the form across Europe, through initiatives such as the launch of a European culture train to the Viareggio Carnival in Northern Italy, and Cultural Exchanges by European Cultural Heads to see carnival first hand in the Caribbean.

In 1986 Pascall became National Coordinator of Caribbean Focus for the Commonwealth Institute and the Governments of the West Indies. This year-long initiative was one of the largest Caribbean festivals and Black-led cultural programmes of its time, involving fifty-five festival committees across Britain. In addition, Pascall negotiated with British Rail, commandeering a 7X carriage train 'the first cultural exhibition train in British history', re-fitting it into a Caribbean museum and gallery space. The train also ran educational workshops and travelled to eighteen British cities in twenty-one days.

A cultural and political activist before the emergence of Black representation in the House of Commons or House of Lords, or indeed before race equalities rights or policies had been established, Pascall was one of the highest profile Black people in England. When called upon, he frequently found himself at campaign HQ, fighting against individual or community injustices, at enormous personal cost and sacrifice.

Pascall's activism has been recognized by a number of awards: British Local Radio Award, Manpower Services Commission Award for Best Community project, BBC Radio London: Ethnic Minority Health Project (1980); Alex Pascall: Broadcaster of 1981, The Society of Black Lawyers, presented by Lord Scarman; The Caribbean Times Award, 'For services rendered to the Black community in Britain' (1984) and an OBE (Order of the British Empire) in 1996.

Pascall continues to fight for equality and social justice for the community, serving as Executive Member of the National Union of Journalist, and Chair of its Black Members Council. In 2005 Pascall was elected a National Union of Journalists Member of Honour (Life Member).

Alex and Joyce Pascall (also from Grenada) constitute one of the most formidable 'power couples' for cultural and political activism, establishing Good Vibes Records & Music in 1979 to maintain artistic freedom and autonomy, publishing rights and copyright for themselves, and other artists whom they have represented over the years. Joyce Pascall has also served as researcher, policy advisor and project manager on a host of creative projects and political campaigns with Alex.

Their daughter Deirdre is an accomplished musician and music producer, who tours internationally, and has collaborated with her father on projects such as his recent musical: *Common Threads* (2003). The Pascalls' son Iyandele, is a senior editor for British current affairs television broadcasts, recently covering the Obama campaign in the USA.

Sir Trevor McDonald was born in 1939. He came to London in 1962 as a reporter for Radio Trinidad, covering the Independence Conference for Trinidad and Tobago by presenting conference reports every night to an eager public waiting back home. As a result, he was invited to join the BBC's Caribbean Service, part of the Overseas Service, as a producer in 1969; this acted as an important bridge between the emergent Black community in London and their countries of origin. McDonald joined ITN in 1973 and was ITV's first Black reporter, working as a sports correspondent, then diplomatic correspondent, eventually becoming the sole anchor of the ITN's flagship news programme *News at Ten* in 1992. He was awarded an OBE the same year, shortly afterwards publishing his autobiography, *Fortunate Circumstances* (1993), going on to write the biographies of cricketers Vivian Richards and Clive Lloyd.

Between 1999 and 2005, ITV's *News at Ten* moved in the schedules and was axed several times, McDonald believing he had given his last news broadcast in December 2005. However he was brought out of retirement in January 2008 to re-launch a new ITV *News at Ten* to great fanfare.

Trinidadian-born McDonald has ironically become a 'British institution', with polls identifying him as 'the perfect newscaster'. His news delivery is authoritative and his inteviews as diplomatic correspondent have maintained a gravitas equal to the task of interrogating world leaders such as Saddam Hussein, Nelson Mandela, Yasser Arafat, George Bush, Bill Clinton, Ronald Reagan, Muammar Gaddafi, Condoleezza Rice and Benazir Bhutto. McDonald was knighted in the Queen's Birthday Honours List in 1999.

Chancellor of London South Bank University, McDonald also holds an honorary award from the University of Plymouth. A popular host at many awards ceremonies, he has been a regularly presenter of the National Television Awards. With an established status and secure within the public's affections, in recent years McDonald has ventured into comedy and light entertainment, hosting *This is Your Life* (2007) for Simon Cowell, *Have I Got News For You* (2006) and *News Knight with Sir Trevor McDonald* (2007). McDonald is an honorary vice-president of the charity Vision Aid Overseas (VAO), which provides optical care in poor countries.

Dame Jocelyn Barrow's career reflects her deep commitment to community relations and social justice. She was a founder member and later general secretary of the Campaign Against Racial Discrimination, which was responsible for campaigning for the introduction of the 1968 Race Relations Act, and a member of the Community Relations Council from 1968 to 1972. In 1972 she was awarded the OBE for her work in the fields of education and community relations.

Dame Jocelyn's international role as the most senior Black member of the European Commission, sitting on the Economic and Social Committee among others, was foreshadowed by her position as vice-president of the International Human Rights Year in 1968. Dame Jocelyn was the first Black Governor of the BBC (1981–88) and deputy chairman of the Broadcasting Standards Council (1989–95). She became a Dame of the British Empire in 1992.

Her commitment to African Caribbean heritage in the UK came full circle for Dame Jocelyn when she chaired the Mayor's Commisson on African and Asian Heritage (MCAAH) (2005). As early as 1972 she was instrumental in the establishment of the North Atlantic Slavery Gallery at the Maritime Museum in Liverpool. Dame Jocelyn has also been Governor of the Commonwealth Institute, Council Member of Goldsmith's College, University of London, and Vice-President of the United Nations Association. She is National Vice-President of the Townswomen's Guild. An honorary doctorate was conferred upon Dame Jocelyn from the University of York in 2007. Baroness Howells was inaugurated as Chancellor of the University of Bedfordshire in 2009.

Oliver Tambo became president of the African National Congress in the 1980s. During his exile from South Africa, he settled in London. In 1979 Oliver Tambo was the first leader of a liberation movement to be honoured by a Special Committee of the United Nations; this marked the beginning of the formal recognition of African liberation movements by the UN.

Oliver Tambo was a maths and science teacher who became leader of the South African Government in exile for thirty years (1960–1990), based at 51 Alexandra Park, Muswell Hill, London Borough of Haringey. From this unassuming suburban house, an unassuming Tambo and his wife Adelaide effectively ran the South African Government in exile, using the house as a base from which to inform the world about the injustices of Apartheid upon the Black people of South Africa, and to develop international alliances. From his London home and HQ Tambo successfully established anti-Apartheid offices in twenty-seven different countries. In today's South Africa, Oliver Tambo is regarded as on a parallel with Nelson Mandela for his role in the overthrow of the Apartheid system.

Tambo returned to South Africa in 1991, being elected national chairperson of the ANC. By the time of this bittersweet return many friends and loved ones had passed on through 'the struggle' and time itself. Oliver Tambo had lived to see his years of exile vindicated and the cusp of a hopeful future for a new generation of South Africans. Unfortunately, he was not to live to see the first free elections for the Black people of South Africa, Nelson Mandela as President of South Africa or his formidible wife Adelaide Tambo become one of the first Black MPs in the new government. The honourable Oliver Tambo died in 1993 following a stroke.

In October 2007 Tambo had a monument and memorial site dedicated to him in the North London park in which his three children played. The previous year, in October 2006, Tambo, the co-founder of modern South Africa had South Africa's main airport re-named after him.

Left: **Tambo** (*left*) shakes hands with Ken Livingstone, then Leader of the Greater London Council, at an anti-Apartheid rally in Trafalgar Square, 1985. The Black American community leader Jesse Jackson is in the centre.

Below: Rally outside the house in New Cross where thirteen young Black people died in the arson attack of January 1981. After the fire, John La Rose and others set up the **New Cross Massacre Action Committee** to support bereaved parents and to demand a full police investigation. The committee organized the Black People's Day of Action in 1982 to demonstrate against the lack of measures taken by the police in the early investigation of the fire. It turned out to be one of the largest ever demonstrations of Black people in Britain. After a public meeting held at Deptford Town Hall (below right), a procession led by the parents of the victims marched to the house in New Cross on the anniversary of the fire. They marched to the chant, '13 dead and nothing said', commenting upon the absence of any official statement of compassion or condolence from government and royalty, in line with other national disasters (particularly those involving children and young people).

Opposite above: Parents of some of the victims of the **New Cross massacre** at a memorial service held at St Mary's Church, Lewisham, in January 1987.

Councillor **Jean Bernard**, Brixton, 1989, eight years after the first riots which devastated the borough. The **Brixton riots** or 'uprisings' were the culmination of a police/community relations crisis that went back many years; above all, they were a reaction to insensitive methods of policing which alienated an entire class of Black young people, in attempting to deal with a criminal minority in this highly diverse community. The injustices created by blanket police operations, which treated the innocent as if they were guilty, generated solidarity among young people, and later the whole community, who were already sharing the experiences of racism and social exclusion from schools to the world of work. The report of Lord Scarman, who led the public inquiry into the causes of the riots, validated much of what young people had been saying for years about their unfair treatment at the hands of the police. The report also documented the social, economic and environmental problems of the area, which have gradually improved with inward investment by companies.

Demonstration against the death of **Colin Roach** in police custody, January 1983. Colin Roach's suspicious death at Stoke Newington police station was another example of the abuse of the so-called 'Sus' laws, under which an individual could be charged with suspicious conduct. They were intended as a deterrent to crime but in practice, because of their vagueness and the biased way in which they were enforced, became a civil liberties nightmare for Black youth. The death of Roach was only one in a long line of Black deaths in police custody. Other victims included Trevor Morville and Tunde Hassan, who also died at Stoke Newington police station.

The mother of **Cherry Groce** protests outside Stoke Newington police station about Groce's shooting by police in her own home in 1985. The shooting triggered the Brixton riots. John La Rose, publisher, quotes the frequently heard statement of youth outrage: 'They are killing our mothers now.'

Above left: **Cherry Groce** being pushed by her solicitor, Paul Boateng, outside the Old Bailey during the Broadwater Farm youth trials, 1986. Cherry Groce was shot by police as they burst into her house in Brixton in 1985, looking for her son. This act, combined with the continued harassment of (mainly Black) youth by the police, triggered the second Brixton riots of September 1985 (*above right*), four years after violence had previously rocked the borough.

A burnt out furniture store in Greasham Road, Brixton, 1985.

A demonstration of the **Broadwater Farm Defence Campaign**, 1985 (*above left*). A week after the Brixton riots of 1985, a middle-aged Black woman, Mrs Cynthia Jarrett, died from heart failure after being pushed by a policeman searching her house in an illegal police raid. The police had entered her house without a warrant, using keys taken from her son while he was in police custody; he had been arrested for a simple motoring offence and no longer lived at home. This incident, one of many cited by the Institute of Race Relations throughout the 1980s as evidence of the abuse of police powers to enter homes in the Black community, triggered the Tottenham riots of 1985 in which PC Blakelock was killed. After the riots the Broadwater Farm Defence Campaign was set up to defend local youth against police reprisal. In 1988 this campaign was co-ordinated by **Janet Clarke** (*above right*).

The Africa Centre at the heart of Covent Garden, opened by Kenneth Kaunda, President of Zambia, in 1964, has provided a window into Africa for both Black and White Londoners for nearly forty years. It has hosted speakers from all over Africa, including exiles, leaders and future leaders of African states, and acted as the prime location for the organization of political events and as the meeting point for rallies and demonstrations. In 1994 the Organization of African Unity proposed to support the centre in its mission to create a 'flagship for Africa in Europe' and to develop its conference and leisure facilities in a new architectural scheme. This picture taken on 13 April 1970 shows, left to right, Mrs George, Miss Waller, Mrs Wilson, Mrs Adu, Mrs Oguumowo, Chief Mrs Jones, Chief Mrs Manuwa and an unknown woman.

A language class at the **Africa Centre** in the early 1960s. Since its inception, the Africa Centre has enriched the intellectual life of the capital, with academics and intellectuals discussing their work and teaching and giving master classes. African women have played a significant part in the workings of the centre. In 1986, the late Sally Mugabe, political activist and wife of the president of Zimbabwe, hosted 'Focus on African Women'. The centre's book fairs and art exhibitions have made a major contribution to awareness of African culture in the UK.

Rt Revd Desmond Tutu addressing the **Nelson Mandela Freedom March** to London in Hyde Park, 1988. This rally was typical of the anti-Apartheid movement at the height of its activity in the 1980s as it focused on the demand for Mandela to be released. The movement itself was born in 1959 as a response to the brutal racist regime in South Africa. It protested against the Sharpeville Massacre of 1960 and all the atrocities and outrages that followed with a mixture of demonstrations, lobbying and economic and cultural boycotts. The photo below shows demonstrators at an anti-Apartheid rally in London in 1982.

Scenes from the **Notting Hill Carnival** (*left* 1987; *above and below* 2009,). The Notting Hill Carnival was founded by Claudia Jones in 1959 after the Notting Hill riots to foster better relations between the Black and White communities. Throughout the 1950s and '60s, the Black community was under physical attack from racist gangs and faced hostility from a White community whose insecurities were being fed by misinformation about the new 'alien culture' in its midst. Today Carnival celebrates Britain's cultural diversity.

Carnival is a festival originating in the West Indies, where slaves used masquerade, costume, dance and spectacle as the only opportunity for political comment, encoded through humour and caricature. Today carnival in the West Indies marks Lent, the gathering of crops, independence from colonial rule and the emancipation from slavery. Slaves who participated in carnival in the West Indies drew their inspiration from much earlier African traditions which deployed masquerade and spectacle for political commentary in festivals such as 'Gelede' from the Yorubas of Nigeria.

Although the **Notting Hill Carnival** began on a small scale (the 1961 Carnival took place in the Lyceum ballroom on the Strand), it is now the biggest and most famous street festival in Europe, attracting crowds in excess of a million and celebrating the ethnic diversity of British society. It is co-ordinated by a Carnival and Arts Committee, whose officers span the worlds of the arts, business, community work, broadcasting and politics. Public funding from local authorities and arts institutions signifies the recognition of the role that the Carnival plays in the economic and cultural life of London.

Claire Holder is a former Chief Executive of the Notting Hill Carnival Trust. Holder, barrister, ran the event for thirteen years, from 1989, and was awarded an OBE for her cultural contribution. Holder had been involved with Carnival since 1973, when she started making costumes for the Ebony Steel Band. In 2009 the Notting Hill Carnival came under the auspices of London Notting Hill Ltd, organised by Michael Williams, Director. In recent years, the need to realize the Carnival's commercial potential has often clashed with the demand to preserve its dynamic and subversive essence and its spiritual value. So while some recognize how much the Carnival contributes to tourism and the opportunities afforded to Black and other businesses, organizations such as the Association for a People's Carnival decry the commercialization and cultural dilution of Carnival, its hijacking by big institutions and its appropriation by arts administrators, museums and academics. By bowing to market forces, has Carnival benefited big business more than the community? The argument – like Carnival – still rages. In 2009 the Carnival attracted an estimated audience of 2.5 million, and the generation of £100 million to the London economy (© London Notting Hill Ltd, official website, September 2009)

[The Notting Hill Carnival]… is about people commemorating their ancestors' freedom from slavery.' (Claire Holder)

The Ethnic Media Group is the largest minority ethnic media group in Europe, with a total readership of over 100,000, and an annual income of £4.5 million.

Michael Eboda, former Editor of the *New Nation*, and his colleagues were responsible for a management buy-out of Ethnic Media Group, from Trinity Mirror (Trinity had previously bought the ethnic media titles from South News). EMG's oldest title is the *Caribbean Times*, which is twenty-seven years old and which had formerly been under the ownership of proprietor Arif Ali. Launched in 1996, the *New Nation* newspaper is today Britain's number one selling Black newspaper.

Michael Eboda, who originally trained in commercial law before being appointed Editor of the *New Nation*, was a businessman, who took advantage of the growing market in sportswear. In 1989, Eboda returned to study, to undertake a post-graduate diploma at the London College of Printing, due to its established ties with the world of journalism. Although his father had studied economics at LSE, Eboda believes that he has most been influenced by his Aunt, Mrs Animashaun, a successful business contractor. 'It was in reality my Aunt who supported the family, encouraged me and provided a strong, dynamic role model. All credit must go to my Aunt. I love and respect her.'

The 1990s saw Eboda working on popular national titles such as the *Observer*'s and *Sunday Times*' *Health* and *Style* magazines, and the *Guardian*. It was in the mid 1990s that Eboda was first invited to join the *New Nation* as sub-editor, eventually being asked to edit the paper under the ownership of the Ethnic Media Group (1997).

Eboda has a strong sense of family history, through his grandmother. His own research into his family DNA has revealed a family origin in West Cameroon, Palestinian Territories, Madagascar and Lebanon. 'I was fortunate enough to be raised in Nigeria for eight years, between the ages of fourteen and twenty-two.' Michael Eboda is convinced that this experience had an enormous grounding influence upon him, and has equipped him to face the challenges he was later to encounter within education and the world of work. 'Research which we conducted, demonstrated that 80 per cent of the 100 most influential Black people in Britain, confirms my own experience, that those who are successful were either educated abroad for most or some of their education. Within three months of arriving in Nigeria, I decided that I would study Law.'

Today Michael Eboda continues to contribute to national newspapers, journals and his own media consultancy. According to Eboda, 'In a struggling competitive industry, revenues are becoming harder to come by, and it pays to be continually looking at new ways of doing things!'

ACKNOWLEDGEMENTS

I give my special thanks to all those who have made this book possible and whose participation suggests that they too have seen the need to tell these human stories in a way with which people can more clearly identify:

West Africa magazine, the keeper of the torch in relation to the history of Black London since 1917, both African and West Indian. I extend my special thanks to its editor, Maxwell Nwagboso, deputy editor, Desmond Davis, general manager, Kaye Whiteman, and illustrator and photographic archivist, Tayo Fatunla, whose historical appreciation led their support in the research of this book and whose own knowledge was a spur to enquiries even further afield.

Mr Arif Ali, original proprietor of the *Caribbean Times* since 1981 and the *West Indian Digest* since 1971, who had the foresight to maintain an archive and whose Hansib publications are a must for all researchers of the Black experience in modern Britain. Special thanks to Mr Ross Slater, news editor of the *Caribbean Times* and *New Nation*, for his early and continued support, and Mr Tetteh Kofi, managing editor of the *New Nation* for the Ethnic Media Group's continued commitment to the project.

The West Indian Ex-Servicemen's (and Women's) Association and its members have been an invaluable historical resource in areas which extend far beyond the military. Posthumously, I would like to thank Mr Kelly, a debonair ex-serviceman and civil servant, whose testimony was particularly moving. Also I thank Mr Webb, the current president, Mr Phillpotts and Mr Flanigan, education and publicity officers, whose knowledge is encyclopaedic.

Colonel Christine Moody and Cynthia Moody, keepers of the torch of the earlier history of Black London, whose own outstanding achievements and dedication to the legacy of the Moody family have been an inspiration.

The London Transport Museum's Hugh Robertson and Felicity Premru have enabled me to include a significant chapter on employment history and the early pattern of modern immigration. I am grateful to them.

Thanks to Mr Christopher Shokoya-Eleshin of Shokoya-Eleshin Construction Ltd; Terence Pepper of the National Portrait Gallery; Mrs Watley-Barrow of the Barbados Museum and Historical Archive; Mr Gbenga Sonuga, former senior archivist and director of the Calabar Museum and Lagos Arts Council, Nigeria; Mr Julian Watson and Ms Francis Ward; Mr C.B. Mears and Mr W. Ryder for their contributions to the history of Black people in Greenwich.

Finally, I would like to thank my sisters Elizabeth and Josephine Okokon, who are probably unaware of the extent to which their support and encouragement have carried me through this project.

REFERENCES, BIBLIOGRAPHY & SOURCES

The following is a credit of all sources and information used to create some of the biographies included in *Black Londoners: A History*. Unless otherwise stated all pictures are courtesy of the contributors.

THE ARTS, ENTERTAINMENT & SPORT

Orlando Martins p.16: Interview with Gbebga Sonuga (formerly of Lagos Archives, Nigeria); Orlando Martins' Order of Service.

Ronald Moody p.17: Interview with Colonel Christine Moody; Interview with Cynthia Moody.

Isaac Julien p.20: Interview.

Chris Ofili p.22: Personal interview; 'Victoria Miro Gallery: Chris Ofili', *The Guardian*, 13 January 2005. Picture: courtesy of Contributor: © George Ikonomopoulos/TO VIMA.

Bayo Akinsiku a.k.a. Siku p.23: Personal interview; Ahmed, Murad, 'Religious superheroes come back fighting in a Manga comic Bible', *The Times*, 18 February 2008; Bland, Archie, 'The ascent of manga: Japan's hottest export goes global', *Independent on Sunday*, 4 December 2008.

Dr Augustus Casely Hayford p.25: Personal interview. Picture: courtesy of contributor and INIVA (International Institute for Visual Arts).

Nadia Cattouse p.26: Personal interview.

Esther Bruce p.27: Bourne, Stephen, and Bruce, Esther, *Aunt Esther's Story* (Hammersmith and Fulham Ethnic Communities Oral History Project, 1996); Interview with Stephen Bourne; Picture: courtesy of Bourne.

Elisabeth Welch p.28: Interview with Stephen Bourne, friend; Pines, Jim, *Black and White in Colour: Black People in British Television Since 1936* (BFI Publishing, 1992); 'Singer Elisabeth Welch Dies', BBC News, 16 July 2003; Bourne, Stephen, 'Elisabeth Welch: Black diva whose roles ranged from Cole Porter's "Nymph Errant" to Derek Jarman's "The Tempest"', *The Independent*, 16 July 2003; Martin, Douglas, 'Elisabeth Welch, 99: Cabaret Hitmaker', *The New York Times* 18 July 2003. Picture: courtesy of Stephen Bourne.

Earl Cameron p.29: Pines, Jim, *Black and White in Colour: Black People in British Television Since 1936* (BFI Publishing, 1992); 'Earl Cameron', *The Royal Gazette*, 1 September 2008; Moniz, Jessie, 'London hit me hard', *The Royal Gazette*, 20 March 2007; Earl Cameron <http://www.imdb.com/name/nm0131565>; Earl Cameron (1917–) <http://www.screenonline.org.uk/people/id/475450/index.html>; Picture: courtesy of the *Caribbean Times* Archive, Mr Arif Ali and Ross Slater/Hansib Publication Ltd.

Rudolph Walker p.30: Personal interview.

Nina Baden-Semper p.30; Personal interview

Patricia Cumper p.31; Personal interview.

Menelik Shabazz p.32: Personal interview; Shepherd, Claire, 'Menelik Shabazz – UK, Black Filmmaker seeks "reel-changes" in Cinema and TV', *Black Filmmaker Magazine* website; 'Menelik Shabazz profile', *Black Filmmakers Magazine* Monthly Film Club, © 2008 Institute of Contemporary Arts.**Burning an Illusion** p.32: Picture: courtesy of the *Caribbean Times* Archive, Mr Arif Ali and Ross Slater/Hansib Publication Ltd.

Ital Lions p.34: Picture: courtesy of the *Caribbean Times* Archive, Mr Arif Ali and Ross Slater/Hansib Publication Ltd.

Brinsley Forde p.34: Picture: courtesy of the *Caribbean Times* Archive, Mr Arif Ali and Ross Slater/Hansib Publication Ltd.

Rudolph Dunbar p.37: Interview with Professor Ian Hall, nephew; Picture p.37: Humphrey Newmar, *Caribbean Times*, courtesy Hansib Publication Ltd; Picture p.38: courtesy of Professor Ian Hall.

Professor Ian Hall p.39: Personal interview.

Tunde Jegede p.40: Personal interview.

Gabrielle p.41: Picture: courtesy of the *Caribbean Times* Archive, Mr Arif Ali and Ross Slater/Hansib Publication Ltd.

Dizzee Rascal p.42: Personal Interview; Simon Hattenstone, *The Guardian*, 24 March 2004.

Baron Leary Constantine p.44: Interview with Randolph Beresford; Picture: courtesy of the *Caribbean Times* Archive, Mr Arif Ali and Ross Slater/Hansib Publication Ltd.

Harold Ernest Moody p.45: Interview with Colonel Christine Moody; Interview with Cynthia Moody; Picture: courtesy of Colonel Christine Moody.

Ian Wright p.46: 'Ian Wright transfers to BBC', BBC News, 22 January 2001; Ian Wright <http://www.imdb.com/name/nm0942442>; Tryhorn, Chris, 'TalkSport signs Ian Wright', *MediaGuardian*, <http://www.guardian.co.uk/media/2007/feb/14/commercialradio.radio>, 14 February 2007; Arlidge, John, 'The Observer Profile: Is this Mr Right?', *The Observer*, 13 January 2002; '"Jester" Ian Wright attacks BBC' BBC News, 18 April 2008; Baker, Andrew, 'Ian Wright quits pundit role at BBC', <http://www.telegraph.co.uk/sport/football/international/england/2297635/Ian-Wright-quits-pundit-role-at-BBC.html>, 18 April 2008; *Ian Wright –Wright Across America*, Synopsis, Studio: Liberation Entertainment, DVD Release Date: 21 Jul 2008.

Albert O. Williamson-Taylor p.47: Personal interview.

Lennox Claudius Lewis p.48: *Caribbean Times* Archive, courtesy Hansib Publishing Ltd; Rendall, Jonathan, 'Quiet Storm', *The Sunday Telegraph*, 7 December 1997; Hauser, Thomas, 'People know I was the last true champion', *The Observer*, 2 April 2006; 'Lennox Lewis answers your questions', BBC News, 21 December 1999; 'Hatton must win in four – Lewis', BBC Sport: Boxing, 2 December 2007; 'Lennox Lewis', <http://www.hbo.com/boxing/bios/lennox_lewis.html>, 20 February 2007; Hall, Sarah 'McCartney wealth put at £713m', *Guardian Unlimited Money*, 20 April 2001; Picture: courtesy of the *Caribbean Times* Archive, Mr Arif Ali and Ross Slater/Hansib Publication Ltd.

MILITARY

Donald Adolphus Brown p.50: Picture: courtesy of Greenwich Local History Library.

West India Regiment p.51: Picture: courtesy of West India Ex-Services Association

Constance Goodridge-Mark p.52: Personal interview; Busby, Margaret, 'Connie Mark, Community activist and Caribbean champion', *The Guardian*, 16 June 2007; 'Connie Mark Honoured', <http://www.itzcaribbean.com>; Goodwin, Clayton, 'Obituary: Connie Mark, Champion of Jamaican culture', *The Independent*, 19 July 2007; Mark, Connie, 'Union Jack', BBC *Video Nation* Archive <http://www.bbc.co.uk/videonation/articles/u/uk_unionjack.shtml>, 28 August 1997.

Colonel Charles Moody p.53: Picture: courtesy of Colonel Christine Moody.

Group Captain Osbourne p.55: Interview with Laurent Phillpotts; Picture: courtesy of West India Ex-Services Association.

West India Ex-Services Association p.55: Interview with Laurent Phillpotts; Interview with Hector Watson; Interview with Allan Kelly; Interview with Neil Flanigan; Picture: courtesy of West India Ex-Services Association.

Allan Kelly p.55: Personal interview; Picture p.56: courtesy of West India Ex-Services Association; Picture p.56 (funeral): courtesy of the Kelly Family, with our special thanks and gratitude.

Hector & Edithna Watson p.57: Personal interview.

Neil Flanigan p.57: Personal interview.

Laurie Phillpotts p.58: Personal interview.

Richard Sykes p.59: Picture: courtesy of West India Ex-Services Association.

Nadia Cattouse p.59: Personal interview.

HEALTH, WELFARE & SCIENCE

Dr George Rice p.61: Picture p.61: courtesy of National Portrait Gallery; Picture p.62: courtesy of National Portrait Gallery and Greenwich Local History Archive.

Surgeon Major Africanus Horton p.62: Picture: courtesy of the *Caribbean Times* Archive, Mr Arif Ali and Ross Slater/Hansib Publication Ltd.

Mary Seacole p.63: Source: Seacole, Mary, *The Wonderful Adventures of Mrs Seacole in Many Lands* (London, 2005); Picture: History Oniks.

Dr Harold Moody p.65: League of Coloured Peoples, *The Keys: Journals of The League of Coloured Peoples* 1933 –1951; Vaughan, David, *Negro Victory: The Life Story of Dr Harold Moody* (London, 1950); Interview with Colonel Christine Moody; Interview with Cynthia Moody; Picture: courtesy of Colonel Christine Moody.

Colonel Christine Moody p.66: Personal interview; Interview with Cynthia Moody.

Kura Anne Mary King-Okokon p.67: Personal interview.

Adelaide Tambo p.70: *Ham and High*, 11 October 2007; McSmith, Andy, 'Oliver Tambo: the Exile', *The Independent*, 15 October 2007; Associated Press, 'Mandela leads tributes to Adelaide Tambo', <http://www.guardian.co.uk/world/2007/feb/01/southafrica.nelsonmandela>, 1 February 2007; *Who's Who? of Southern Africa* (98ed, 2005); Smith, Alex Duval, 'Adelaide Tambo 'Ma Tambo' to the ANC in exile and a champion of women, the elderly and disabled in South Africa', *The Independent*, 2 February 2007; 'City of Cape Town New offices for Adelaide Tambo Subcouncil 2008/08/04', <http://www.capetown.gov.za/en/Pages/NewofficesforAdelaideTamboSubcouncil.aspx>; 'Woman of a changing world', *The Sunday Independent (South Africa)*, 4 February 2007; 'South Africa Holiday: Adelaide Tambo', <http://www.southafricaholiday.org.uk/history/le_adelaide_tambo.htm>; BlackModz, 'A woman of style and moral substance: Adelaide Tambo' <http://blackmodz.blogspot.com/2007/02/woman-of-style-and-moral-substance.html>, 4 February 2007; Picture: courtesy of the Tony Stevers Archive & Collection.

Dr Elizabeth Okokon p.70: Personal interview.

Dr Christopher Balugun-Lynch p.72: Personal interview.

Dr Mabel Ali p.74: Personal interview.

Charles Ifejika p.75: Personal interview; Finn, Widget, 'Starting out', <www.independent.co.uk>, 8 February 2004; 'Contact Lens Cleaning & Soaking Fluids', <http://www.college-optometrists.org/index.aspx/pcms/site.college.What_We_Do.museyeum.online_exhibitions.contact_lenses.fluid>; Ifejika, C.P., and McLaughlin-Borlace, L., Lucas, V.J., Roberts, A.D., Walker, J.T., *Efficacy of a contact lens cleaning device and its enhancement of the performance of contact lens care products*, Centre for Applied Microbiology and Research; Hume, E.B., and Zhu, H., Cole, N., Huynh, C., Lam, S., Willcox, M.D., *Efficacy of contact lens multipurpose solutions against serratia marcescens*, Institute for eye research.

Noreen Goss p.76: Personal interview; Picture: courtesy of the Noreen Goss Photographic Archive & Collection.

Dr James Adjaye p.77: Personal interviews 2007 & 2008.

TRADE, INDUSTRY & ENTERPRISE

Black Tailor in Whitechapel p.81: Picture: courtesy of Museum of London Photographic Archive.

Madam Ewa Henshaw p.81: Picture: Gbebga Sonuga, formerly of Lagos Archives, Nigeria.

Sir Edward Asafu Adjaye p.82: Picture: Courtesy of *West Africa Journal*, Mr Desmond Davies, *West Africa Journal* Archive.

George Dryden p.83: Picture: Rod Leon, *Caribbean Times* 16/5/90, Hansib Publishing Limited, courtesy of the *Caribbean Times* Archive, Mr Arif Ali and Ross Slater.

Len Dyke p.84: Picture: Rod Leon, *Caribbean Times* 16/5/90, Hansib Publishing Limited, courtesy of the *Caribbean Times* Archive, Mr Arif Ali and Ross Slater.

Dounne Alexander p.85: Personal interview; *Airways Magazine* interview; Events & Exhibitions, Dounne Alexander Walker, University of the Arts London, 2007 Events Archive; 'Britain's black achievers revealed in historic exhibition', Press release, London College of Communication, 19 September 2007; 'Dounne Alexander: Profile', <http://www.grammasintl.com/html/profile_da.asp>.

Joy Nichols p.85: Picture: courtesy of the *Caribbean Times* Archive, Mr Arif Ali and Ross Slater/Hansib Publication Ltd.

Pearl Connor-Mogotsi p.86: Interview with Noreen Goss, close friend; interview with Joe Mogotsi, widower; Picture: courtesy of Noreen Goss.

Isobel Husbands p.87: Personal interview.

Christopher Shokoya-Eleshin p. 88: Personal interview; 'The Search is on for Liverpool's Most Successful Entrepreneurs: Liverpool nominations for the Inner City 100 Launched', Press Release, Royal Bank of Scotland (<www.rbs.com>) 29 March 2001.

Alake of Abeokuta p.90: Picture: courtesy of the National Portrait Gallery.

Margaret Busby p.91: Personal interview.

Albert O. Williamson-Taylor p.92: Personal interview; Hartman, Hattie, 'Piecing It Together', *The Architects' Journal*, 21 February 2008; 'Zaha Reveals Barcelona Spirals', *The Architects' Journal*, 11 May 2006; Waite, Richard, 'Heatherwick Selected for Shanghai Expo', *The Architects' Journal* 27 September 2007; 'Breaking News Daily', *The Architects' Journal* 16 November 2006; Vaughan, Richard, 'Designer Sought for Mobile TATE' *The Architects' Journal*, 26 July 2007; Waite, Richard, *Engineering Growth*, *The Architects' Journal*, 16 November 2006; Thompson, Max, 'Olympic Win for Henighan Peng', *The Architects' Journal*, 18 October 2007.

David Adjaye p.95: Personal interview; Lange, Alexandra, 'Don't Call David Adjaye a Starchitect', *New York Magazine*, 15 July 2007; Dyckhoff, Tom, 'Behind the façade', *The Guardian*, 8 February 2003; Hill, David, 'David Adjaye's MCA/Denver Opens', *Architectural Record*, 26 October 2007; Slessor, Catherine, 'Denver's new MCA celebrates radical art and architecture', *Architectural Review*, 1 April 2008; Milmo, Cahal, 'David Adjaye: Downfall of the Showman', *The Independent*, 24 July 2009.

David Thompson p.97: Personal interview.

Trevor Robinson p.98: Personal interview; <www.quietstorm.co.uk>.

Terry Jervis p.100: Personal interview.

Noel Uche p.102: Personal interview.

Alexander Amosu p.103: Personal interview.

CIVIC & POLITICAL

Lord Taylor p.107: Personal interview; 'John Taylor, Lord Taylor of Warwick', *Who's Who*; 'The Peers: Nearly all-male, nearly all-white, nearly all-Christian', BBC News Online: Special Report, <http://news.bbc.co.uk/1/low/special_report/house_of_lords/59793.stm>, 25 February 1998; Picture: courtesy of the *Caribbean Times* Archive, Mr Arif Ali and Ross Slater/Hansib Publication Ltd.

Olaudah Equiano p.108: *The Interesting Narrative of the Life of Olaudah Equiano or Gustavus Vasa, the African, Written by Himself*, 1789; Picture: *The Interesting Narrative of the Life of Olaudah Equiano or Gustavus Vasa, the African, Written by Himself*, 1789.

Free Natives of the West Indies p.110: Picture: Engraving by Agostino Brunias, 1790, courtesy of the Barbados Museum and Historical Society.

Mary Prince p.111: *The History of Mary Prince, A West Indian Slave*, 1831.

Amy Ashwood Garvey p.112: *Oxford Dictionary of National Biography (ODNB)*, <www.oxforddnb.com> (Oxford, 2004).

Claudia Jones p.113: Interview with Ranjana Ashe; Picture: courtesy of the *Caribbean Times* Archive, Mr Arif Ali and Ross Slater/Hansib Publication Ltd.

Lord & Lady Pitt p.114: Pictures: courtesy of the *Caribbean Times* Archive, Mr Arif Ali and Ross Slater/Hansib Publication Ltd.

Bernie Grant p.115: Interview with Mrs Grant; 'Labour MP Bernie Grant dies', BBC News, 8 April 2000; 'Bernie Grant: A controversial figure', BBC News, 8 April 2000; Speech given by Bernie Grant M.P. to the House of Commons of the British Parliament on 19 December 1995 on Africa Reparations Movement; Letter to Mr Julian Spalding, Director, Art Gallery and Museum, 10 December 1996 on African Religious and Cultural Objects, <http://www.arm.arc.co.uk/CRBBletter1.html>; Bernie Grant Archives at the University of Middlesex, Middlesex University, Bernie Grant Centre, Tottenham, London; Picture: courtesy of the *Caribbean Times* Archive, Mr Arif Ali and Ross Slater/Hansib Publication Ltd.

Gertrude Paul p.115: CRE File; CRE Executive Office, Note on Commissioner's Correspondence 11/6/80; Letter of Appointment to Gertrude Paul from William Whitelaw, Home Secretary 25/3/82; *Caribbean Times*, courtesy of Hansib Publication Ltd; Picture: Terry Austin-Smith, courtesy of the *Caribbean Times* Archive, Mr Arif Ali and Ross Slater/Hansib Publication Ltd/Courtesy of Lambeth Press Office, London Borough of Lambeth, Lambeth Town Hall, Brixton Hill, London SW1 1RW).

Linda Bellos p.116: London Strategic Policy Unit, *Black Councilors in Britain*, foreword by Ansel Wong (Association of London Authorities, 1988); Ali, Arif (ed.), *Third World Impact* (Hansib Publication Ltd, 1986); Anthony, Andrew, 'Yes, we were bloody angry', *The Guardian*, 15 February 2006; Woodward, Will, 'OBE to fighter for equality', *The Guardian*, 30 December 2006; Hibbert, Katharine, 'Best of Times, Worst of Times: Linda Bellos', *Times Online*, 25 February 2007; Picture: Stefano Cagnoni (Report, London), courtesy of the *Caribbean Times* Archive, Mr Arif Ali and Ross Slater/Hansib Publication Ltd.

Merle Amory p.116: Picture: Andrew Wiard, 'Report' 411, courtesy of the *Caribbean Times* Archive, Mr Arif Ali and Ross Slater/Hansib Publication Ltd.

Gloria Mills p.117: Picture: Joanne O'Brein/FORMAT, courtesy of the *Caribbean Times* Archive, Mr Arif Ali and Ross Slater/Hansib Publication Ltd.

Lord William Morris p.117: Picture: courtesy of the *Caribbean Times* Archive, Mr Arif Ali and Ross Slater/Hansib Publication Ltd.

Diane Abbot p.118: House of Commons Profile; Abbott, Diane, 'A Race Against Time', <www.guardian.co.uk>, 10 July 2008; 'Opening Up Politics', <http://news.bbc.co.uk/1/hi/programmes/this_week/4873968.stm>, 11 April, 2006; Picture: Andrew Wiard (Report), Asian Times Award, courtesy of the *Caribbean Times* Archive, Mr Arif Ali and Ross Slater/Hansib Publication Ltd.

Ambrosine Neil p.119: London Strategic Policy Unit, *Black Councilors in Britain*, foreword by Ansel Wong (Association of London Authorities, 1988); Ali, Arif (ed.), *Third World Impact* (Hansib Publication Ltd, 1986); Picture: courtesy of the *Caribbean Times* Archive, Mr Arif Ali and Ross Slater/Hansib Publication Ltd.

Rudolph Daley p.119: London Strategic Policy Unit, *Black Councilors in Britain*, foreword by Ansel Wong (Association of London Authorities, 1988); Ali, Arif (ed.), *Third World Impact* (Hansib Publication Ltd, 1986); Picture: courtesy of the *Caribbean Times* Archive, Mr Arif Ali and Ross Slater/Hansib Publication Ltd/courtesy of: Lambeth Press Office, London Borough of Lambeth, Lambeth Town Hall, Brixton Hill, London SW1 1RW.

Valda James p.119: Personal interview; London Strategic Policy Unit, *Black Councilors in Britain*, foreword by Ansel Wong (Association of London Authorities, 1988); Picture: Humphrey Newmon, *Caribbean Times*, 19/7/88, courtesy of the *Caribbean Times* Archive, Mr Arif Ali and Ross Slater/Hansib Publication Ltd.

Randolph Beresford MBE p.120: Interviews with the late Mr Beresford; Beresford, Randolph, and Johnson, Christopher A., *A Journey Through Life : From Guyana to Ghana* (EnTra Publications, 1995); London Strategic Policy Unit, *Black Councilors in Britain*, foreword by Ansel Wong (Association of London Authorities, 1988); Ali, Arif (ed.), *Third World Impact* (Hansib Publication Ltd, 1986); MBE citation; Picture: J.A. Love, *Caribbean Times*, courtesy of the *Caribbean Times* Archive, Mr Arif Ali and Ross Slater/Hansib Publication Ltd.

Dr John Roberts QC p.122: Personal interview.

Baroness Amos p.124: Personal interview; Cathcart, Brian, 'We are deeply concerned: Again', *New Statesman*, 4 July 2005; <http://www.indymedia.org.uk/en/actions/2005/g8/>; Picture: courtesy of Valerie Amos/Cape Town 2007 World Economic Forum on Africa.

LONDON INTERNATIONAL

Dr Kwame Nkrumah p.126: Nkrumah, Kwame, *The Autobiography of Kwame Nkrumah*, (Thomas Nelson & Sons, 1957); Padmore, George, *Pan-Africanism or Communism? The Coming Struggle for Africa* (Dennis Dobson, 1956); 'Kwame Nkrumah's Vision of Africa' BBC World Service, 14 September 2000; Lee, Paul, 'Documents Expose U.S. Role in Nkrumah Overthrow', <http://www.seeingblack.com/x060702/nkrumah.shtml>, 7 June 2002; Picture p.126: Sport & General Press Agency Limited, courtesy of Desmond Davies, *West Africa Journal* Archive; Picture p.127: Nkrumah, Kwame, *The Autobiography of Kwame Nkrumah*, (Thomas Nelson & Sons, 1957)

Eleazar Chukwuemeka (Emaka) Anyaoku p.128: *Who's Who 1897–1996: One Hundred Years of Biography* (A&C Black Ltd, 1996); Picture: courtesy of Desmond Davies, *West Africa Journal* Archive.

Mabel Dove p.128: Picture: courtesy of Desmond Davies, *West Africa Journal* Archive.

Rt Hon. Nnamdi Azikiwe p.129: *Who's Who 1897–1996: One Hundred Years of Biography* (A&C Black Ltd, 1996); Fryer, Peter, *Staying Power: The History of Black People in Britain* (Pluto Press, 1984); Okokon, Susan, *Race, Censorship and Propaganda* (1998); Foray, Cyril P., *Encyclopaedia Africana Dictionary of African Biography, II* (Reference Publications Inc., 1979); Picture: courtesy of Desmond Davies, *West Africa Journal* Archive.

Mrs Azikiwe p.129: Picture: courtesy of Desmond Davies, *West Africa Journal* Archive.

Sir Edward Asafu-Adjaye p.130: West Africa Archive 1996/7; *Who's Who in the World*, (Marquis Who's Who Inc, 1975); Ewechue, Ralph (ed.), *Makers of Modern Africa*, (Africa Books Ltd, 1981); *Who's Who 1897–1996: One Hundred Years of Biography* (A&C Black Ltd, 1996); Picture: courtesy of Desmond Davies, *West Africa Journal* Archive.

H.V.H. Sekyi p.131: Picture: courtesy of Desmond Davies, *West Africa Journal* Archive.

Sir Seretse Khama p.132: West Africa Archive; Duffield, Michael, *A Marriage of Inconvenience: The Persecution of Ruth and Seretse Khama* (Unwin Paperbacks, 1990); Picture: courtesy of Desmond Davies, *West Africa Journal* Archive.

Dr Hastings Banda p.133: Picture: courtesy of Desmond Davies, *West Africa Journal* Archive.

Mrs Banda & Prince Phillip p.133: Picture: courtesy of Desmond Davies, *West Africa Journal* Archive.

Haile Selassie p.134: Sources: Nkrumah, Kwame, *The Autobiography of Kwame Nkrumah*, (Thomas Nelson & Sons, 1957); James, C.L.R., *Abyssinia & The Imperialists* (1936); Fryer, Peter, *Staying Power: The History of Black People in Britain* (Pluto Press, 1984); Picture: courtesy of Desmond Davies, *West Africa Journal* Archive.

Mrs Kweaie Armah & Ghana High Commissioners' wives p.135: Picture: courtesy of Desmond Davies, *West Africa Journal* Archive/The Commonwealth Secretariat Libraries, with special thanks to Miss Murtagh, Ms Theodora Adu Apeanyo and Martin Coppins.

Mrs Asafu Adjaye p.136: West Africa Archives; *Who Was Who* (A & C Black Ltd, 1996); Picture: courtesy of Desmond Davies, *West Africa Journal* Archive..

Black schoolboys p.136: Picture: courtesy of Desmond Davies, *West Africa Journal* Archive.

Paul Boateng p.137: 'UK Envoy calls for Urgent Citizen Advocacy on Trade' <http://allafrica.com/stories/200803181246. html>, 17 March 2008; Profile: Paul Boateng, BBC News, 29 May 2002; 'British High Commission in South Africa', News Release, 16 July 2007; 'Methodist Serves as Britain's first Black Cabinet Minister', *The Times*, 13 October 2006; The Secretary of State for Foreign and Commonwealth Affairs quoted, 1 November 2005, in Hansard debates; Picture: courtesy of the *Caribbean Times* Archive, Mr Arif Ali and Ross Slater/Hansib Publication Ltd.

Adelaide Tambo p.138: Picture: courtesy of Desmond Davies, *West Africa Journal* Archive.

Winnie Mandela & Commonwealth Secretariat p.139: Reddy, E.S., *Apartheid: The United Nations and the International Community* (Vikas Publishing House PVT Ltd, 1986); 'Why the Generals Feared Saro-Wiwa', *The Guardian*, 25 October 1997; Chris McGreal in Lagos, *The Guardian*, 13 November 1995; Shiner, Cindy, 'Fatalism Overtakes Weary Opposition', *The Guardian*, 13 November 1995. Picture: courtesy of Commonwealth Secretariat, West Africa Archive, 1996/7.

Herbert Yearwood p.140: Picture: courtesy of Ms Gibbs and Mr Williams of the Barbados *Nation News*, 2006.

CHURCH LEADERS

Isaac P. Dickerson p.143: Greenwich Local History Archive; Picture: courtesy of Greenwich Local History Archive and the National Portrait Gallery.

Revd Samuel Adjaye Crowther p.144: Anderson, G. (ed.), *Biographical Dictionary of Christian Missions* (Macmillan Reference, 1998; Aldred, Joe, 'Birmingham Black Christianity of 1800–1900', March 2006; Yoruba Mission papers in the Church Missionary Society Archives held at Birmingham University Library; C.M.S. (Y) 4/3 10 Samuel Ajaye Crowther (1925); Onwuka, Dike K., 'Origins of the Niger Mission 1841–1891', (A paper read at the centenary of Mission at Christ Church, Onitsha, 13 November 1957); Page, Jesse, *Samuel Crowther: The Slave Boy Who Became Bishop of the Niger* (S.W. Partridge & Co., c.1892); Project Canterbury: <http://anglicanhistory.org/>; Picture: Page, Jesse, *Samuel Crowther: The Slave Boy Who Became Bishop of the Niger* (S.W. Partridge & Co., c.1892).

Bishop James 'Holy' Johnson p.146: Stock, Eugene, *The History of the Church Missionary Society: Its Environment, Its Men and Its Work* (CMS, 1899); Ayandele, Emmanuel, 'Holy, Johnson, Pioneer of African Nationalism, 1836–1917* (Routledge, 1970); Lipschutz, Mark R., and Rasmussen, R. Kent, *Dictionary of African Historical Biography*, 2nd edn (University of California Press, 1986); Ewechue, Ralph (ed.), *Makers of Modern Africa*, 2nd edn (Africa Books, 1991); Brockman, Norbert C., *An African Biographical Dictionary* (ABC-Clio Inc, 1994).

Isaac Oluwale p.147: Brockman, Norbert C., *An African Biographical Dictionary* (ABC-Clio Inc, 1994); Picture: courtesy of the National Portrait Gallery.

George Makippe p.148: Picture: courtesy of the National Portrait Gallery.

Rt Revd Wilfred Wood p.149: Personal interview; 'New Bishop Of Croydon', Press Release, Diocese of Southwark, 25 March 2003; 'Retiring bishop slams Big Brother', BBC News, 31 July 2002; 'A report on the development of the Committee for Minority Ethnic Anglican Concerns (CMEAC), the former Committee on Black Anglican Concerns (CBAC)' (Church House Publishing, 2003); Picture: courtesy of the *Caribbean Times* Archive, Mr Arif Ali and Ross Slater/Hansib Publication Ltd.

Paul Keynes Douglas p.150: Picture: © Anna Arnone, *Caribbean Times*, Hansib Publication Ltd, courtesy of the *Caribbean Times* Archive, Mr Arif Ali and Ross Slater/Hansib Publication Ltd.

Garth Moody p.150: Interview with Dr Christine Moody; Interview with Cynthia Moody; Picture: courtesy of Dr Christine Moody.

The Rt Revd Dr John Sentamu p.151: Biography, Office of the Bishop of Stepney – thanks to Margaret Pattinson; Picture: Humphrey Newmar, courtesy of the *Caribbean Times* Archive, Mr Arif Ali and Ross Slater/Hansib Publication Ltd; Picture p.152: courtesy of John Barton and *Arun Arora* Communications Adviser to the Archbishop of York, York Minster.

TRANSPORT

Joe Clough p.154: Picture: courtesy of London Transport Museum.
B. Johnson & J. Joff p.155: Picture: courtesy of London Transport Museum.
Cynthia Palmer p.156: Picture: courtesy of London Transport Museum.
Ken Harper p.156: Picture: courtesy of London Transport Museum.
Mrs A. Hart p.157: Picture: courtesy of London Transport Museum.
London Transport Catering p.158: Picture: courtesy of London Transport Museum.
Mrs Merna Miller p.159: Picture: courtesy of London Transport Museum.
Black Female Bus Inspector & White Colleague p.159: Picture: courtesy of London Transport Museum.
London Underground p.160: Picture: courtesy of London Transport Museum.

EDUCATIONALISTS & WRITERS

Students 1940s p.162–3: Picture: courtesy of Desmond Davies, *West Africa Journal* Archive.
Nigeria House p.164: Picture: courtesy of Desmond Davies, *West Africa Journal* Archive.
Gloria Lock p.164: Personal interview; Lock, Gloria, *Caribbeans in Wandsworth* (Wandsworth Borough Council, 1992).
Beryl Gilroy p.165: Picture: Peepaltree Press.
John La Rose p.166: Johnson, Linton Kwesi, 'John La Rose, Obituary', *The Guardian*, 4 March 2006; Hutchinson, Shaun, 'A Black British Icon', *The New Black Magazine*, 2008; 'John La Rose: Radical bookseller and publisher who campaigned for social and racial justice - particularly in education', *The Independent*, 22 April 2006; John La Rose Tributes, <http://www.georgepadmoreinstitute.org/john-la-rose-tributes>; Picture: courtesy of John La Rose, New Beacon Books.
Andrew Salkey p.166: Picture: courtesy of John La Rose, New Beacon Books.
Professor Paul Gilroy p.167: Picture: courtesy of the London School of Economics, Press Department.
Jessica & Eric Huntley p.169: Rose, John La, *Foundations* (New Beacon Books, 1966); Report on the Second Annual Huntley Conference, 'Writing the Wrongs: Fifty years of Black Radical Publishing in Britain', held at the London Metropolitan archives on 17 February 2007; *Untold London*, London Metropolitan Archives, 28 August 2008; Major accessions to repositories in 2005 relating to Publishing, The National Archives.
Ben Okri p.170: Brown, Ben, '*Starbook* by Ben Okri' *The Observer*, 19 August 2007; 'Ben Okri (Nigeria, 1959)', <http://international.poetryinternationalweb.org/piw_cms/cms/cms_module/index.php?obj_id=408&x=1>, 9 October 2007; Flynn, Julia, 'Has Ben Okri lost touch with reality?' *The Telegraph*, 13 September 2007; Cripps, Charlotte, 'Cultural Life: Ben Okri', *The Independent*, 8 February 2008; Sethi, Anita, '*Starbook*: a magical tale of love and regeneration', *The Independent*, 26 August 2007; Picture: courtesy of the *Caribbean Times* Archive, Mr Arif Ali and Ross Slater/Hansib Publication Ltd.
Kwame Kwei Armah p.171: Personal interview.
Jocelyn Jee Esien p.173: Personal interview.

NEWS & NEWSMAKERS

J.E. Casely Hayford p.176: Picture: History Oniks.
Alex Pascall p.177: Personal interview; Motions from London Freelance Branch to ADM 2000; National Union of Journalists Freelance Branch © 1999 NUJ & contributors; Information About Alex Pascall, Chronicle World - Changing Black Britain Food for Thought, Institutional racism in print?; Hodgson, Jessica, 'There may be 200 black and Asian journals, but national newspapers are almost an ethnic minority-free zone', *MediaGuardian*, 20 May 2002; Profile GVRM Artiste /Lecturers, Alex Pascall, OBE 2004 © Good Vibes Records and Music Ltd, 2004. Picture: *Third World Impact* (Hansib Publications Ltd, 1986)/courtesy of the *Caribbean Times* Archive, Mr Arif Ali and Ross Slater/Hansib Publication Ltd.
Sir Trevor McDonald p.178: Profile, courtesy of ITN; McDonald, Trevor, *Fortunate Circumstances: Trevor McDonald* (Weidenfeld & Nicolson, 1993); *Caribbean Times* Archive, courtesy Hansib Publication Ltd; Newsworthy Career of Sir Trevor, BBC News, 15 December 2005; '*News at Ten* Returns to ITV', <www.itv.com>, 31 October 2007; 'Sir Trevor McDonald's Second Coming', 14/01/2008; Grice, Elizabeth, 'Sir Trevor was "stunned but absolutely delighted," at his award', *The Times*, 12 June 1999; 'How Sir Trevor McDonald became a British institution', *The Times*, 24 October 2007; Picture: courtesy of the *Caribbean Times* Archive, Mr Arif Ali and Ross Slater/Hansib Publication Ltd.
Dame Jocelyn Barrow OBE p.179: 'Dame Jocelyn Barrow : A Curriculum Vitae', Focus Consultancy, 1997; 'University of York honours Nine', University of York, Communications Office, <http://www.york.ac.uk/admin/presspr/pressreleases/hongradsjuly07.htm>, 6 July 2007; 'Mayor's Commission on African & Asian Heritage report published 19-7-2005, 355', Press Release, London, GLA Website; 'Barrow Dame, Jocelyn Anita Barrow, DBE', *Burke's Peerage & Baronetage* 107th Edition, *Burke's Landed Gentry* 19th Edn (Burke's Peerage Partnership); Picture: courtesy of Deputy Vice Chairman, Broadcasting Standards Council/*Caribbean Times* Archive, Mr Arif Ali and Ross Slater/Hansib Publication Ltd.
Oliver Tambo p.179: 'Reddy, E.S., *Apartheid: The United Nations and the International Community* (Vikas Publishing House PVT Ltd, 1986); Magubanae, Bernard Makhosezwe, *The Political Economy of Race and Class in South Africa* (Monthly Review Press, 1979); Picture: © Sando Moore, courtesy of the *Caribbean Times* Archive, Mr Arif Ali and Ross Slater/Hansib Publication Ltd.
Oliver Tambo & Ken Livingstone p.180: Picture: courtesy of the *Caribbean Times* Archive, Mr Arif Ali and Ross Slater/Hansib Publication Ltd.
New Cross Fire p.180: Cashmore, Ernest, and Troyna, Barry (eds), *Black Youth In Crisis*, (George Allen and Unwin Publishers Limited, 1982); La Rose, John, 'The Tottenham Insurrection 1985'; 'The Cynthia Jarrett Inquest', Michael La Rose, *New Beacon Review* Nos 2 & 3, November 1986; , Michael, 'The Cynthia Jarrett Inquest', *New Beacon Review* Nos 2 & 3, November 1986; Ali, Arif (ed.), *Third World Impact* (Hansib Publications Ltd, 1986); *Caribbean Times* Archive, courtesy of Hansib Publications Ltd; Picture: courtesy of the *Caribbean Times* Archive, Mr Arif Ali and Ross Slater/Hansib Publication Ltd.

Town Hall Protest p.180: Picture: courtesy of the *Caribbean Times* Archive, Mr Arif Ali and Ross Slater/Hansib Publication Ltd.

New Cross Service p.181: Picture: courtesy of the *Caribbean Times* Archive, Mr Arif Ali and Ross Slater/Hansib Publication Ltd.

Brixton police, p.181; Picture: Humphrey Newmar, *Caribbean Times*, courtesy of the *Caribbean Times* Archive, Mr Arif Ali and Ross Slater/Hansib Publication Ltd.

Colin Roach p.182: Cashmore, Ernest, and Troyna, Barry (eds), *Black Youth In Crisis*, (George Allen and Unwin Publishers Limited, 1982); La Rose, John, 'The Tottenham Insurrection 1985'; 'The Cynthia Jarrett Inquest', Michael La Rose, *New Beacon Review* Nos 2 & 3, November 1986; , Michael, 'The Cynthia Jarrett Inquest', *New Beacon Review* Nos 2 & 3, November 1986; Ali, Arif (ed.), *Third World Impact* (Hansib Publications Ltd, 1986); *Caribbean Times* Archive, courtesy of Hansib Publications Ltd; Picture: courtesy of the *Caribbean Times* Archive, Mr Arif Ali and Ross Slater/Hansib Publication Ltd.

Cherry Groce Protest p.182: Picture: Photo News Service, Press Room, Central Criminal Court, Old Bailey, London EC4, courtesy of the *Caribbean Times* Archive, Mr Arif Ali and Ross Slater/Hansib Publication Ltd.

Cherry Groce in Wheelchair p.183: Cashmore, Ernest, and Troyna, Barry (eds), *Black Youth In Crisis*, (George Allen and Unwin Publishers Limited, 1982); La Rose, John, 'The Tottenham Insurrection 1985'; 'The Cynthia Jarrett Inquest', Michael La Rose, *New Beacon Review* Nos 2 & 3, November 1986; Michael, 'The Cynthia Jarrett Inquest', *New Beacon Review* Nos 2 & 3, November 1986; Ali, Arif (ed.), *Third World Impact* (Hansib Publications Ltd, 1986); Picture: Photo News Service, Press Room, Central courtesy of the *Caribbean Times* Archive, Mr Arif Ali and Ross Slater/Hansib Publication Ltd.

Brixton Riots/Uprising/Insurrection p.183: Cashmore, Ernest, and Troyna, Barry (eds), *Black Youth In Crisis*, (George Allen and Unwin Publishers Limited, 1982); La Rose, John, 'The Tottenham Insurrection 1985'; 'The Cynthia Jarrett Inquest', Michael La Rose, *New Beacon Review* Nos 2 & 3, November 1986; , Michael, 'The Cynthia Jarrett Inquest', *New Beacon Review* Nos 2 & 3, November 1986; Ali, Arif (ed.), *Third World Impact* (Hansib Publications Ltd, 1986); Picture: D. Hoffman, 28/9/85, courtesy of the *Caribbean Times* Archive, Mr Arif Ali and Ross Slater/Hansib Publication Ltd.

Burned furniture store in Greasham Road, Brixton Riots p.183

7am: Shooting of Black mother, Mrs Cherry Groce by Inspector Douglas Lovelock p.183, Picture: Humphrey Newmar, courtesy of the *Caribbean Times* Archive, Mr Arif Ali and Ross Slater/Hansib Publication Ltd.

Broadwater Farm Defence Campaign p.184: Cashmore, Ernest, and Troyna, Barry (eds), *Black Youth In Crisis*, (George Allen and Unwin Publishers Limited, 1982); La Rose, John, 'The Tottenham Insurrection 1985'; La Rose, Michael, 'The Cynthia Jarrett Inquest', *New Beacon Review* Nos 2 & 3, November 1986; Ali, Arif (ed.), *Third World Impact* (Hansib Publication Ltd, 1986); *Caribbean Times* Archive, courtesy of Hansib Publications Ltd.

Dolly Kiffin, head of the Broadwater Farm Youth Association, p.184: Picture: Humphrey Newmar, *Caribbean Times*, courtesy of the *Caribbean Times* Archive, Mr Arif Ali and Ross Slater/Hansib Publication Ltd.

Black and Asian Protesters with Broadwater Farm Youth are Innocent and Enough is Enough Banners p.184: Picture: courtesy of the *Caribbean Times* Archive, Mr Arif Ali and Ross Slater/Hansib Publication Ltd.

Janet Clarke p.184: Picture: courtesy of the *Caribbean Times* Archive, Mr Arif Ali and Ross Slater/Hansib Publication Ltd.

The Africa Centre pp.184-5: The Africa Centre: 'Flagship for Africa in Europe'; Whiteman, Kaye, 'The OAU and the Africa Centre', *Matchet's Diary*, 4–10 July 1994; Picture: Courtesy of The Africa Centre Archive.

Nelson Mandela Freedom March to London, with the Right Reverend Desmond Tutu p.185: Reddy, E.S., 'Apartheid: The United Nations and the International Community', UN Special Committee against Apartheid (Vikas Publishing House Ltd, 1986); Magubanae, Bernard Makhosezwe, *The Political Economy of Race and Class in South Africa* (Monthly Review Press, 1979); *Caribbean Times* Archive; Picture: © Anna Tully, courtesy of the *Caribbean Times* Archive, Mr Arif Ali and Ross Slater/Hansib Publication Ltd.

Anti-Apartheid March p.185: Picture: courtesy of the *Caribbean Times* Archive, Mr Arif Ali and Ross Slater/Hansib Publication Ltd.

Carnival File, Grove Welcomes You to The 1987 **Notting Hill Carnival**, p.186: Picture: courtesy of the *Caribbean Times* Archive, Mr Arif Ali and Ross Slater/Hansib Publication Ltd.

Enslaved 'Cotton Pickers', Carnival 2007. p.186: Picture: Dr Elizabeth Okokon.

'Eastern Promise' Carnival 2009. p.186: Picture: Dr Elizabeth Okokon.

Claire Holder p.187: 'Ramona Andrews speaks to Claire Holder', Carnival Inside Out, 2001; Muir, Hugh, 'Financial turmoil threatens to engulf Notting Hill Carnival: Row erupts over accounts for last year's event', *The Guardian*, 9 August 2003; Picture: April 1989 Carnival Pull-Out, Humphrey Newmar, *Caribbean Times*, courtesy of the *Caribbean Times* Archive, Mr Arif Ali and Ross Slater/Hansib Publication Ltd.

Michael Eboda p.187: 'Editor's anger at stop and search', BBC News, 24 February 2003; Picture: History Oniks.